TALL TALES

and wee stories

Billy Connolly

TALL TALES

and wee stories

TWO
ROADS

First published in Great Britain in 2019 by Two Roads
An Imprint of John Murray Press
An Hachette UK company

This paperback edition published in 2020

6

A CIP catalogue record for this title is available from the British Library

Paperback ISBN 978 1 529 36136 0
eBook ISBN 978 1 529 36135 3

Typeset in Celeste by Palimpsest Book Production Ltd, Falkirk, Stirlingshire

Printed and bound in Great Britain by Clays Ltd, Elcograf S.p.A.

John Murray policy is to use papers that are natural, renewable and
recyclable products and made from wood grown in sustainable forests.
The logging and manufacturing processes are expected to conform
to the environmental regulations of the country of origin.

Two Roads
Carmelite House
50 Victoria Embankment
London EC4Y 0DZ

www.tworoadsbooks.com

Contents

Introduction

'I've got a lot to say. And sometimes it comes out in the wrong order. Please don't worry about this. I personally couldn't give a fuck. So don't let it get you down. There's a bit of profanity. But I like that. And I'm rather good at it, too.'

I've always loved telling stories. It's the most natural thing in the world for me. When I was a musician and folk singer, I would chat to the audience between songs. I wouldn't tell jokes, as such, I told wee stories.

Once, in the early days, when I'd forgotten the lyrics to an old Jimmy Driftwood song, I stopped singing and started riffing on the story of the song to cover my arse. The audience loved it. They laughed and cheered when I'd finished and I thought to myself, *oh, this is interesting!*

So, I was a storyteller long before I was a comedian. It was something I learned at school and later in the army, but most of all from my time as a welder in the shipyards on the Clyde. When we stopped work for a cup of tea, and the heavy machinery fell silent, the stories always flowed. They could be rough, rude, cruel even, but they were always funny. And there were some brilliantly funny men there, much funnier than me, real patter merchants who could've made a life out of comedy. But I guess I had a banjo and that gave me a ticket out.

Being a comedian has always been a bit of a mystery to me, because I actually very rarely get funny ideas away from the stage. I can't churn out jokes like some people can. I wouldn't know how. But I can always tell stories. And the comedy seems to emerge out of the stories as I tell them.

As you're about to see, my stories usually don't come in a conventional shape. They're kind of lumpy and strange. They might appear to have a beginning, middle and end, but often they don't – it's an illusion. They're a merry-go-round of memories, observations, fantasies and ad-libs that somehow fit together and mean something. That's the way I like it because that way they're as imperfect as I am. They're not story-shaped; they're me-shaped.

The thought of going out on stage scares the life out of me. It always has. I'm riddled with anxiety and self-doubt every time. What the fuck am I going to say to these people?

But the nerves are good for me, they force me to work harder. And if I didn't – if I got complacent – then it could fall flat and I'd make an arse of myself. But when it's good, there's no better feeling. I love it when I pick up on a ripple of laughter. I try to build on that, to try something new. And I love the sense of trust that comes with that: an audience who are willing to stick with me wherever my story goes.

I don't really 'prepare' as such. There's no special technique and I've never done homework. I never write anything down. All I have when I step out on stage is a wee list of headings like this:

Parachutists
Alcohol
Marijuana
Army

Scrotum
Holiday
Cameras
Shampoo

And every time I take a step back for a sip of water, I'll glance at the list on my wee table and see two or three things, and then I'll go on to talk about them. And sometimes they'll come out jumbled up in a very weird and unexpected order, and that creates something new that's as surprising to me as it is to you.

I will give you an example. I might have a story about parachuting. And maybe the previous night, halfway through, that led me unexpectedly into talking about, say, welding. Then the next night I might start by talking about welding, and see where that leads me. Then, on a whim, I might stick something new in the middle of that, and see how that affects the next thing. That is the way I operate. I get lost and see where it leads me.

I love losing my way. I love getting lost in cities and small towns and all kinds of places, wandering off down long and winding streets and wee lanes and exploring the area, turning corners and seeing what's there. And I love getting lost in my stories for the same reason. It's how I discover things, how I learn things, how I imagine things. It keeps things fresh and it keeps them funny and it keeps me amused.

I must admit that I didn't always feel this way. There was a point in the past when I thought that maybe I was mentally ill, and so I went and asked some Buddhists – in Lockerbie, of all places – about all this stuff going round and round in my head in such a rapid and chaotic way. And they just said, 'Enjoy it. Sit back and enjoy it. Watch it like a train going past.' So that's what I now do. And that's what I recommend that you do, too.

Sometimes I'll drift away. You mustn't worry about this. And sometimes I won't drift back. Don't worry about that, either. Just enjoy where the ride takes you. I always do. Once a guy yelled out at the end of my show: 'Billy! What happened to the guy in the toilet?' And I said: 'Right enough – I forgot about him. Tell you what, though – if you come to Manchester tomorrow night I'll finish the story there!' But the next night I got to the end of the show and I heard this desperate wee voice: 'Billy! You promised . . . what happened to the guy in the toilet?'

By the way: apart from all the stories about people and places I've known and things that I've seen and experienced and thought about, you'll also see a lot about bodily functions: pissing and shitting and vomiting and belching and farting and all of that kind of stuff; and maybe some of you will wonder why it's there. It's there because it's natural rather than fabricated, and it genuinely makes me laugh. I love the vulnerability of it. Sex, sitting on the toilet, needing to pee, trying not to fart, being sick, suffering from haemorrhoids or an itchy bum in a crowded room – when your trousers are down, you're vulnerable. When you're vulnerable you're funny.

You'll also notice that there's an awful lot of swearing in the pages that follow. I don't apologise for that. It's not 'bad language', it's ordinary language. I don't understand the snobbishness about swearing. I grew up swearing. Everybody around me swore. It's part of our culture. It can be poetic, it can be violent, and it can be very funny. It's the rhythm of how we speak, and the colour of how we communicate – at least when we're being honest and open and raw. So, if you're likely to be offended by the swearing, you may as well fuck off now.

But I hope the rest of you will enjoy reading what's here. I've been asked many times to put my stories down in a book and I've always refused. It didn't seem right because as long as I was still performing live then I was still playing around with my stories – pulling them apart, twisting them around, improvising and improving. But in December of last year I decided to retire from live stand-up. I'm not as young as I was and standing on stage for two hours or more had finally become too much.

So, this feels like the right moment to put these stories down, once and for all. I'm glad what I said up on stage is now captured on the page. You'll hear my voice in your head while you're reading. And if you miss seeing my drunk walks or wildebeest mimes – it's your turn now. Get together with your pals and try them yourselves for a laugh.

Books have always meant a great deal to me. When I was young, people used to have all kinds of advice as to how the working class could free themselves from factory life and all of that frustration, but for me the true secret tunnel, the hidden escape route, was in the library, reading books. I used to buy as many of them as I could from Oxfam when I was skint as a teenager. I even had a spell as a messenger boy for a bookshop – John Smith's in Glasgow – and in between delivering books to readers all over the city, I used to sit out the back and read a pile of them for myself. It was magical. A book, it's nice and quiet and very civilised. Yes, you can scribble a comment in the margins if you must: *'My thoughts exactly!'* but no one else will see it. It's a purely private matter.

So it's very nice to think that now you have my own book here in your hands. It's always been a pleasure talking to you. I hope now it'll be a pleasure reading me.

Billy Connolly, June 2019

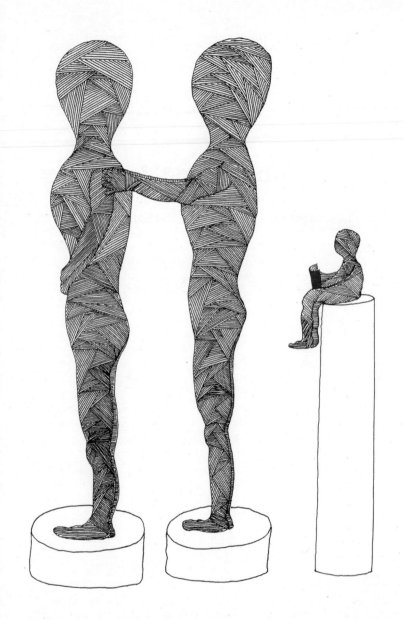

1.
Childhood & Family

'I was brought up as a Catholic. I've got A-level guilt.'

ANDERSTON, GLASGOW

Believe it or not, I usually don't enjoy performing in Glasgow very much. It's because it's my hometown, which is really difficult when you're a comedian because you can't lie in your hometown. It's essential when you're a comedian that you lie well, but when you're performing in your hometown – and especially in Glasgow where they don't hang back – they *know* when you're lying.

You know, you can say, 'Oh, there was a wee guy in my class at school and he was this and he was that . . .' and somebody in the audience will say, 'Hey! Hey! *I* was in your class and I don't fucking remember *him*.'

Do you know Tony Roper, the actor? He's a funny guy. Because Tony comes from Anderston, in Glasgow, and I was born there, he thinks I'm an Anderston guy. I left when I was four. And yet he keeps asking if I know certain people. I have to say, 'Tony – I left when I was *four*, for Christ's sake!' You don't know anybody when you're four! But he keeps doing it, because it's where he comes from.

Because nobody in Glasgow comes from Glasgow. They come from Partick and Govan and Maryhill and Anderston and the Gorbals and stuff.

I met him for lunch a while ago and we're rabbiting away about this. Anderston used to be a very, very cosy place – not anymore, it's devastated now, but when I was wee it was like a nice village, very warm. People all knew one another.

I'll give you an example. My sister Flo and I were playing in the street, and we got lost. Well, we weren't *lost* – we knew where we were – but nobody could find us. She was five and I was three. She used to look after me all the time. I was always crying. I cried for the first ten years of my life: '*Waaaah!*' 'Come on, Billy.' '*Waaaah!*' 'Come on, you're all right.' '*Waaaah!*'

Anyway, we lived on the top floor of this tenement building there. Across the road lived this family called the Cumberlands, who were nice people, I guess. There were eleven girls and a boy in their family, and the boy was the youngest. You could see what had happened. The guy – who was quite a legend in those parts – had been shagging his brains out trying to get a boy! The woman ends up like a wet chamois.

So, what happened was this. On Friday night, me and Flo were out playing in the street. It was the end of the week so Mr Cumberland came home from his work with his wages. He goes in, says to his wife, 'There you are, there's the wages, I'm away out for a pint.' But his wife says, 'Nae fuckin' danger, you going out for a pint. I've been on ma feet all day looking after the fuckin' weans, making fuckin' sausage and tatties and peas and fuckin' mince. Ah've got a child under ma arm an' Ah'm painting the door with ma fuckin' leg, an' every time Ah go to sit doon there's a fuckin' baby sittin' there, an' Ah'm feedin' the dog an' Ah'm tryin' tae knit a fuckin' pullover at the same fuckin' time. *So now you get those children in here tae bed before you go for any bloody pint!'*

So he goes, 'Okay. Okay, give me peace, give me peace!' And he staggers out the house. 'Aw, right, how many weans have Ah got? Twelve.' He goes into the street and he says: 'Right, fuckin' you, you, you, you, you . . .' He rounded up the first twelve children he came across. Two of whom were me and my sister.

And we were washed and put to bed. I was there, tucked in with all the others, looking around, going: *'Waaaah!'* My sister's going: 'We're all right, we're all right, I've been in here before.' *'Waaaah!'*

Meanwhile, my aunt, who brought us up, is going berserk. She's out with a policeman, because we were down at the docks – she thinks we're off to Shanghai in a kitbag with some fucking pervert.

The only reason they found us is that they found two Cumberlands crying in the street. 'We can't get in the house! The bed's full!' So, they took them in and that's when we *both* started going: *'WAAAAH!'*

A VISIT FROM THE PRIEST

The priest used to come around visiting the houses, you know, to see how everybody was doing. And they were always wee lonely men. They always looked cold, priests – cold-looking men, who'd come creeping about.

And people would say 'Here's a *priest* coming! Put that television off! Right, get to yer rooms, come on, *hurry*, get in yer damned rooms! The priest is coming up the bloody stairs! *Get in yer damned rooms!!*' And, you see, priests think the world is full of broken televisions. Everywhere they go, they're not working.

You see, a guy once told me, the Queen thinks the world smells like paint, because ten feet in front of her, there's always a guy going – *brush-brush-brush* . . .

I lived in the tenements, and there was a kinda *warmth* about the whole thing. I've always seen tenements as kind of vertical villages. People say, 'Oh, the *deprivation!* Oh my . . . !' Nonsense. When you're a wee boy it's not like that. It felt great, there were all these nice neighbours. And they had big wooden toilet seats then, you know – luxuries!

You didn't lose the power of your legs reading the Sunday paper. Maybe it's my age, but it seems I can't walk halfway across the room when I've been on the lavvy. *'Heeelp!'* Pins and needles, can't pick up the damn things. 'Oh my God!'

The only other time I've felt like that was in America. I'd had a drink called a 'Zombie'. Have you ever drunk Zombies? It's kind of muddy-coloured. I would advise you to do it. It's an *extraordinary* concept: you get drunk from the bottom up. You're perfectly lucid, talking away: 'Oh yeah, been there. Yeah. Have you got the time? Oh, is that British time . . . ?' You're being very terrific, jet-setting and urbane – until you need to go to the toilet and your legs are pissed. 'Excuse me, I'll just go to the toilet—' *Crash!* And you can't get up, you see.

Chic Murray once told me, he fell in the street, and a woman said to him, 'Did you fall?' He said, 'No, I'm trying to break a bar of chocolate in my back pocket.'

But a priest came to the house, and our mother said to us,

'There's a coat there, to keep you warm.' Because, you see, in a tenement, it's a bit, y'know, a bit *poor-ish*, and in the winter you throw coats on the bed, for the kids. 'Oh God, the very thought!' But it was actually brilliant, because you could *wear* them in the dark and go about playing games. 'Right – you wear the fur coat now, I'll wear this big thing . . .'

And the priest's in, having the corned beef sandwiches and the custard creams. 'Have another crumpet, Father, that's what they're there for. Come on, get it down!' 'Thank you very much, Mrs Connolly.'

But there's bedlam in the room behind. '*Will you be quiet!* Will you try to be *quiet* in there. I can hardly hear myself think in here. I'm trying to talk to Father Flanagan in here. The noise is *deafening*!'

'It's him, Mummy! It's him again. He's taken more than his fair share of the coat.'

'Ha-ha-ha, what are you talking about, "*coat*"? There's no *coat* in there. I don't know – she has a fertile imagination, Father. The coats are all in the *cloakroom.*'

Bloody 'cloakroom'. She thinks it's a dance hall she's in.

'The coats are in the *cloakroom*, and well you know it. Down on the mezzanine floor. Near the luncheonette, next to the breakfast bar. It's an *eiderdown*, you stupid girl. "Coat?" Ha-ha-ha, I don't know where they get it! She must have thought it was one of them duvet jackets. *Eiderdown!*

'What were you were saying, Father . . . ? What were you saying about God, there, Father? What was that? All right, enough. Here, have another custard cream, that's right. Oh, you don't say?'

Bedlam, bedlam, bedlam.
'Will you *STOP* that, in there? I won't tell you again.'
'It's him, Mummy, it's him again!'
'What's he doing this time?'
'He's shoving his legs through the sleeves of the *eiderdown*!'

THE WORST YEARS OF YOUR LIFE

I hated school. And I hated most of my infant and primary school teachers; I absolutely detested them. It was mainly down to their method of teaching, which revolved around beating the shit out of you and shouting a lot.

I used to sit in my seat and think, 'Oh, you wait till I leave school. I'm comin' back here an' you're getting' it. They'll never know it's me – I'll have a boiler suit on an' a bunnet!'

And those janitors. Oh, how I wanted to sort out a few of them. Animals, but cowardly with it. 'Oh, it's nothin' tae do with me, Headmaster, but I saw him playin' football an' breakin' a window. If you ask me the kid's a thug. Good for nothin' an' he'll come tae nothin'.'

I was five. There I was, all snotters and troosers that were too big for me, condemned for life according to the janny. I hated those bastards. They never seemed to grasp the fact that being a janny was hardly a great achievement, and yet they were quick to brand tiny kids as losers. God knows what that made them. As far as I remember half of them were bent anyway. A trail of Smarties into the boiler room. That sort of thing.

Moving to secondary school was quite a traumatic experience

for me, because I was shocked to discover that almost everybody there had dry noses. I couldn't believe it. Previously I'd been accustomed to this green ice rink of a place, inhabited by all different kinds of snottery people, so I guess in that one sense, secondary school was a bit of a progression. In all other ways, however, it was just as shite as the previous schools. Lots of hitting and shouting in the name of education. I hated the whole affair.

I was always particularly shit at mathematics, but I didn't care a jot. I still don't care. I don't give a shit.

One of the maths teachers had a thin leather belt that he actually named 'Pythagoras'. And he'd hit you with it if you got your sums wrong. One day, my cousin John snuck into the classroom and cut it up into tiny pieces. It didn't bother the teacher; he just brought in a new belt, wrote 'Pythagoras 2' on it and asked who wanted to try it out. Most of us tried it out and none of us were any the wiser about mathematics.

The teachers all gave up on me very quickly. They sent me outside to count the railings for an hour or two. 'Don't come back until you know how many there are!'

Algebra was a complete mystery to me. 'Connolly: a plus $1b$?' 'You're taking the piss, right, sir? You can't count letters! You can only count numbers, silly. Unless of course I was absent the day we did the B times table. One B is B, two Bees is a couple of Bees, three Bees is a couple of Bees plus the one we spoke about before . . . ?'

I'm down on record at my old school as saying, 'Why should I learn Algebra? I've no intention of ever going there.'

The whole thing was a mystery to me.

I mean, is there anything more useless, or less useful, than algebra? I have never used algebra since the day I left school. Nobody's ever asked me to use it. I've never seen anybody use it. I've never heard of anybody who once used it. And I would hate anybody who fucking *tried* to use it.

Can you imagine, going along the street, and a tourist comes up: 'Excuse me, I wonder if you could direct me to the Tower of London?' 'Certainly. Have you got a pencil? Thanks. Right: Let *x* equal the Tower . . .' 'Oh fuck it, I'll ask someone else.'

I've always worked on the principle that people who are good at mathematics and all that make good employees, and people with a bit of imagination make good employers. Because you can always employ somebody to work out the Pythagorean theorem.

THE SCHOOL OUTING

In Scotland – or in Glasgow anyway – every year, once a year, when you're a wee boy at school, they take you into the countryside for the day. It's supposed to do you a lot of good.

They put you in a bus and wheech you out there, and then you all get off the bus and they say, 'Okay, boys, pay attention! Right. See that *green* stuff over there? Grass. Okay? See the *brown* and *white* things walkin' aboot on it? Cows. Don't break them. I'll be back here in half an hour.'

The teachers all shoot off to the boozer.

So, this wee boy, he'd been away on the school outing, and he came back about five o'clock in the evening. His father was coming in from his work. 'Oh, hello, son. How d'you get on at the school trip, eh?'

'Oh, it wuz gud. Dead dead gud. Ah loved it. Dead dead gud. Great.'

'What did you do?'

'Oh, it wuz dead dead gud. We went in the bus an' we got a paper bag with an orange an' an apple an' a pork pie. An' we ate them all an' Harry Johnson vomited oot the windae, hahaha!'

'Aw, what did ye do in the *countryside*?'

'Oh, it wuz great. Ah loved it. There wuz a big field, an' there wuz all coos in it. An' they wuz eatin' the grass an' doin' jobbies. At the same time. They're very clever things, coos, y'know? An' there wuz pigs over here in another field, an' they were eatin' rubbish an' fartin' all over the place. I never liked them very much, they're smelly. An' there wuz another field over here, an' it wuz all full of chickens in the wee hooses they lived in an' everythin'. They were my very favourites, I think. An' there wuz a field just roond the corner an' that wuz full of fuckers. An' then, over here there wuz a field with horses in it, an' wee ponies an' a donkey, it wuz dead gud. An' then roond this other corner, there wuz a field an' it was all full of sheep an' tha—'

'Hey, hey, hold it, hold it. D'ye think we cud go back a couple of fields, son?'

'Okay. Where wuz it – the pigs an' that?'

'Nah, nah, nah, I think it wuz further on than that.'

'Oh, the chickens? Oh, they wuz ma very, very favourites.'

'No, I think it was actually the next field tae that.'

'Oh, the fuckers? They were awright.'

'The fuckers, you say?'

'Aye. Fuckers.'

'Well, wh-what are fuckers?'

'Well, the teachers said they were heifers but we knew what she meant!'

STUDENT TEACHERS

I was brought up as a wee Glasgow Catholic. As a consequence, I went to a really weird school: Our Lady of Perpetual Pre-Menstrual Tension. It was fucking hard going, let me tell you.

We used to just pray for student teachers to come so that we could destroy them. I'd have been about eight or nine at the time. I remember they were always big Irish guys. Big Irish priests. Poor big buggers. Marist Brothers: Brother Bartholomew, Brother Matthew and Brother the Other and Brother This and That.

They were all . . . kind of fat people. I don't know why. Big fat red guys. Big clean hands, big fat fingers.

I was always very good at that sort of 'saxophone fart' noise. You know the one? *Bmmmrrrrrrr!* Starts high, goes low and then steady: the changing tone is totally believable. The teacher would be writing on the board. *Bmmmrrrrrrrr!* He'd look around, look back, resume writing. *Bmmmrrrrrrrr!* Look around, look back, resume writing. *Bmmmrrrrrrrr!* It would be driving the poor guy insane. But the third day, he had a headband with wing mirrors on it, flipping chalk over his shoulders: 'Ow!'

And then it started again: *Bmmmrrrrrrrr!*

About a week he took of this – a week and a half, maybe – and I'll never forget the day he cracked. It was in geography. There was a map of Africa over the blackboard and he had a pointer. He was going, 'This is the Niger here. This is the Nile. Right? Are you listening here? This is the White Nile and the Blue Nile and the Niger. And now this is the Zambezi. These are the main rivers in Africa. Now, just over here—'

Bmmmrrrrrrrr!

He stood absolutely still. And then an almost imperceptible shudder started all over his body. And then the first sign of something awful happening: his neck changed colour. From that jolly cherry red, it went a kind of slatey grey colour.

'Psssst, hey, look – his fuckin' *neck's* changed colour!'

'Oh yeah, so it has, his fuckin' neck's changed colour there!'

I don't know if it was Africa that did it, but he changed his grip on the pointer and he slowly turned around. He said:

'CONNOLLY – YA *BASTAAAAAARRRD!*'

I thought, 'Fuckin' hell.'

I threw up the lid of my desk and I heard the thing clattering off it. When I brought the lid down again, I didn't know he was running behind it.

'Aaaaggh!'

BANG! SLAP!

'YA! BA! STARD! YA! IGNORANT! BA! STARD!'

There's a teacher running in from next door, and the janitor, and they pulled him off me. But he was still throwing his arms and legs about, trying to get at me: 'I'll KILL him! He's a *bastard*! A fuckin' *bastard*!'

He was *purple* now.

And the class was going: *'Ea-sy! Ea-sy! Ea-sy! Ea-sy!'*

And Mr Clarke, the teacher from next door, came in, and he said: 'He's all right, now, boys. He's in the first aid room, having a cup of tea. His brother's just driving him home.'

Nee-Naw-Nee-Naw . . .

A SWIM IN THE NORTH SEA

When we were at school, they would occasionally risk letting us out beyond the four walls and into the world, or at least somewhere near Glasgow. It was probably so that they could repair everything we'd wrecked. Sometimes, during the day, they would take us to factories and stuff, and for, you know, a wee boy, that's good, that's very interesting.

But there was a teacher there who didn't like me, because I couldn't play football. And, it's true, I'm not very good at football. And he would say, 'Come on, Connolly, ya big fucking jessie!' That's what you're called, if you can't play football.

'Come on, ya big bloody jessie! Tomorrow we are going swimming . . . in the *North Sea*.' And we did.

Now, Aberdeen has a beach, because it's got sand. But there the similarity to beaches ends. That's the *North Sea*, for Christ's sake! That's the Arctic Ocean when it's around the corner. Because the Arctic comes down and then it becomes the Atlantic and splits that way and it's the North Sea.

On the horizon there's oil rigs. 'Now hear this. All employees must wear a survival suit at all times. You wouldn't last two minutes if you fell into the North Sea. Failure to wear the survival suit will result in instant dismissal.' Forty miles away, women are taking their children's clothes off. 'In you go, ya big jessie!'

I had to get stripped. There were fish looking up in the water saying, 'There's a fucking pale *blue* guy coming in!' Standing there, skinny, muscles like knots and a midget's penis.

And my swimming costume, it was that knitted cotton stuff, with a belt and a fucking pocket, the reason for which escapes me completely. None of your Speedos' 'second skin'. This was more your second cardigan. A big woolly number, you know? If you were stupid enough to go in above your waist, they grew. It was *absorbent,* it could drag you to the bottom. You had to grab armfuls, when you were coming out, the crotch was away down here. People could look in and see your willy – if you *had* one, but, in the North Sea, you *don't.*

I read a piece on sumo wrestlers in one of those in-flight magazines. Cliff Michelmore – an old broadcaster, authority on everything – had written it. Apparently, sumo wrestlers have such exquisite control of their bodies, they can withdraw their testicles at will. *Wheech!* So you aim a hefty boot, and they go – *Wheech!* 'Is that the best you can do?'

I could do it when I was twelve. One foot in and I see the whole fucking lot disappear! An ugly gaping wound. Whole thing shot up to my lungs. I had to get it out with a chimney sweep's brush.

This is why Scottish guys don't look sexy on the beach; it's all flopping around here. You go to the Mediterranean or Caribbean and people are wandering around with a *huge* thing – like a baby's arm hanging out of the pram. There's your warm water, lap, lap, lap.

'Connolly – in the water!'

'I'm going, I'm going!'

'Come *on*, you big bloody jessie, get in there!'

I ran down and put my foot in, and my heart stopped. I'd never felt cold like that before, and I heard this weird noise: '*Whoooaaaahooo! Whooooouuuuuaaaaiiii!*'

What the fucking hell was *that*?

It was *ME*!

You know the way, when you get a fright? You know, if you go through a dark room and an icy hand touches you, the inside of your leg or something? You don't go, 'Oh, what, my goodness! Oh, what was that? Oh gosh!' Nah. You go: '*Whooooouuuuuaaaahhhh!*'

It's something you're not in control of. '*Whoooaaaahhhhh!*' You can hear it. Normally you can't hear yourself, you kind of feel it, but that you can hear like it's some other bugger. '*Whooahhhh!*'

It's something deeply primal. Something from when we lived up trees. It's stamped on your DNA or something. '*Whooooouuuuuaaaahhhh!*'

It's closely related to the '*Blueyooouuuuuhhh-ooo-uuuuooooooohhh!*' Do you know, the noise you get when you shove a freshly boiled potato up a donkey's arse? It's *exactly* the same noise. '*Whooo-ahhh-oooohhhh!*'

So, the other guys are saying, 'Go in further, ya big fucking jessie!'

'*Oooouuuaaaaahhhaaaaooo!*'

And I wandered in, up to my knees. And I lost the will to live.

'Billy!'

'Uhaaaooah?'

'Look over there.'

'Uhhuuoopp?'

'Look over there!'

'Uhhhoaappp? Oooooohhhhh!'

There was a guy in a speedboat, a bastard.

'Brrrrrrrrrrrrrrrrrrrr!'

'Uhhoooooooop!!'

Waving – 'Uuhooooooooohh!!'

Coming towards me. I didn't want to run, in case I fell in. 'Uuaahuuhooohh!' The wave from it inexorably slid in my direction.

I hoped it would go away.

It got bigger.

'Uuaaaoooohh!'

I will never forget that wave going up the inside of my thighs.

'Uuhoooaaaaaahh!'

And it kissed the underside of my scrotum.

'Aaaaaaaaaaaaaaaarrrggghhh!!!'

A VISIT FROM THE CARDINAL

I'm going to tell you a story. The scene is a Roman Catholic primary school in Glasgow.

The teacher is standing in front of the class, who are all

about seven and eight years of age. She says: 'Right, children. Today is a very, very important day in the history of this school, isn't it?'

'Yes, Miss!'

'John, why is it an important day?'

'Please, Miss, a Cardinal's comin' to see us all the way from Rome!'

'That's right. Sit doon, John. Jeannie, what's so special about this Cardinal?'

'Miss, he used to be a pupil at this school when he was a wee boy!'

'That's right. This Cardinal was a pupil at this very school – and in this very class – when he was a little boy. And he's coming all the way from Rome, with the Pope's permission, to see us. And it's a very important day in the history of the school, and I want you to be on your best behaviour. There's only one thing I want you to remember: how to address a Cardinal. We call him "Your Eminence". We don't call him "Father", like a priest, or "Your Grace", like a Bishop. It's "Your Eminence". What do we call him?'

'YOUR EMINENCE, MISS!'

'Yes, that's right. Now, it won't be long till he's here. And I must say your parents have turned you out beautifully. You're a credit to them.'

Then the magic moment arrives. The door opens. And he swishes into the room. He's got on the vestments, the hat, the whole number.

'Morning, children.'

'MORNIN', YOUR EMINENCE!'

And he hoovers across to the desk. 'Oh, it's a great privilege having you here, Your Eminence, it really is a great day in the history of this school, thank you.' 'Oh, that's fine, that's fine. Do you mind if I speak to the children?' 'Oh, carry on, Your Eminence.'

So, he wanders away over, and he says to the first wee boy: 'Hello, son.' 'Hello, Your Eminence.' 'And what are you going to do when you're a big boy?' 'Ah think Ah'd like to be an engineer, Your Eminence.' 'Oh, did you hear that, boys and girls?'

'YES, YOUR EMINENCE!'

'The boy wants to be an *engineer* – that's *good*, isn't it?'

'YES, YOUR EMINENCE!'

'Because engineers look after the world that God gave us. They drill for oil, they get energy from moving water, they build bridges – they're very *clever* men! Well *done*, son, sit down.'

'Hello.' 'Hello, Your Eminence.' 'What's *your* name?' 'Peter McGuire, Your Eminence.' 'And what do *you* want to do when you're a big boy, Peter?' 'I think I'd like to be a plumber, Your Eminence.' 'A *plumber* indeed! Why do you want to be a plumber?' ''Cause my daddy's a plumber, Your Eminence.' 'Did you hear *that*, boys and girls?'

'YES, YOUR EMINENCE!'

'He wants to follow in his father's footsteps. Does that remind you of anybody?'

'. . . No, Your Eminence?'

'What about *Jesus*?'

'OH *YES*, YOUR EMINENCE! FORGOT, YOUR EMINENCE!'

'Well, *don't* forget it *again*, will you? He's *nailed* tae the wall tae remind you, for Christ's sake.'

Meanwhile, there's a wee boy at the front. The teacher whispers: 'Connolly, what are you doin'?'

'Ah'm, er, lookin' fer ma dinner money.'

'You're a *liar* – get your hand out of your pocket before you hurt yourself, you *stupid* boy! *And stop picking your nose!*'

'Aw, okay.'

And of all the people to pick on, the Cardinal picks on him. 'Hello, son.' 'Hi.' 'And what are *you* going to do when you're a big boy?' 'Ah, *fuck off*!'

Well! The mayhem and madness that follows could not be described! Sporadic fighting broke out in the back row. '*Ah, come on!*' '*Ooof!*' '*Agghh!*' Chairs were going through the window. The teacher fainted – big blue knickers up in the air: '*Whuuuupppp!*'

'WHAT DID YOU SAY TO ME?'

'I said "fuck off" – are ya deaf as well as daft?'

Well, people were throwin' each other back to get out the door.

'YOU SCOUNDREL! YOU HORRID, *HORRID* BOY! *I* used to be a pupil at this school. *I* sat at that self-same desk. But *I* didn't sit there interfering with myself and being rude to the guests. *No!* I worked extremely *hard.* And I won a scholarship to a *posh* school, where I worked even *harder* and went to *college* and became a *priest.* Five years later I was a *parish* priest. But did I rest on my laurels? *No such thing!* I *haunted* the libraries of this land, reading *everything* I could get my hands on, and writing in the margins: "My thoughts *exactly*, how *true.*" They made me a *Canon*! They made me a *Monseigneur*! I went to *Paris* to study. I was there for *five years.* I became a *Bishop*! Ten years later I was an *Archbishop*! They sent for me from *Rome*! I went to the *Vatican* to study at the feet of the *Holy Father*! They made me a *Cardinal*! I was on the jury who elected the last POPE! And you're telling *me* to fuck off? *YOU FUCK OFF!*

MUSIC LESSONS

As I've already mentioned, I hated school and I particularly hated music lessons. I think that would later become all too apparent in my playing. But I really hated my music teacher. She was bloody terrible. She was a psychopath.

She was totally addicted to the song 'Marie's Wedding'. Every single music lesson would be dominated by 'Marie's Wedding'. You'd be sitting there, with big holes in your jumper, and your wellies on, your nose stuffed up with snot, singing, 'Step we gaily on we go.' Every damned time.

She believed in all the modern teaching methods: like grabbing you by the back of the neck and smashing your nose into your desk, that sort of thing. And you had to sing all the time. 'Come *on*, Connolly!' she'd scream. 'Sing "Step we gaily on we go"! SING IT!' It was terrifying.

But she had a special trick, a special technique: she used to divide the class into four sections, and each one sang 'Marie's Wedding' at different times. She was really pleased with herself for devising that little idea. So, we rehearsed like that for about a year. And then came the big day: 'Marie's Wedding' for the school concert.

And it started with the row who sat at the window – that was all the Brylcreem crowd, with the clean shirts, all neatly pressed, and badges on their blazers; they were always top of the class or thereabouts. And that was the easiest bit of the song. 'Step we gaily on we go' – nae one else to worry about, nae problem.

Then the second row, they were also quite clever, they were usually fourth or fifth in the class, somewhere around there, up to tenth in the class, they were quite smart but also a wee bit scruffy. Still no challenge in the song.

I was in the third row. That was the 'stupid but saveable' row.

But the fourth row, they were just a joke. They were already singing something else when the song started. They were the serious rejects. They didn't get lessons or anything. They would've beaten the teachers up if they'd tried to teach them anything. So, they were left alone to sit there and squeeze each other's boils.

Wullie the Boilsucker sat in that row. Oh, what a character he was. He was born when he was twenty-two, this guy. He'd sit there muttering, 'Anyone want tae see ma willy?' The place would be in uproar, with teachers jumping out of windows to get away from him. Even the pigeons were afraid of this guy.

Anyway, the music teacher, she'd go, 'Right, class!' And the first row would be off: 'Step we gaily on we go . . .' And the second row would be waiting to come in, and they usually got it right, because it's easy enough when you're coming in second. So, on it went: 'All for Marie's wedding . . .'

But by the time it came to our turn, somebody had just

spoken to me, and I'd forgotten who started the song. We were looking up and down the line, starting and stopping and starting and stopping, and by this stage the fourth row had come in, singing a completely different song: 'You can throw a silver dollar . . .'

It was a disaster, an utter disaster, and there were generous beatings all round, which really encouraged us all.

But in the usual music lessons, in every other one, we got a thing called 'Musical Appreciation'. And that meant this teacher played 'Marie's Wedding' on the piano, and you didn't need to sing – just listen. That made it even harder to appreciate.

She'd build up to it. She'd play several other tunes, leading up to the climax: 'Marie's Wedding'. Always 'Marie's Wedding'. And on the one just before 'Marie's Wedding', which was always 'Soldier's Joy', she'd lean over the piano and make sure that everybody was appreciating. 'Connolly!' she'd shout. '*Appreciate!*' I mean, what were you supposed to do?

She was a fat woman. Big-bosomed. And when she leaned over to check on you, she used to make mistakes, because half of her body was playing the tune. That's the only time I appreciated anything that she did.

Ah, school days. Thank God they're over!

CAMPING

Going camping is a very healthy pastime. And it teaches you all sorts of useful things, like how to light fires with bits of wood and stuff like that, so you can go off and live in wee tents, get wet and light more wee fires. It's great for building the character.

So, when we were young, we used to go camping, myself and four other scruffs. We used to go camping in Partick – which is a quaint fishing village on the Clyde – and there was a guy called Shug Gilchrist who led the party off on the bus. When I say he led the 'party' – today it would be called a gang, but back then it was just a bunch of blokes who'd all get the Red Bus to Loch Lomondside.

Shug was known to be a very practical man. For example: Shug was one of those people who used to drink in this Glasgow pub called the Saracen Head in Gallowgate – otherwise known as the Sarry Heid or just 'Sarry'. The barman there was this huge guy called Angus, who'd pass pints over the heads of everybody who was standing at the bar, thus spilling beer and cider all over them and drenching their clothes. Well, most people just muttered and moaned and put up with this, but Shug came up with a novel solution: he started coming in with a pacamac, a plastic raincoat that folded up into an envelope, and he'd put it on and button it right up to his neck, so that he could stand at the bar and drink away without getting his clothes drenched by Angus. That was why we tended to regard Shug as a natural leader.

We didn't go camping in the normal way of things, with the anoraks and the wee woolly hats and the heavy boots and that. It was more your plastic mac and a bottle of wine and a good suit with the winkle-pickers. We all used to wear winkle-pickers then. That was the style. And when it rained, they used to turn up at the front. We looked like extras for

Kismet. But we'd all get on the bus and sit at the back, drinking this terrible cheap wine called Fiesta – a horrible wine that made your teeth pink – and generally make a complete mess of ourselves.

We'd also sing songs. Shug Gilchrist used to lead off the singing, too, but he didn't know the words to any of the songs. He liked country and western music, and so he'd sing in that style: 'Oooh-appa-leechee-ee-ow-ow . . .' He just made noises that sounded vaguely like words. And we'd all join in: 'Oo-acheee-ow-ah-gan-deeda . . .' And everybody else on the bus is going: 'Aw, give us a break, man. That's horrible, that is, it's hurting ma ears!' And thanks to the terrible Fiesta wine, we're all peeing out the windows intermittently, much to the consternation of passing motorcyclists: 'Ah, get a grip, that's terrible that!'

The real campers sat in the front seats of the bus. They wore anoraks and wee bobbly hats. They all sat together in a row, these hand-knitted campers, with their rucksacks full of mince and wee packets of boil-it-yourself potato stuff. And they'd all sing as well, but proper old camping songs, and all their wee bobble-hatted heads would be nodding in unison.

So, we'd eventually get to Balloch, and the knitted people would get out first. 'La-la-la-la-la-diddy-da!' Those of us at the back were having difficulties just standing up. But they always disappointed me when they walked away, the proper campers, because they walked ordinary. I'd hoped they'd walk like wee puppets, with their woolly hats, but they just walked off like anybody else.

And then we'd get off the bus. We'd come staggering down

the steps: 'Aha! Here we are, eh? Ah told yuz, didnae Ah? Nae bother, eh? Nae bother at all! Magic, eh? Aye, magic. Er, where are we?' And Shug would say, 'We're in Balloch, y'know? Balloch, Loch Lomond and all that!' So someone else would say, 'Where do we do the campin' bit and all that?' 'I dunno,' Shug would say, and he'd point at the knitted people and say, 'Ask them.'

We'd start shouting over to the proper campers: 'Hey, Jimmy! Hey! Hey! Hey, *you*, Jimmy!' They'd turn around and see us and say, 'Ooh no, it's those bad boys – run!' We'd be shouting, 'Wait a minute!' But they were already off – *shoom!*

It wasn't long before we're shuffling around in the dark, shouting out: 'Hullo? Hul-lo-o?' We'd be staggering through fields and all that, getting bitten by midges.

And eventually, more by luck than judgement, we'd come to the Luss Hotel. Oh, the Luss Hotel is a lovely spot. There's a campsite across the road from it. There's these guys there with Australian Bush hats and the machetes and the bando-liers for the bullets and all that, wandering about, and they camp in dormobiles – it's very strange.

We used to go into the hotel and we'd finish the wine standing around in the toilet. For years I thought that was the lounge. Then we'd go up to the public bar and get a pint of heavy. We'd drink that and fall straight down on the floor, crawling around out of our minds with all the drink. The barman would be looking over the counter, bewildered, wondering what had happened to the water he'd put in the beer.

I remember outside the hotel, Shug was standing in the middle of the road, and the rain was pouring down, and he was singing one of his plaintive airs: 'Oooh-sanaweech-o-avaah . . . onacappy-wee-a-chay . . .' And the four of us were lying on the grass verge – *thinking* that we were standing beside him, singing: 'Ony-toddy-a-oo-ooh . . . bada-biddy-be-ay . . .'

Shug is standing there in his plastic mac and a bunnet, which he always wore because he had something wrong with his jaw, and it stuck out – his bottom teeth were in front of his top teeth, his bottom lip was like a wash-hand basin. If he didn't wear the bunnet when it was raining, he would have drowned. If you happened to speak to him when he'd forgotten his bunnet he sounded like a whale.

We were all singing – 'Ah-ba-cheera-we-al-all' – when a big farmer came along the road. *Clump-clump-clump.* He'd got the big sensible shoes on, like the ones your mother got you for the school dance. My mother used to take me to the Co-operative shop and force them on my feet, and as these women were jamming them on and breaking my toes they'd be saying to my mother approvingly, 'smart but casual'. But this big farmer, he had the sensible shoes and the big tweed suit on – big jaggy tweed that would ruin a lesser mortal in about a week – and a wee dumplin' hat, knee-length troosers and big woolly socks, with a dent in the backs of his legs where his dog walks. And he had one of those big round farmer faces.

So, he goes up to Shug and says: 'Hal-looooo!' Nearly blew his bunnet off. Shug says, 'Eh, w-wait a minute there, pal.' The farmer says, 'This is ma ground here!' Shug goes: 'Ah, well, Ah don't know much about that. Any risk of we campin' in your ground, eh? No, this grey ground – that's a road. I wanna bit of green ground, ye ken?' And the farmer goes: 'Ah, that's all right, son, on you go.' So, Shug goes, 'Aw, thanks very much!' Then he collapsed alongside the rest of us on the verge.

That was the kind of camping we used to do. And it's true what they say. It really was very character-forming.

CHILDREN

I think children are remarkable, and I do have a very deep and real love for them. I could watch them for hours and hours. They're brilliant wee things.

And they're awful clever, because they can pee and shit and fart, cough, hiccup, laugh, cry and burp. All at the same time. They sort of explode. Boom! You're just about to phone for an ambulance and then you hear them laughing. Fuck!

They're extraordinary, aren't they?

Ours sleep in bed with us, because I was reading a book about China and it said there were no incidents at all of cot death in China. Because there are no cots in China. So, we thought, let's try it for a wee while, having them sleep with us. And it's great, with their wee warm bodies asleep there. Except they have no sense of direction. There's something wrong with their compass. They can't point the same way as everybody else. They have to sleep *across* the bed. They take it in turns: 'Right, you go over there, I'll spread out over here.' So if you're looking for a wee cuddle in the middle of the night, these fuckers are in the middle.

And being the ageing hippy, I said to Pamela, my wife:

'Look, it's obviously the window, the light from it or something, that's making them sleep like that. They're pointing at
the window. Let's *all* lie that way tonight.' So, I changed all
the bed around.

I'm like that. Before this, I pointed it north. I read a thing
about James Galway, the flute player, where he said he pointed
his bed due north, so I thought, 'Right!' I got my compass
out, started moving the bed. Didn't make a bit of difference.
I still cannae play the flute.

But I moved the bed again, and we're all lying in the direction of the window. And the babies just turned around in the
direction we'd been trying to get them to sleep for ages.
Bastards!

I'll tell you a thing you must never do if you're pregnant.
Or if you're going to be pregnant. Or if you're going to have
a little baby round to stay for a while, or whatever. If there's
going to be a baby in your life.

Don't buy one of those intercoms at Mothercare that lets
you hear the baby in the next room. Because the babies
pretend to be dead. They do! They are bastards and they do
it on purpose. And they start very, very, young. God knows
who tells them, but they fucking do it.

We had one of those intercoms. Ours was in the bin *years*
ago. We used to sit in the living room, reading a book or
whatever, and you could hear the wee speakers on the wall,
you could hear the babies breathing contentedly. 'Ah . . . hah-
hah . . . hah . . .' And you'd look at the wife, point at the
speakers and smile at how cute it sounded. 'Hah . . . uh . . .
hah . . . hah-hah . . .' And then suddenly the sound would

stop. You'd be reading away and then pause, look up, and listen: nothing. Not a sound.

And you'd say, 'Er, when did you change the batteries on that thing?' 'An hour ago.' '. . . Aaaghh!' And as soon as your arse is off the chair: 'Ah . . . Hic. Hah-hah . . .' '*Bastard!* STOP it!!'

BESIDE THE SEASIDE

I was walking along – not the seaside, like the sand and all that – the road that's next to the seaside. The 'plaza', or the fucking 'esplanade', or 'promenade' . . . thing. Because I hate sand. I'd go miles and miles to avoid sand.

If I *liked* lying in sand, I would go on holiday to the fucking M25 and lie around there, or some building site. I *hate* sand. It just fucking sticks to me and makes me uncomfortable. I've got very fair skin, you know, that kinda pale blue skin. It doesn't suit the sun, and it doesn't suit the sand.

My wife can *lie* on sand, she can just lie down and relax. She can pull on Shetland wool sweaters straight on to her skin. *Eaauuugghh!* I have to leave the room! I can't do that.

And I've never understood oil and sand together. When you're lying down, you look like a fucking doughnut! And you can't get it off.

On the fancy beaches – you know, like Barbados, St Tropez and all that – they've got the showers, usually stuck to a tree: *Ssshhhhhhhhhhhhhhh.* And that gets the sand off your shoulders and that, your chest, your back. But that's not where you're really worried about.

You can't get it off the uncomfortable bit. Because there's children nearby. And they've all been taught about perverts.

'*Daddy!* There's a man *masturbating* over there!'

'Where is the dirty bastard – I'll fuckin' sort him right out!'

'PUT THE CANDY DOWN AND MOVE AWAY FROM THE CHILD!'

You can't wash down there. So, you have to walk home with sand in your crotch. And it sandpapers your scrotum all the way home. *Scrrrr-scrrr-scrrr-scrrr-scrrr.* Your willy's like a lobster with its throat cut.

I've loathed the seaside since I was a wee boy. We used to go on holiday to the River Clyde. It flows through Glasgow down to the coast. And, you know, for working-class people, it was the second fortnight in July, Glasgow Fair. And it was freezing and raining all the time.

If you know anyone from Glasgow, ask them if you can see their holiday photographs from their childhood and you'll see these people in raincoats, on the beach. They're the only people I know who did that – raincoats on the beach! Raincoats on the beach: sou'wester, wellies and a bucket and spade, the rain pissing down.

And your father would make you do 'beachy' things, rain or no. '*Dig a hole!*' 'Why?' 'JUST DIG A HOLE OR I'LL TAKE MA HAND TAE YOU!' 'Oh, fer fuck's sake!' And you'd pour water into it and it goes away. 'It just went away, Dad!' 'POUR MORE IN!' 'Okay . . .' 'MAKE A *DAM* – BE A *REAL* BOY! MAKE A DAM, AND MAKE A BIG *PUDDLE!*' 'Why?' 'DON'T ASK ME WHY OR I'LL *HIT* YA ONE!' It was misery and I loathed it.

And then I grew up, and I got away from the beach.

But then I would fall in love from time to time, and they'd want to go to the beach. And I would make excuses not to go.

But then I got married and had children. And down to the fuckin' beach we went. Making sandcastles and big boys would run over them – 'Fuck off!' – water and tunnels and flags and shit. And they got to about twelve or thirteen, and they didn't want to go there anymore. Fucking brilliant! We left the beach.

Then I got divorced. Married Pamela. Three girls. Back to the fucking beach we went. More sandcastles. Big puddles. 'Where does the water go, Dad?' 'Oh, I dunno, keep pouring it, it'll be fine.' More sandcastles, big boys running over them – 'Fuck off!!' – more puddles, *dig-dig-dig*.

So now Scarlett, my youngest daughter, gets to thirteen, and she doesn't want to go to the beach anymore. Certainly not with me. 'Fucking YES! We've left the beach!'

But my oldest daughter has had a baby. Fucking back we go! 'Grandad'll take you to the beach!' *Dig-dig-dig* . . .

I'm condemned to live on the beach for the rest of my life!

MY GRANDFATHER

You would have loved my grandfather. He was the grumpiest man alive.

A very straight-backed sort of guy, a former soldier. Even

when he was very old he'd still stride about as though he was going on parade.

I used to go out and see him on my motorcycle over at Eastwood, in Glasgow, where he lived, and he would always give me a big welcome: 'Hallo, son!' And then, before I knew where I was, I'd find myself back out on the pavement again. He'd flung me out. The shortest meeting of all so far was seven minutes.

He was ninety-six and he just couldn't be bothered. He lived alone. He didn't like visitors. He didn't like me particularly. He didn't like anybody particularly. He was just bored with everybody, and he didn't want anybody in his house. So seven minutes was the record.

I introduced him to Pamela. I'd just met her and I took her over there. I said, 'You'll love him.' I said, 'Now, look: check your watch before you go in.' 'Why?' 'Just check it and see. Seven minutes is the record.' 'What do you mean?' 'Just see.'

So we go in, and he was very nice. 'Hallo, son! And this must be the lovely Pamela! Hallo, darlin', how're you doin', come away, you must have a cup of tea – sit on the couch there, I'll get the teas away in the kitchen.'

There was a lot of banging and crashing going on in the kitchen. And he's shouting and bawling. *'Who left this here??'* He lived alone. And in no time at all he appears again – no teapot, no tray, no cups, no biscuits.

He comes over to me and he says, 'Well, I'm sure you're a very busy man . . .' And we're back on the fucking street!

I said to Pam, 'Quick, look!' 'Five and a half minutes.' 'Yes! We broke the record!'

He had scurvy. He was the only British person to have scurvy in the twentieth century.

He was in this hospital called the Southern General in Glasgow, and I went to see him. And I'd got him this big tartan dressing gown. Although he was a McLean, it was a Royal Stewart dressing gown. I couldn't resist it, it was in a sale. Big gaudy thing. He was like the King of Scotland sitting there.

And I said, 'How are you doin', Grandad?' He said, 'Ah, I don't like it in here – there's a lot of *old* people in here.' He's ninety-six!

Then he said to me, 'How long did it take you to drive here?' I said, 'About fifteen minutes.' He said, 'Well, you'd better set oot before it's dark . . .'

UNCLE FREDDIE

My Uncle Freddie, he was a very lucky chap. He was awfully lucky. He was always winning things.

Until he went to the First World War. He didn't do too well there.

As he was leaving to go to the war, and was bidding farewell to his mother, he said, 'Well, cheerio, then, Mammy,' and his mother said, 'Well, cheerio, son.'

They were people of very few words.

He said, 'Yes, cheerio, right enough, Mammy.' She said, 'Aye, you're right there, son.'

But then she said, 'Oh, hold on a wee minute – I nearly

forgot.' And she went into her drawer and brought out a wee package. And she said, 'Son, it has come to my notice that some of the lads who are going to fight on foreign fields are not returning. As a matter of fact, vast amounts are copping their whack daily. So, I would like for you to take this wee prezzie. It is your father's watch.'

And she gave him his father's watch, which he put in the top pocket of his waistcoat, which he always wore under his army shirt, because it was made of jaggy material and gave him plukes.

So, he took the watch and put it in the top pocket above his heart. And he said, 'Well, cheerio, Mam.' And away he went to the war.

And they were all fighting one day in France. The British and the Germans were tearing lumps off each other and shooting away. They'd been playing football against each other a couple of days before, but this day they were shooting. They were playing a game called 'Cop Yer Whack'. And several cops were being whacked, I can assure you.

And there was this sniper, a German sniper, up a tree. And he saw my Uncle Freddie getting a third light for his cigarette. And he says to his mate, 'Ha-ha, Franz, here's a cracker here!' His mate says, 'Oh, you go on, Hans, you have a go at him.'

Bang!

And the bullet went *juuussshhh – thump!*

Hit him right in the chest. And it would have gone right through his heart, but it didn't.

It hit his father's watch. Skited off, shot up his left nostril, and blew the top of his head off.

COUSIN JOHN

I remember when I toured in France, hitchhiking, with my cousin John. You would have loved my cousin John. He was lovely. He's dead now. You wouldn't like him now. But you would have loved him then.

He was one of those guys that people liked to call a loony, you know? He was a bit of a nutter. But I'm always suspicious when people do that: 'Oh, you'll *love* him, he's a *loony*!' You go: 'Oh, fuck.' But he was a great guy – very bright, very funny.

I'll give you an example. He could be quite frightening. Do you remember – most of you will be too young – there was a campaign in petrol stations: 'Put a tiger in your tank'? Well, just after that, there were other campaigns: 'Make your car look like a racing car.' There were numbers and things you stuck on. And one that never quite took off was: Bullet Holes. You peeled them off a card and stuck them on your car. You looked like you'd just driven past Al Capone, you know?

John had them. On his glasses.

He used to quite frighten people. 'This is my cousin John.' 'Oh, Jesus Christ!' But he was a lovely guy.

He taught me so much. Useless stuff. Like, he taught me how to slice up a banana inside the skin. I've had endless fun with that.

We were living in a youth hostel in Dunkirk in France and when you had food you'd keep it in these cubicles in the kitchen that were open to everybody. You could just steal stuff. We'd steal a banana and he'd get a sewing needle. And he would hold the banana as vertically as you can hold a banana, and he'd come down an inch and push the needle in and – *swish-swish-swish* – across, horizontally, and then he'd pull it out, then down half an inch and he'd do it again, then down half an inch and do it again, until you got to the bottom. Then you put it back where you got it.

And you'd wait for the owner to show up. Which he eventually did. And as soon as he'd lift the banana and went to peel it you'd turn away, and he'd do that: *plun-plun-plun-plun-plun!* 'Fuck's sake!' And you'd say, 'What is it?' 'The banana was sliced inside its skin!!' And he spends the rest of his life trying to prove it to you.

Another thing John used to do, which I found great: he would steal an egg and he'd get the same needle, or one very like it, and he'd put a hole in the top of the egg. And a hole in the bum. Then he would blow the egg into a frying pan. *Phhhhhhhhhh.* Then he would get a sheet of toilet paper – you know that hard stuff that hurts your arse? – and he would write on it, 'Sorry, I was starving!' Then he'd roll it up real tight, shove it inside the egg, and put it back where he got it.

But maybe my favourite . . . For some reason he had a dislike of people who went to bed with their socks on. And you know in these hostels you sleep in dormitories? Well, we would lie there waiting, watching people going to bed, and eventually he would see somebody and go, 'Billy, nine o'clock, blue socks . . .' 'Right, okay.' We'd wait until the guy was sleeping, we'd creep up and roll the sheets back from his feet, to expose the socks, take one sock off, and put it on top of the other one.

You'd see the guy in the morning, looking for his sock. 'What the fu—? Has anybody seen a blue sock?' Eventually he puts on his hiking boots with one bare foot and one not. And he hobbled off.

I've always wondered how he got on when he got home and was undressing. 'Jesus Christ! How did that get on there?'

John was great. He was a funny man.

He had a French phrasebook that he'd got from his father, who fought in France during the war. You never saw women like it, the bewildered expressions, when he whispered in their ear, 'We have reason to believe there are Germans hiding in your cellar.'

AUNTIE AGNES, UNCLE HARRY
AND OTHER RELATIONS

My eyes have a tendency to do something strange sometimes. They dart to the left and stay there for a long time. My eyes would have been normal but for what happened when I was young: my Auntie Agnes knitted me a balaclava.

My Auntie Agnes was always knitting. She was a big fat woman, married to my Uncle Harry, who was a thin, demented creature. He'd been in a Japanese prisoner of war camp and he was never the same again. He was drunk his whole life, he wore shiny suits and ties with racy pictures of women on them. A strange demented man, very thin, with oily hair.

I was always getting a slap on the head because he would steal bread off our table when we were having dinner and shove it under his shirt or in his pockets. It was a legacy of his prisoner of war days. And that would baffle me. I'd do a double take and then say, 'Uncle Harry's stealing bread.' *Slap!* 'Quiet!' 'But-but he *did!* He stole the bread and put it up his jersey!' *Slap!* 'Quiet!'

He was the nicest man you ever met. Well, *you* never met him, but he was the nicest man you never met. He was such a sweet person. Always drunk out of his brain. He was obviously in terrible pain and was basically thought of as a nutcase. He needed psychiatric help, but he was working-class so they'd just say, 'Ah, he's a fucking headcase, he's daft, leave him alone.' If you're a toff you get the proper psychiatric help. If you're an officer: 'Oh, yes, instant psychiatric help for *you*! Him, he's just fucking *daft*, leave him alone!'

And we never had many parties in our house. We had a few – two or three – but we weren't really a party kind of family, we were a bit solemn. But we had a lot of uncles and aunties, and when we *did* have parties they'd sing. They'd close their eyes and sing in this weird way: '*Ahhh, edeyfuhhhh.*' You know those songs with no words? '*Oooh, eddyfuuuhhh, wheniddallll enskinydehoo.*' And they'd only open their eyes to point at you: '*Anyfuhhh*'– open eyes, point, smile, close eyes again – '*Faaahhdeeeaaaayyy.*'

And I used to love watching them. They were a brilliant race of people. Uncle Bobby, he would sing 'Here in My Heart' and it would take about a fortnight! '*Heeeerrrreeeeeeinmahaa aaaah . . . Ahmsoooooloooooooooneleeeeeeeeee . . .*' There were people sleeping in corners. Some would be going out shopping and coming back. '*Saaaaaayyyythaaaatyeeeeeewcurrrrrrrr . . .*'

And my auntie, my Irish auntie, she would sing like someone playing a saw. But Harry was brilliant, he knew lots of really dirty songs and nobody ever pulled him up for it because they couldn't recognise any of the words, he was always so pissed.

'Hey, Harry, give us a song.'

'*Ohhhh, whatshegotunderthemuftywaftyshupandgivehera-tum . . .*'

And all my wee aunties are smiling and nodding and going: 'La-la-la-la-la!'

Uncle Harry. The best guy.

You would have loved Uncle Harry. I thought he'd joined some kind of secret society when I was a wee boy. He never spoke to me in English once. He just spoke to me in a series of grunts and farts and clicks and secret signs. You'd open the door and go, 'Oh, it's Uncle Harry!' And he'd be winking, tapping his nose and pointing at you: 'Ah-ha, spt, sshhh, tic-tic.' I thought I was privy to something really special.

My Auntie Agnes was a nice woman, but there was a peculiar smell coming from her. She emanated this odour. It was my sister who noticed it first. She said, 'There's a funny smell off Auntie Agnes.' So naturally I gave her a good smelling when she wasn't looking, and sure enough there was a very peculiar smell coming from her. But you couldn't pinpoint what it was. I've only ever smelt the same smell once, and it was drifting out of a doorway in Hong Kong. I was going to go in and see what it was but it was dark, I was kind of scared actually.

She would come to our house on Sunday nights, her and

Harry, every Sunday like clockwork. And she would eat all of our expensive biscuits – you know, the ones with the silver paper on them – so on Sunday afternoon my father would put me and my sister to work, wrapping McVitie's Digestives in Bacofoil, to act as decoys and slow the process down a bit. But she wasn't fooled for a second: 'That's a fucking McVitie's Digestive!' She'd throw them away and we were in danger of being beheaded by these fucking oatmeal Frisbees flying at you.

But after all that was finished, we'd be sent to bed, my sister and me – I'd got a brother, Michael, too, by then, but he was still only a baby and was lost in his baby things – and once we were in bed you could hear them all laughing, all the adults, next door. And you wished you were in there with them.

The women would knit and talk, and the men would drink and smoke and talk, and if there was a bit of gossip the knitting suddenly got really fast: 'What? A *sailor*? The di-rty bitch!' – *click-click-click!* – 'Him not ten minutes dead and she's going about with a sailor? Well, Jesus Christ!' The needles are melting with all the activity.

They had the knitting patterns balanced on their knees as they went: *click-click-click*, 'K2Tog, P&P.' K2Tog is 'knit two together', P is 'plain and purl'. I can speak fluent Knit, because I went out with a girl who liked to knit, and I pretended to look interested in a vain attempt to get her knickers off.

But these relations of mine, they'd all be knitting and talking:

'What are you knitting, Elizabeth?'

'I'm knitting a wee bedjacket for Alex's new wee girl.'

'Oh, that's lovely – what's her name?'

'Isobel.'

'Oh, that's terrific. I love the shoulder.'

'It's a raglan, I'll show you how to do it. And what are *you* doing?'

'Oh, I'm knitting wee booties for Alec's wee boy.'

'Ah, that's nice.'

And Agnes would be there. She had this great hairy string she was knitting with. This brown thing slowly emerging. No pattern. 'What are you knitting, Agnes?' 'Dunno yet.'

She would knit things for me. But she always used this jaggedy-arse wool that would drive you insane with the itchiness of it. If she made you a pullover you had to wear your jacket underneath it, otherwise it would rip the skin off your chest. And she just made it any old way – the collar was where your shoulder should be. People at school would think you were deformed.

She's the one who knitted my gloves. The joined-up gloves. And because I was in bed at the time, she knitted them to fit my jacket. And they fitted perfectly – but just not with me in it! I'd get up in the morning and be told:

'Wear them! Your Auntie Agnes knitted them for you!'

And I'd say, 'But they're too wee – look!'

'She *made* them for you, you ungrateful wretch!'

'I look stupid!'

'You *always* look stupid!'

'Thanks *very* much!'

I'd away to school looking like I'd got the hands of a

kangaroo, stuck out in front of me. I couldn't point without twisting my whole body around. My granny thought I was deformed. 'Give your granny a cuddle, son.' I'd be struggling to move my arms. 'He's no right!' 'No, I'm okay!' 'Aw, he *thinks* he's okay, the poor wee bugger!' 'Really, I'm okay!' 'Of course you are, son! Oh, Jesus Christ, it's nae fair! He'll be going to school on that bus they take the dinners in. I've seen them, the wee daft weans, I've seen them licking the windows of that bus! They're no right. Your heart goes out to them!'

Well, one night my Auntie Agnes knitted me a balaclava from this jaggedy-arse wool. This is the wool from around a sheep's arsehole. Fifty pence a hundredweight. It drives you fucking insane. Now, as an adult, if you imagine waking up with a balaclava on, think of your reaction. And you're an adult; I was just a wee child!

She put it on me while I was asleep in my bed! As an act of kindness!

Can you imagine waking up in bed with a balaclava on that you didn't have on when you went to bed? You would remember, wouldn't you, if you'd put a balaclava on at bedtime? Your wife would say, 'What the fuck are you putting a balaclava on for?' And you'd be alarmed and upset if you woke up to find that a balaclava had been pulled over your head while you were asleep: 'Who put this on me?' you would say, as you hurriedly dragged it off.

Well, I was only seven. I wasn't even sure what a balaclava was. Especially one made of jaggedy-arse wool. I didn't even know I had a balaclava on. I just thought that lots of things were eating my head! When I woke up I went insane.

'Aaaaggghhh! Giant ants are eating my head!' And I leapt out of bed, naked but for a jaggedy-arse balaclava, and ran into the living room: *'Giant ants are eating my head!'*

And my granny said, 'I told you – he's not right!'

But I can hear you thinking: 'What's all this got to do with his eyes, by the way?' Well, the reason my eyes would shift to the left is that my Auntie Agnes had knitted the hole in my balaclava off centre, so the only way I could see out of it was to shift my eyes over to the left.

And people now say, 'But why didn't you just pull the hole to the front?' Because she'd knitted *ears* in the fucking thing – *that's* why! It was anchored to my bloody head!

MY FATHER'S CAR

He was a nice enough guy, my father, but we never got on very well. Because, well, some people just don't – fathers and sons. And when your son's a comedian it's particularly hard, I think. Especially my kind of comedy. He never approved, you know. He was very keen on Catholicism and all that stuff, so we didn't really hit it off, what with me 'making a fool of Jesus' and all of that. And I didn't buy him a house or a car like 'stars' do. He never wanted any of that stuff.

He never even drove until very late in life. Like a lot of men of his generation, he never really got into it. He never had the money, and then when he *did* have the money he didn't have much of the inclination to drive. He was a bit scared, actually.

But towards the end of his life, he phoned me up and said, 'I've just bought a car, do you want to come up and have a look?' And when he told me what it was, I thought, 'Oh my God.' It was one of those fibreglass, three-wheel cars: a Reliant Robin.

Now, they're probably brilliant, you know, and I've got no right to run them down, but they do have certain failings. Like in the winter, when you're driving in the snow, everybody else makes *tracks* in the snow, and between the tracks there's a mound of icy crap. But in a Reliant Robin, that crap's for you and the wheel in the middle. And there's a great danger as you press the accelerator that you'll feel the ground against the sole of your foot.

Anyway, he was coming to dinner at my house. He wore a range of glasses, my father. He had several pairs of glasses for different purposes and they all used to sit on his chest. He had glasses for the telly and glasses for reading and glasses for cooking and glasses for listening to the wireless, you know? All kinds of tasks.

But he came to my house in his new car and he was late, and so – I'd been starting to panic – I went out and said, 'What kept you? The dinner's drying up in here.' He says, 'Aw, Jesus! I drove here wearing my *reading* specs!' I'd feared he'd been in an accident. I was expecting carnage and smoke on the roads. But he was late because of him wearing the wrong specs. There was a wee steamy bit on the windscreen where his nose had been.

So, I said, 'Come in, come in!' And just as a joke, as a mere whimsy, I said, 'You should get one of those prescription windscreens.' I just made it up. I said, 'You should get your optician to get you one of those prescription windscreens so you can just forget your glasses and just drive.'

But the problem was, I was walking in front of him when I made this joke, and he never saw me laughing, so he took me seriously. And so, suddenly all excited, he says, 'Oh! Can you get them? What a *great* idea!' So, I said, 'Er, aye, I-um – I read it in a magazine, I think.'

And you see, it was too late now to deny it; I didn't want to hurt his feelings. If I'd said then, 'No, no, it was only a joke,' he would have said, 'Oh, that's just great – first you make jokes about Jesus, now you're making fun of my eyesight! Oh, this is fucking wonderful! What a laugh you must be!' So, I just said, 'Aye, um, I read it in a magazine, er, it was just a thing, um . . .' 'Oh, oh,' he said, 'get the magazine! Bring the magazine up for me. Have you got it here?' So I said, 'Er, well, I think it's, um, upstairs – you go in for your dinner and I'll have a look.'

So, I was upstairs pretending to look around in the room, rumbling furniture about trying to sound busy. Then I came back down and said: 'Oh, sorry, no, I cannae find it, I'll have to get it for you later.' 'You *do* that,' he said really excitedly. 'You give us a phone as soon as you find it. What a *brilliant* idea!'

Well, he bugged me for weeks and weeks and weeks and weeks. 'Have you found that magazine yet?' I'd say, 'No, er, still looking.' He'd say, 'Well, hurry up and find it, cos I've told all the guys at work. And I've got seven names here – they want them as well.' I thought, 'Oh noooooo! Oh GOD!' The whole thing was completely out of control.

But after a bit longer it sort of petered out. With no result it just dwindled away. He must have realised eventually that there was something amiss, so he never brought it up again.

And after his death, I was thinking about him sitting in his Reliant Robin, no glasses on, seeing absolutely perfectly, looking very happy with himself. And then I thought, 'What if he tried to sell it?'

I started imagining all sorts of scenarios of him having this special windscreen and trying to sell the car. Letting people have test drives. And them saying, 'Mr Connolly, I don't understand it – every time I drive your car I get these terrible headaches!' Or people on the motorway saying, 'Jesus, will you look at the size of that man's *head*!!!' Or people looking in the rearview mirror and suddenly seeing this huge great head: 'AAAAGGGGHHHH!'

2.
Scotland & Beyond

'There are two seasons in Scotland: June and Winter.'

VISIT SCOTLAND

You should go to Scotland. I'm sick and tired of meeting English people who say: 'You know, I've been everywhere, but I've never been to Scotland,' as if I should be fucking delighted to hear it. Go – it's a lovely place.

And don't just go to the usual places. You know, people go to look at Edinburgh Castle, and then they go to look at a couple of mountains, and then they come back. Go further afield for a change. Go to Fife and Dundee and Aberdeen and Glasgow – you'll love it, there are lots of nice places.

And don't do what people always come to me and do. They say, 'Oh, I went up to Scotland once and it was raining.' Of course it was fucking raining! Where do you think Scotland is – the fucking Pyrenees? Take a raincoat, you stupid fucker!

The mountain rescue are sick of it – going up and down Ben Nevis and saving people in fucking khaki shorts and sandshoes. Where do they think they've gone, Benidorm?

Anyway, let me tell you about Fife, where metal is located. It's opposite Edinburgh. It's the other side of the River Forth. It sits between the River Forth and the River Tay. The River Tay is at Dundee, Edinburgh down below and that sticky-out bit on the right-hand side is the Kingdom of Fife. And it's a great place.

If you go across the Forth Bridge from Edinburgh, you're into Fife. If you come the other way, you're back in Edinburgh. You can go two ways on the Forth Bridge. Yeah, it saved us building two fucking bridges, didn't it? Because we're very mean.

You've probably heard that before. There's a nasty rumour that copper wire was invented by two Scotsmen fighting over a penny. My father once dropped fifty pence, bent down to pick it up and it hit him on the back of the neck. He used to wake up at night to see if he'd lost any sleep. Yes, and we've the most crowded taxis in the world: 'What? Four pence for seven miles? You fuckin' highway robber!'

No, Fife's a great place, you would like Fife. Everybody likes Fife, it's great. St Andrews is in the north. St Andrews is kind of posh and it's got the golf and all that, and a university. It's full of posh folk. A lot of them are called Alisdair. Alisdairs always spell it for you: 'Could you sign it "To Alisdair" – d-a-i-r. Alisdair.'

'Alisdair? Have you seen Farquhar?'

'Oh, yes. Farquhar is over there with Finlay. Finlay and Anderson – they're talking to Campbell.'

'Are they really?'

'Yes. Campbell is talking to Robertson, and Robertson is talking to Farquhar and Farquhar is talking to Fettes. There's nobody with first names round here anymore.'

And it's nice agricultural land up there. It's really pretty. Seasidey places, nice fishing. You should go. Pittenweem and all those nice wee villages, you go in and get pissed on the coffee – they put whisky in their coffee and you get totally trousered. Come down and there's Dunfermline, and Kirkcaldy – fabulous town, where they used to make linoleum, great place! Making linoleum is a kind of smelly thing; they were going to change the name of Kirkcaldy to Whatsthatfuckingsmell. It's the first thing people said when they got off the train.

Now, the linoleum industry went down the pan, and they've got a million reasons for that. My personal one is that no one could pronounce 'linoleum'. They used to go into shops and say:

'Hello, can I have a roll of linoliment, thank you.'

'I'm sorry, what was that?'

'A roll of linomineint.'

'A romint and only one?? We don't sell romints.'

'I never asked for a fucking romint! I said a roll of limo-minum!'

'Look, I think I'm going to have to ask you again, at the risk of appearing rude. I'm awful sorry about this.'

'God knows it's simple enough: a romaminomium!'

'You've got me there.'

'For God's sake! A romum- oh, fuck it – give us a carpet!'

And that's what happened.

FAMOUS SCOTS

A few years ago, I was summoned to the Office of Births, Deaths and Marriages in Edinburgh. And I happily attended. They wanted to talk to me because they were doing an exhibition to encourage people to come and look into their family backgrounds and to use their facilities to do it. They'd got ten famous Scottish people and they had researched their backgrounds, and you could go there and look at it and see what you thought.

Ten famous Scots. There was Sean Connery, me, and eight other guys. I just say that to irritate Ewan McGregor. And Brian Cox – how do you fucking like *that*?

No, of course, there are lots of other famous Scottish people. One of them is Alan Cumming.

I once did a gig in Hollywood for BAFTA – the British Film and TV Academy – presenting Britannia Awards to Americans who'd been in British movies. It was a nice night; it went very well. And the following year they got Alan Cumming to do it, so I had to show up and hand over to him – that's the way they do it. And I'd always been dying to meet him anyway, because I think he's amazing. Plus, he comes from Carnoustie on the east coast of Scotland, and I had a holiday there when I was ten and I was dying to tell him. Not only that, but Carnoustie is also very close to Arbroath, and I lost my virginity in Arbroath, and I was dying to tell him that as well.

So, I met him and we got on like a house on fire. And as we were chatting away, I said, 'I believe you come from Carnoustie?' He said, 'Yeah.' I said, 'I had a holiday there when I was ten and I had a lovely time.' He said, 'That's nice.' Then I said, 'And I lost my virginity in Arbroath.' And his answer to that will go to my grave with me. He said, 'I passed my driving test there.' I said: 'I think I won.'

But the Births, Deaths and Marriages was great. They'd charted our lives and our ancestors, and they'd made a great job of it. There was a woman called Morrison, I think it was, who was the historian there, and she took me through the history of my family, from Galway and the Isle of Mull and all of that, and it was all very interesting. And at the end of it she said, 'What do you think?' I said, 'I'm delighted.' She said, 'You're not disappointed?' I said, 'Why would I be disappointed?' She said, 'Well, some people, when they realise their whole family are peasants, they get disappointed.' I said, 'I'm *delighted* about that. I love peasant stuff. I love peasant food, music, literature. There's no reason why I'd be disappointed about that.' She said, 'That's a very refreshing attitude.' I said, 'I'm a very refreshing kind of person, Mrs Morrison.'

I said, 'I can't believe people get disappointed.' She said, 'Oh, last week we had a big fat middle-class woman in here' – she just said 'a woman', I added those other bits; there's a bitchy side of me I'm going to have to do something about – 'and she was really disappointed to find out that her great-great-granny's name was Fanny Kissing.' I said, 'Why was she disappointed? It's my hobby!'

But if you ever get a chance you should go to that place – the Office of Births, Deaths and Marriages – because it's brilliant. It's got brilliant stuff.

The historian changed into white gloves at one point. I thought she was going to do an Al Jolson impersonation, but it was to go and get this incredibly rare certificate. It was the birth certificate of Mary, Queen of Scots. I actually got to hold it in my hand.

I was trembling, it was a magnificent thing. I couldn't believe it. She was executed just around the corner from where I was standing. It was extraordinary.

And then she went and got another one. Rob Roy MacGregor. What a prick. He was a spy for the English against the Scots, and a spy for the Scots against the English. He was a murderer and a thief, he was almost seven feet tall, and it's said he could tie his bootlaces standing up. He must have been the most peculiar shape.

Now, I dislike him especially because of the movie *Rob Roy*. If you've seen it, you'll remember a scene where someone has stolen his cattle and he and his men are up in the hills looking for them. And one of them jumps over a fence into a field and says: 'Ah, there's nae cows here, Robert . . . Wait a minute.' He finds a cow shit, and he picks it up and takes a big bite out of it, spits it out, and says: 'They've been gone two hours, Rob!'

I am here to inform you: the people of Scotland do *not* tell the time by eating shit! My grandfather lived to the age of ninety-six; I never once saw him reaching into his waistcoat pocket, pulling out a piece of dog shit, having a bite, and saying, 'Fuck, is that the time already?'

SCOTTISH BLUES

What you must understand about Scottish people – well, not 'must' understand, but I'm going to tell you anyway – is that we're not white.

I hear people on television saying, 'We, as black people, resent the fact that you white people . . .'

But I'm *not* a white person.

I'm fucking pale blue. It takes me a week of sunbathing to turn white!

And the Irish tend to be pink, I find. They run to the pinkish.

We're more your powder blue.

FAUX SCOTTISH

I look at singers, on the telly, and I look at *Scottish* singers, and I think, 'What are you *doing*?!'

You see, I'm a Scottish person. Right? You probably noticed. And I'm looking at these Scots on telly. These sort of singing shortbread tins. It's the whole nation that they're singing about in this garbage:

Ohhhh, the mountain's over here, and the river's
  over there.
Salmons in the river, and I'm roaming in the
  gloaming.
Ho, ho, ho, ho!
Bonny purple mountains,
And the sun is going up . . .

FUCK OFF!

I don't even begin to understand that. Because the folk music is actually wonderful – the real thing – but they avoid that like the plague in order to sing this . . . *stuff*!

And it's all written down in London, by strange wee men

who have never even *seen* Scotland! And one of them got found out about five years ago. He wrote a song called 'The Blue Misty Hills of Tiree'. But if you've ever *been* in Tiree, it's like a bloody *billiard* table! 'Oohh, the misty blue hills . . .'

Of all the shortbread people, I think Harry Lauder was the worst of the lot. He was a music hall performer, he was incredibly popular and was impossible to avoid when I was growing up. He'd trill these horrendously twee faux-Scottish ditties like 'A Wee Deoch-an-Doris' and 'I Love a Lassie' and he had this awful fake laugh: *'Ha ha ha! Ho ho ho!'* I was allergic to the fucker. I used to parody one of his songs, 'Keep Right on to the End of the Road', and declare: 'Friends, Romans, Countrymen: I come to bury Lauder, not to praise him!' God, he used to drive me crazy.

And there's also this never-ending line of Highland *weird* people. I mean, I'm not saying they're mad or anything like that, I think, but they're definitely weird. The Highland people are actually an amazing race of people. Lyrical, nice people. But there's a section, who keep turning up on television in Scotland, with a Bri-Nylon shirt and a space in their teeth, and the wee badger handbag there. 'Mountains and rivers and bonny Morag and the roaming in the gloaming . . .' And it's a very strange affair.

And then there's the Gaelic ones. You've probably seen them. They say 'hello' to you all the time, when they're singing:

'Hyah-hi-lo-oh . . . Hyah-hi-he-hi-ho-loh . . . Hi-ay-lohhhh . . . Hiyah-ha-ha-ho-loh . . . Hey-Hi-ho-oh-loohhhh . . .

'This is a song they do, when they're mashing up the Harris

Tweed, to send it off to . . .' And I say, 'Then why are you wearing a Bri-Nylon shirt?'

'Heri-Hiyoooolohhh . . .'

It's absolute nonsense!

And we seem to produce in Scotland a kind of religion that's very strange, too. It's the most patronising thing in television (except for the weather).

Television treats you as if you are four years of age: 'Now here is the weather. This is the country where you live. And this is a wee cloud!' I really feel brassed off when they do that. They stick clouds and lightning on the board. *You don't need to do that!* I know what a cloud looks like! Just tell me, I'll understand!

But, anyway, that kind of singing, you know? Women sing kind of weird up there, they've spoiled a lot of great songs. Robert Burns wrote some real crackers, and they spoil them with that strange *'Waaaah-haaaay'* way of singing.

Because ordinary people sing okay. No, really. And the whole thing is organised by people who've got second names instead of first names. 'Crawford, have you seen Finlay?' Who *are* these people? They're aliens! The surname clan has taken over! 'Kendall, have you seen Finlay? Oh, he was with Crawford and . . .' What are you *talking* about??

And the women dancers are great, y'know, they're all giving it a bit of that. Winsome and buxom. And the men are getting a bit light in their loafers. But for me, it's a bit strange. Ballroom dancing's getting the same way, with people doing that camp sort of prancing. What are they *doing*? If you did *that* down a Glasgow dance hall, you'd last about ten minutes!

And these people do it with an elastic suit on! What's that about? What's that Paso Doble? Nobody actually does the Paso Doble, except them. And drunk people on holiday in Spain.

THE SCOTTISH NATIONAL FOOTBALL TEAM

Many years ago, Scotland used to reach the finals of the World Cup quite regularly, and, quite regularly, they'd get stuffed. And it got to be really boring.

We'd always qualify. We'd always treat Wales really badly. They never got in, we always got in – and we always fucked it up when we got there.

And my theory was, and still is: we're the wrong fucking shape. Because everybody else has got *big* thighs, and they're *shiny* people – they're big fucking shiny footballers! Long hair, tanned, glamorous footballers with big shiny thighs. But we're wee guys with thin pale-blue legs.

And these big shiny footballers, they run in that confident kind of way, like dancers. Whereas we run out with our wee little legs looking like schoolboys searching for the loo.

And there's no apparent plan. It's like the Boys' Brigade. They obviously haven't been formally introduced. They obviously don't know each other. And I thought at the time, 'Wouldn't it be better, maybe on the bus to the game, if you had a wee fucking *talk* about it? A casual chat, y'know?' Like: 'If you give the ball to me . . . I'll give it to him. Then he can give it to him . . . And maybe he can give it to . . . Alec – do *you* want the ball? Aye? Well, *he'll* give you it. Nae problem. And after that you can give it to him, and he can give it to him over there.'

If I was the manager, I would go into the dressing room and I'd say:

'Now, listen, lads. You are the cream of Scottish football. We've scoured the country, we've found you, and we've put you all together. This is the Grand Plan. You are the very best. And out there are the best from every other country on earth. But *you're* the cream of Scottish football, so I wouldn't dream of telling you how to play. You're better than I am, obviously. I never made it this far in my own career. But when you get out there, and you get the ball – try and enjoy it. Get a feel of it – it's a fucking *good* ball. You've got *lovely* boots on. The grass is in *beautiful* nick. So have a little play – *enjoy* the ball. And when you're fed up with it, try and give it to somebody you know. And if you could all run in roughly the same direction, all to the better. And if you run out of ideas and things to do with the ball – just stick it in the fucking net every now and again. All the best!'

But this seems to elude them. There's no plan. Whereas you see these South Americans, and the striker is walking around casually, hands behind his back, and then you see an idea form in his head, a little stratagem, and he suddenly moves, which invariably leads to the fucking net going *Boing!* and the crowd going *'Yeahhhhh!'*

But our mob are all running around and shouting at each other: 'Willy! *Willy!* Willy! Over here! Over *here!* Oh, Willy, for fuck's sake, *over here*!!'

It won't do.

And how come goalkeepers never admit liability for anything? Every time the ball whistles past them they're straight out of their goal, arms raised, shouting at anyone and everyone: 'Hey! HEY! Fer FUCK'S sake! What's going on? That bastard kicked the ball! Who the fuck does he think he is?'

And when they arrange that wall for a free kick, nobody listens to the goalkeeper. They're all *groping* themselves. The goalkeeper's going: 'Willy – over here! Bobby! Bobby – over there! Charlie! Charlie! Over—' *Biff-whish!* 'Oh, fer fuck's sake!'

I like watching goalies. When you see a photograph of the keeper he's always sailing through the air. Belly up. Tipping a ball over the bar. It's a beautiful balletic pose. But he's done that twice in his life. Most of the time, in contrast, he's like this: motionless, arms folded, chewing gum, then jumping up and down, left arm windmilling, then right arm windmilling, then jumping up and down again, then motionless again, arms folded, chewing gum, now with the ball flying past his earlobe. I don't know how they put up with that for their whole careers.

But I also watch the crowd. Usually much, much, more interesting than the game. I especially like the South American crowds, because their players foul properly and the crowds just enjoy it. They get their fucking foot right in there, and half of the crowd explode with a 'YEAH!' and the other half go mad with a 'NOOOOOO!'

But after that you get this amazing choreographed chanting and handclaps and it's very tribal. Some unseen signal triggers them all off: '*Ahh-aaaay-eee-aay-oohh-ay-hoh-ah-hay-ee-ha!*'

'What the fuck was *that?*'

It's like over five hundred people are sent this unseen signal and they're off: 'Ooo-aaayy-Oo-ay-a-ay-ay-oo-ay-o-ay-ay . . .'

And they all know it perfectly. There's no one on the periphery kind of learning it. They all just do it.

We surely could improve at that. Even if we keep losing on the pitch!

A SCOTTISH PARTY

I like parties. You don't get eyes like this reading the *Melody Maker.* I've been to a few parties in my life, let me tell you. And a couple of New Years ago, I was invited to a party in Glasgow, which I must tell you about. And this is the truth.

The guy who invited me was in this place called Springburn, which is a kind of working-class area – quite nice, it used to have a horrible bit, but they rolled that up and sold it to Zambia. And the kids are still playing in the street there in their wellies, wondering when the rain's comin' back. But this house was in the kind of middle-of-the-road Springburn.

I went with a pal of mine. It was Hogmanay in Scotland, you know, New Year – something the same as your Christmas, but without God to knacker the proceedings. You just get well into the bevvies: *'Yeeeeeuuuuurrrrrrgggghhh!'*

So, we got to the party. And it's wall-to-wall people. And it's like Gomorrah: *'Yuuuurrrgghh!' 'Hic!' 'Giz a large one!' 'Danny Boy!' 'Yay!'* And Scotsmen have this great habit of singing about Scotland when they're still there. They're

singing: 'Though I'm far across the sea . . .' No, you're not –
you're in the living room! 'Shut up, you – it's the only song
yer father knows right through!'

There's other guys at the party. Three hundred of them
and they're all singing different songs at the same time. And
there's always the guy who doesn't know the words of any
of them, but joins in anyway making funny noises. Always
country and western: 'Habee wajay amego wahdoon—' 'What
are you singin' aboot??' 'Ay don't know.' 'Have a large one.'
'Okay!'

And there's two guys in the corner. They're sittin' there:
'Bprrrr . . .' 'Don't be sick, Willie.' 'Hup . . . Hup . . . Ah'm aw
right, Ah'm aw right . . . A-Ah'll be aw right . . . A-Ah'm na
well . . . Jus' get me a drink, that'll sort me oot.' 'Now don't
be sick – remember Ah told you that, okay?' 'A-Ah'm
aw right . . . Ah'm as right.' 'That's ma Auntie Agnes's new
carpet – Don't. Be. Sick!' 'A-Ah'm okay . . . Hup . . . Ah'm aw
right . . .'

I'm talking to the guy who owns the house. It's just an
ordinary wee house, you know the type. Three geese going
up the wall there. The ostrich at the mantelpiece, nodding
away. The whole number of little crinoline ladies from the
seaside, the mantelpiece just crowded with things. Quite a
nice house, though. I mean it's not the sort of place with
adverts in the ashtrays, it's a bit upmarket, quite pleasant.

But there's a picture on the wall of a guy in a Highland
Regiment outfit – the bagpipes, the kilt, the whole thing. He
looks like he's posing for a shortbread tin. And I said to the
guy who owns the house, 'Is that you?' 'Aye! That's me, son!

Ah was that soldier!' 'Really?' 'Aye! Ah was a fine figure of a man, Ah'll tell you that!' I said, 'Aye, you were that, indeed. Do you still play the pipes?' 'Oh, Ah havenae played them in a few years, like. Mind you, they're in the cupboard, there.' So, I said: 'Get 'em out.' He's thrilled: 'Aye, just a jiffy!'

And his wife rolled her eyes and went, 'Oh, fer Christ's sake! Oh *nooooo!*'

And your man's legs were just a blur. Into the lobby, door open, loads of stuff coming out the cupboard – ladders, prams, cots, *things*. 'Ah-ha! Here we are!' And out comes this flea-bitten set of bagpipes. It looks like an octopus with pyorrhoea. Dust everywhere.

'Here we go!'

Hyoooooaaaaah! Hyoooooaaaaaahhh! Eeaaaaooooooaaagg-ggggggghhh!

You know, it sounds like Glen Campbell: '*Ow-eeooo-aaaggghhhh!*' But this guy manages to get all his pipes and the drones all in tune, and he was actually a good piper. And he comes marching into the room, playing 'The Barren Rocks of Aden'. *Daddleadeleedeeledidlee* . . . And all the loonies go bonkers: 'Eeaseh! Eeaseh! Eeaseh! Eeaseh!' 'We are the champions!!' They're ready for marching over the border, you know?

And there's bedlam. There's people falling through coffee tables, the sound of crunching glass under feet, but yer man's still piping away. The poor guy's wife is in the chair, going, '*Ohferchrissake!*'

Total bedlam.

'*Hu-bbbbrrrrrrr.*' 'Don't be sick, Willie!' 'A-Ah won't . . . A-Ah'm okay . . .' *Deedle-doddle-dee* . . .

So, in the middle of the march past, he does a kind of fancy turn – a spin – and the bagpipes go *whuuuuush!* – and knock his wedding picture off the wall.

SMASH!!!

Crunch! Dee-diddle-Crunch!-Da-da-diddle-Crunch!-Dee-duddle-Crunch!-Daddle-day-Crunch!

And a drunk's come in and he's enjoying the procession. He leans on the mantelpiece, slides right along and smashes all the stuff.

Deedle-deedle-da . . .

'Don't be sick!' 'A-Ah won't . . . A-Ah'm aw right . . .'

Then someone belts the budgie's cage. It's on one of those stand things – the door flies open and the budgie comes out like a rocket: *whooooooooooosh*! It's like one of the Red Arrows going across the sky. 'Ah, Ah'll get it wi' me jacket' – *whishhh* – 'Ah know what you do, you pour salt on its tail . . .' There's feathers drifting doon, the bagpipes are still going like hell.

'*Bppprrrrrr.*' 'Don't be sick.' 'Ah'm aw right . . .'

The budgie, in the middle of all this, has a heart attack. Does a burning Spitfire impersonation.

Scrunch-Scrunch-Scrunch-Scrunch! – Deedeleeedle-dah . . . Scrunch-Scrunch . . .

It's the size of a golden eagle by the end.

Dee-diddy-deedle-daddle-dooooo . . .

Now, someone's been sick in the bathroom. But he's finished all the vomiting, there's nothing left. So he's going through that one now: '*Huh-huh-huuuuuuhh-aaaaahhh! Huh-huh-aaah-ahhh-aaaah!*'

Diddle-deedle-dah . . .

'*Huh-huuuuuaaaaaeeeeehhh!*'

And with the strain of it all, he's farting as well. He's kneeling on the floor with his head down the toilet, '*Huh-huh-huuuuaa*' – *brrrrrriiippp!* And he's panicking in case he shits himself, right? Like: '*Huh-huh-huuuuaaaaa*' – *brrrrrriiipppp-thhhhuuuuuup!*

Diddle-daddle-diddee . . .

'*Brrpppp.*' 'Don't be sick.' 'Ah'm aw right . . .'

Meanwhile . . .

A guy arrives with forty fish suppers in a big parcel. 'Ah thought ya might be hungry, like, so Ah got a wee snack . . .' There's steam all around him. And he's brought them all the way on the bus – burning his willy all the way. But he's arrived, anyway.

And the fish suppers are getting cold, so he puts them in the oven. And there's a pot of soup on the stove. A big pot boiling away. So he bungs the whole thing in the oven, in the parcel, lights the gas and shuts the door.

Deedle-daddle-diddl-o . . .

Meanwhile there's people walking about with blood coming down their faces. Because in the bathroom, the bulb has gone, and there's a bicycle on a pulley – they do that in tenement buildings – and people were going, 'Hey, the light's nae workin'—' BANG!

Deedle-Daddle-dum-dum . . .

'Don't be sick.'

So eventually, the two drunks are sitting there. '*Mm-bah* . . .' 'Don't be sick, now.' 'Ah'm aw right, Ah'm aw right . . . *Mm-ppp-mm-ppp-mmm*—' 'Don't be sick!' '*Mmpp-Mmpp-puh-puh-pu-pu-pu-brrrrraaaaaaaaaaaaaaaaaaaaaaaaaaaaahhhhhhhhh!*'

SPLAT!

'Ah, ferchrissakes it's all over me!' 'But ya said not tae do it on the carpet!' 'That's *mohair!* Ya bastard – Ah *warned* you, didn't Ah?' *'Brrrrraaaaaaaaaaaaaaaahhhhhhhhh!'*

Meanwhile . . .

There's a drunk in the bedroom, naked, lying on the coats. Naked as the day he was born. And there's a woman come storming out: 'Hey! There's a drunk man in there! Naked. Lyin' on all the coats! I told him to get up, he told me to fuck off! I don't like that kind of talk – sort him out, George!' And there's her husband, you know, he's built like a jockey's whip. Looks like a cancer case, y'know? 'Go on, you sort him out, put him in his place!' 'Er, okay . . .'

Meanwhile . . .

The guy by the kitchen is sniffing: 'Hey, there's somethin' *burnin'* in here, in't there!' *Sniff.* 'Keep the women back – *I'll* sort this oot, don't worry about a thing!' He shoots in the kitchen and the flames come belting up, and he pulls out this blazing parcel. Fish and chips covered by black smoke. And he puts out the flames by throwing the whole thing into the soup: *Ka-booooosh!*

The bagpipes are still going. *Needle-eedle-needle-nada* . . .

And the cancer case is away in the bedroom saying: 'Don't talk to ma wife like that again, okay?' His wife's shouting out: 'Come on, sort him out, George, that's not enough!' 'Oh, okay, ferchrissakes!'

Whack.

And the drunk wakes up. And he looks like *me*, y'know? *'Uuuaaaahhh!'* And he comes out of bed like a dervish. And with one mighty leap he lands on the floor. *'Uuuuaaaahhh! Who hit me in the arm?'*

And this drunk did the funniest thing I have ever seen in my life. Completely casually, he leaned over – completely naked – and put on one shoe and kicked George in the balls!

THE OLD FIRM

Now, as you've no doubt heard, and as most people in Britain no doubt know, in Glasgow we have two very famous football teams: Rangers and Celtic. And never the twain shall meet.

And when they're playing each other, the supporters of Celtic go to one end, and the supporters of Rangers go to the other end, they shout at each other for ninety minutes, and then they all go home. It can be quite heavy, right enough: 'Ah, ya Orange bastard!' *'Aaaagh!'* 'Have some o' that, ya Fenian bastard!' *'Ooooh!'*

And it's very heavy. And very good.

This is a story about a wee Glasgow man who made the mistake of his life and went to the wrong end.

He was a wee bit drunk-ish, but he sobered up rapid when he discovered what had happened. But then it was too late. He was too deep into the crowd. And he was surrounded by giant supporters of the opposition. *'Ugghhhuuhhuh!'* They're all growling round him: *'Uggggghuuuhhh!'* They'd never been that close to one before.

So that's the scene.

And he's standing there like that. 'Er . . . N-Nice day for it, eh?' '*Uughhhhhh!*' And his team scores two goals. He went, 'Oh, Jesus *Christ* . . .' '*Uuggghermmuuh!*' And eventually one of them spoke to him.

'*Hey!*' 'Aye? Er, what is it?' '*Go* – get me a *Bovril!*' For some obscure reason, Scotsmen drink Bovril at football matches, and at no other times in their lives. '*Go an' get me a BOVVVVVRIL!*'

So, he said, 'Aye, okay.' '*Ah-ah-ah* – you'll run away, won't ye? Take off one of yer *shoes!*' He takes off one of his shoes. 'Right – go!' So, he limps away for the Bovril.

He comes back and says, 'There's your Bovril.' 'Ta. There's ya shoe.' And there was a big jobbie in it. 'PUT IT ON!' He thinks, 'Oh, Christ Almighty!' *Squelch!* 'Hur-Hur-Hur-Hur!'

Then his team scores another two. 'Oh . . . *Christ!*' And eventually another one of them spoke to him: '*Hey!*' 'A-Aye?' 'Go an' get *me* a Bovril – an' leave yer *other* shoe!' So, the shoe's off, and he's limping away with one shoe full of shit.

He comes back. 'There's ya Bovril.' 'Ta. Here's ya other shoe.' Same again. 'PUT IT ON!!' 'Oh . . . all right . . .' *Squelch!*

So, he's standing there. There's a big space all around him. '*Prooaaar*, Jesus *Christ!*' He's in abject misery. There's flies everywhere. He can see his mates at the other end: '*Yeaaaaahh! We are the Champions!*' 'Pfffff . . .'

And eventually, to his great relief, the game ended. '*Right – on yer way!*' 'Aw right, aw right . . .'

So he waited until most of the crowd were away, then he sort of squidged out of the ground. *Squelch-squelch-squelch-squelch* . . . And he was going down the street, keeping close to the wall. *Squelch-squelch-squelch-squelch* . . . He'd got dogs following him: 'Get away!'

And he came upon a television crew for the BBC. The camera, the whole works, the guy with the sheepskin jacket and the bunnet. 'Hallo! Excuse me, sir, can I have a wee word in your ear an' that?' He says, 'Look, we've been interviewing people here for the television aboot football violence. Can you just come a bit closer here, sir – oh, *no*, Christ, there's a hell of a *smell* aboot here, have I got somethin' on ma shoe?' 'No . . . *I've* got somethin' in *ma* shoe.' 'Oh, okay, er, well, we've been talkin' aboot football violence to a lot of the supporters. Have *you* got anything to say to the viewers aboot it? Any original points of view?'

He says, 'Aye! You're bloody *right* I have!' He says, 'Give us that microphone.' And he stares the camera straight in the eye. He says:

'In my *sincere* opinion, football *violence*, in this country, will *never* end. Not as long as *they* are shittin' in our shoes! And *we* are pissin' in their Bovril!'

SOMETHING TO DO IN THE RAIN

I like the rain. If you're born in Scotland or Ireland, you have to like the rain, because it's there whether you want it to be or not. I mean, these two countries: they didn't get green by mistake.

It pelts down there. And that's sort of a good thing. It makes your skin lovely, and you have a bad hair day every day of your life – so that's another thing not to worry about anymore. You just get yourself a sexy raincoat and get on with it – you get on with life.

I had a campaign a while ago – it obviously didn't work very well – to get the weather people in Britain to stop calling rainy weather 'bad weather'. Because if it rains every day, and they say it's 'bad' weather, you're going to be seriously pissed off most of your life. 'Sorry, ladies and gentlemen, it's going to be yet another crap day tomorrow.' You know, that can seriously affect the national psyche. When people are setting off each day to earn their living, or, even worse, setting off for a nice leisurely day out with the family, they really don't need these characters telling them it's going to be shite out there.

But I do like rain. I taught my children to like it too. They were brought up in Los Angeles, but I taught them how to take their shoes and socks off and just walk around in it and experience it. It's part of life. The fishermen in Scotland always say: 'There's no such thing as bad weather, there's only the wrong clothes.' And they're quite right.

I love it when it rains when I go home to Scotland. It feels natural, it feels normal, it feels right. Rain is okay. As they also say in Scotland, 'The graveyard's full of people who would love this weather.' Right again.

You can do all kinds of things in the rain. You can have all sorts of fun. I used to give people electric shocks in the rain.

It happened when I was young, when I worked as a welder in the shipyard in Glasgow. One of my friends at the time, who was called Alex Mosson – he still is called Alex Mosson, actually – who's since been the Lord Provost of Glasgow and all kinds of grand and important things. But back then he was just a nutcase like me. He was a carpenter.

He and I would go on to the deck of a ship and look for puddles in the rain. And if we found a nice big puddle, we'd nod to each other, and I would go down underneath the deck with my electric welding equipment, directly beneath the puddle, and lurk there with my electric welding gear. And he, meanwhile, would stay standing up above, holding a metal rod, and he'd wait until someone walked through the puddle, then he'd quickly knock twice on the deck with this rod, and I'd go – *fizzzzzzzzzz*. And the guy would go flying in the air. 'Aaaagghh!'

We'd do it quite a few times. We'd swap places, take it in turns to electrify the puddle. Up they'd come – *knock knock* – *fizzzzzzz* – 'Aaaagghh!' You wondered how high they would actually jump. We were going for world records there.

That was one of the funniest things you'll ever see, certainly in the rain.

So, don't despair when it rains. Embrace it. And use your imagination – have some fun in it. It's an opportunity.

TWO SCOTSMEN IN ROME

This wee thing is about two Glasgow guys who went on holiday to Rome.

These two guys were in Rome, and they were going around, being tourists, looking up at all the famous sights: 'Aye, look at that, that's fantastic . . . Look at that an' all, fantastic, I'm intae that . . . I wonder who papered that ceiling, that's fantastic . . .'

And the sun was belting down on them: 'Hey, the sun's beltin' doon on me!' 'Aye, we should go an' get a bevvy.' 'Right.' So, they shot into a wee bar in Rome.

And they go right up to the bar and say, 'Hey, Jimmy, give us two pints of heavy.' And the barman says, '*What?*', in Italian, like.

And they go, 'Two pints of heavy – are you deef or somethin'?'

The barman says, 'Look, we don't have "heavy" in Rome. We've got all sorts of clever things, but we don't have heavy. But look,' and he's pointing at all the different bottles, 'you're welcome to anything you see here . . .' So, they're looking suspiciously at all these unfamiliar drinks. 'Ah, I don't know about any of these things . . . Hey, tell you what – what does the Pope drink?' The guy says, 'Oh, crème de menthe. I've heard he likes a wee glass of crème de menthe every now and again.'

'*Give us two pints of THAT, then!*'

Their two green pints duly arrive. And they look at the drink for a moment, a bit unsure about it, and then nod at each other. 'Aw, if it's good enough for the Big Yin, it's good enough for me, okay . . .' They pour the whole glass straight down their throats. 'Nae bad – it's like drinkin' Polo mints, in't it?' 'When in Rome, eh? D'you get it? When in Rome and that!' They lick their lips and turn back to the barman: 'Give us another two, there you go!'

And they're at it all night. Nothing but green pints.

They wake up in the morning. They're in a crumpled heap in a shop doorway. Their suits are all creased and ruffled up and they've peed their trousers and been sick down their jackets. They've been shouting and hugh-ing all night. *HEUEGH!* And occasionally calling for Ralf: *RALF!* Hughie and Ralph. *HEUUEEGGHH!!! RAAAALFFF!!!* And it's green. Green Hughie. *Hughie Green?*

I'll tell you what, though – just to digress – talking about being sick. How come – this is a great dilemma – how come *every* time you're sick there's diced carrots in it? How come? Because I have *never* eaten diced carrots in my life! You can have lamb madras, a few bevvies, and *HUUGHHIE!!!* Diced carrots. *RAAAALFFF!!!* More diced carrots. Every time. And sometimes tomato skins as well, even though I don't eat bloody tomato skins! *How come?* Now my personal theory is that there's a pervert somewhere, with pockets full of diced carrots, following drunk guys.

But back to Rome.

Back in Rome these two guys are waking up in the morning. They're rubbing their faces slowly, rubbing their weary eyes. 'Christ Almighty! . . . Ooohhhhh, ma *heid!* . . . I think I'm wearin' an internal balaclava!' One of them starts rubbing his body. 'Christ Almighty . . . Oohhh, ma body's so sore . . . AAGGHH! *I CANNAE FEEL MA LEG!*'

'That's *MA* leg, ya bampot!'

'Oh, thank Christ for that! Jeez, what a fright I got there!' He looks over at his friend. 'How are *you?*'

'To tell you the truth . . . I feel kind of funny. I think I've had a tongue transplant. This one doesnae seem to fit.'

'Christ . . . and they say the *Pope* drinks *that* stuff?'

'Aye. Nae wonder they have to carry him about on a chair, eh!'

THE IRISH, THE SCOTS AND THE SWISS

I love Ireland. I go there every couple of years. And my name being Connolly, my grandfather came from there. Connemara, he came from. A village called Ballyconneely, which is nearly 'Billy Connolly' when you put your mind to it.

'What's my name?' 'Ballyconneely.' 'Pardon?' 'Ballyconneely.' 'Aye, that's close enough!'

It's a brilliant place, Ireland. There's something very alive about the people there, something lovely and crazy and intelligent and strange about the whole culture. And it makes me envious because we're the same race, the Scots and the Irish. We're all Celtic people.

The Scots *came* from Ireland – for reasons best known to themselves. 'Come on – I know an even *colder* place. It rains *all the time*! It's fuckin' amazing. Head for the black cloud.'

The Scots have done that all over the world. During the Highland Clearances in the eighteenth century we went to Virginia. It was fucking paradise – the Blue Ridge Mountains and all of that. 'Too hot! Further north, lads.' So, they went up to Hudson Bay – where it was cold enough to freeze your bollocks off. If you had a piss you had to snap it off. If you farted in bed you woke up with an ice cube up your arse.

We went to New Zealand. North Island: beautiful women,

stripped to the waist, long black hair, singing and dancing. 'Nope. Further south!' To Dunedin. 'Drizzle! Ha-ha! This is the fuckin' place! Now you're talking.'

I don't know why it is, but we've done it all over the bloody world.

I think the Reformation had a lot to do with it in the sixteenth century. John Knox, a fucking Weary Willie of a man, and a hypocrite, too. 'THOU SHALT NOT!' This is a race of people who wear skirts and no knickers! We fucking SHALL, pal! Done it before and we'll do it again.

Then we pick up a religion from Switzerland. Fucking *Switzerland*! Calvinism. John Calvin. This dreary prick from Switzerland. Nothing good comes from Switzerland. Cuckoo clocks and fucking Toblerones!

It's impossible to fucking eat a Toblerone without *hurting* yourself. What kind of people are they? And who on earth buys those huge big Toblerones at Heathrow? Perverts who shove them up their arses? Toblerones should come with a wee tool kit. You can't eat the fucking thing. It's a stupid shape. And I'm told they keep them in the fridge! It's so pointy and sharp and offensive. What kind of sick mind thought that one up – an aggressive sweetie. A bar of chocolate that *hurts* you! Only them fuckers – Switzerland.

And they seem to have some kind of deal with hotel chains, because every fridge has a Toblerone in it. And once you spot it and you've eaten your first Toblerone, that's you done – you're a slave to it. Every day you're there in your room, checking out the minibar: 'Have they replaced the Toblerone yet?' You become incredibly addicted. And you start lying to yourself: 'Um . . . I'll, I'll just have one Alp . . .' I think that's the design feature, I think it's supposed to represent the Alps. As if the Alps were all exactly the same size and each one right behind the other. You go to Switzerland and say, 'Fuck, is that the Alps? Is there only the one?' Then you're advised to lean to the side and look. 'Oh, I see!'

So, you'll be lying to yourself, telling yourself: 'Look, I'll have just the one Alp. What harm can that do to anybody?' And you whip out the Toblerone and unwrap it. 'Just the one Alp.' But even as the word 'Alp' has formed in my mind, I've already put two in my mouth. 'Aw, it's wet now, I'd better eat it.'

Then, you're in the second valley. Your teeth have dug down into the second Toblerone valley. And you reach the bottom, you're now at that heavy chocolate base. So now you have two Alps in the tongue side of your teeth, which means that you have a third Alp on the other side, rammed up behind your lip, shoving your lip up your nostril and you can go no further without ripping your nostril off your face.

So you think: 'I'll gnaw through the base, I'll just gnaw my way through it.' So you're gnawing and sawing with your top teeth, licking and sucking as you go, and the chocolate is swirling around in your mouth, with the honey and the almonds, and you're thinking, 'Mmmm, oooh, fuck!' Your heart's pounding with the sugar rush. Then you break through the base, and suddenly the first two Alps shoot up at the roof of your mouth and into your brain, and you're in agony: 'Oooh-aah-oooh-aaa-aahhh!'

And that's exactly how yodelling was invented in Switzerland.

Do you know what I've always wanted to see? The Swiss

Army. Just to see what they do with those wee red knives. I'm sure in Rwanda or some place they'll turn up with their wee knives held up high on their shoulders like rifles. 'Left, left, left, right, left! Squad halt! Knives . . . out! Scissors . . . out! Nail files . . . out! Things for getting stones out of horses' hooves . . . out!'

'Franz?'

'Yes, sir?'

'Where are the enemy?'

'Hang on – I'll get my wee spyglass blade out!'

I just want to have a look at the Swiss Army. I just want to see them once in my life.

NEW ZEALAND

You *must* get your arse down to New Zealand at some point in your life. For the good of your immortal soul.

There's no one there. Not a soul in the place. There are *some* people in the towns – maybe a dozen or six. I was driving my motorbike for three hours one day and two cars passed me. It was like nineteen-forty-fucking-five!

It was fabulous!

It's a brilliant place, you MUST get your arse down there.

But apart from that, there's a town there called Dunedin, which is a *dreary* town. It's got that Scottish Presbyterian feel about it. And there's a few of them around the place. Scottish Presbyterians were a dreary fucking bunch, and they liked taking it to other places.

They went all over Canada. Fucking *dreaaaaaaary,
dreaaaaaaary* – 'Bring out your dead!' – *dreaaaaaaary,
dreaaaaaaary*, fucking dreaaaaaaary.

'Where will we go?' 'I don't know – where's the drizzle?
Follow the drizzle!'

And Dunedin, which is the old name for Edinburgh – I didn't
know that until they told me – is dreary. But I landed there in
a helicopter – very flashy, with a biker jacket and all that,
fucking loving every second of it. Pretending I wasn't bothered,
you know – *yawn!* – while my heart was going: *YESSSSSSSSS!*

There was a reporter waiting for me. You'd have thought
it was 1945 – the guy's got the trench coat with the belt tied
and the trilby hat on the back of the head. Scoop Martin –
Showbiz. And there's a woman with him, so I think maybe
she's the photographer, or she's getting the 'female angle' on
the whole affair, whatever. So, I think they're a team. But as
it turned out, she was just a woman who was walking past
and had stopped to look at the helicopter.

The reporter was getting really pissed off, because he's
asking me stuff and I'm talking to her. And she's joining in!
'Oh, yes, and what did you think of so-and-so? . . . Ah, well,
you know, it's a very interesting point you bring up . . .' And
he's standing there thinking, 'Fer FUCK'S sake!'

But this Weary Willie of a reporter, he eventually says:
'Billy, I've been reading some clippings' – licking the tip of
his pencil (Why do they do that? Why do they lick their
pencil? Do they get off on the graphite or something?) – 'I've
been reading some clippings, and you're often heard to say
that there's always *drizzle* here. Why do you say that?'

I said, 'Put your notebook in your right hand.'

'Sorry?'

'Just transfer it to your right hand.'

He does it. Then I held out my hand with the palm facing upwards, and said, 'Put your left hand out like that.'

He does it. Then he went: 'Oh . . . fuck! Okay.'

AUSTRALIA

Australia is a very strange place if you're Scottish. It's hot and it's scary.

The suntan oils and creams in Australia, the numbers, usually go from one to fourteen. Me, a blue Scotsman, I required number twenty-six. The woman in the shop said, 'Twenty-six? Christ – that's a *bandage!*' I said, 'Fuck it, give us it!' She said, 'You'd be better off with a boiler suit and a balaclava!'

And as for the wildlife in Australia – I really don't know how the people there survive to adulthood! There are so many scary creatures sneaking about the place, waiting to pounce. It's terrifying.

I was in a shop there once and there was a jar, like a honey jar, on the counter, and in it was the biggest spider I have ever seen in my life. It was in liquid, it had been dead for years, but it was still fucking terrifying. So, I said to the woman serving me, 'What's that?' She said, 'Oh, that's the famous funnel-web spider.' I said, 'Oh. Where do they live – out in the bush?'

You know, trying to sound knowledgeable, 'out in the bush', pointing over my shoulder; I thought it was a safe bet to point away from the sea.

She says, 'Oh, no. These funnel-webs, they're local. We caught this one in a garden across the street.' I was living there at the time – I was *near* those fuckers! And then she said this thing that thousands of people have said to me in my life, and they were all lying. She said, 'Don't worry: it won't bother you if you don't annoy it.'

Who the hell annoys these bastards? Is anybody that bored that they get up in the morning and go: 'Aw, I'm so fuckin' bored. I think I'll go and annoy that fuckin' funnel-web spider!'

In my life, there seems to have been lines and lines of little shits who had Alsatians or Doberman Pinschers, foaming at the face, keeping a steady gaze on my bollocks, going, *grrrrrrr!*, and these little shits who were holding them were always saying, 'It won't bother you if you don't annoy it.' But they never tell you what annoys it! Like breathing and stuff like that.

But back to Australia. My tour opened in a place called Townsville. Which was up in the north in Queensland, up in the tropical bit. And I went for a little walk once I arrived there. I was walking along the seaside and there was a big noticeboard there and it said: 'BEWARE'. So, I was being ware. It said: 'STINGERS!' I thought, 'Fucking *stingers*?' Now, I don't know if stingers burrow holes in the ground, drop out of trees or arrive in fucking taxis, so I'm moving around, looking in multiple directions, being very ware.

Then I thought, 'I'd better read on.' And the warning went

on: 'STINGERS, OR BOX JELLYFISH . . .' I thought, 'Oh my God, these fuckers are *gift-wrapped*! What sort of country *is* this?' Imagine being in the water, swimming along, and this box with a pretty bow on it sails into view: 'Oooh, I wonder what's in there?' You open it up: 'Aaaaagghhh!'

But this notice went on: 'IF THE HEART STOPS . . .' I thought, 'What *size* is this fucker?' It said, 'DOUSE THE WOUND LIBERALLY WITH VINEGAR'. Oh, I *always* go swimming with a bottle of vinegar! You're probably the same yourself.

Well, the following morning, I was watching the news, and it said a wee boy had been stung. And then they added: 'And don't go around the rock pools today as we've seen the unwelcome return of the blue-ringed octopus.' And they showed you this bastard. You could see the cameraman shaking as he was pointing his camera at it! This thing's only small, but it's got these weird bright blue things on its legs and it's got this look about it that shouts: '*Fuck off!*' When this bastard stings you, you don't even make it to the phone. You're looking for a stinger to take the edge off the pain!

I'm warning you. Australia is a dangerous place!

IBIZA

I was in Ibiza once. I will never forget it, it's tattooed on the inside of my head.

We checked in – I had two children then – and I was unpacking, and giving everybody a lecture: 'Don't drink the tap water, right? Your daddy's got this under control, okay? Only drink the *bottled* water. I've put the bottle over here, see, now listen to your dad. The bottle's there. *That* one – it says "Evian", see, EH-VEE-ON, Evian. *That's* the water. You even brush your teeth with it. Don't drink any other water, okay? That's good. Now, behave and get about your business, I'm unpacking here.'

So, my son drank the water – slaked his thirst, as was his wont – and then filled the bottle from the tap, unknown to me. A good boy. (We all agreed he was a nice boy, when he got out of the hospital. A sound thrashing was delivered.)

But at the time, it was hot, really hot, and I was really parched. I thought, 'God, I could *die* for a drink!' And it occurred to me, as I said to my wife: 'This'll be a good way to show the children not to drink from the tap.' So, I said, 'Right, are you watching, children? This is me drinking the water from the bottle' – *glug-glug-glug* – 'Oh, *nice* water!'

Then I continued with the unpacking, messing about, farting about – well, *literally* farting about. Not the thing you wish for.

I thought, 'God, I'm gonnae fart.' You don't want to fart all over your family, you know? I thought, 'I'll go out on the veranda.' So, I did the Man-Needing-To-Fart-Getting-Out-Of-The-Room Walk. And then when I reached the veranda I tried to sound really nonchalant, you know: 'Oh, the view's *lovely* out here,' I shouted. 'When you're finished unpacking, you must come out!' *Brrrip!* 'Yeah, it's *fabulous* out here!' *Brriipppp!* 'Yeah, mmm, la-la-la-la . . .' – *Brrrip!* – 'La-la-la . . .' *Brrrip!* 'Today, I'm off to Sunny Spain . . .' *Brrrip!* 'La-la-la . . .' *Brrrip-sgggtttttttttt!*

94

My heart stopped, as I felt that last fart run behind my knee. 'OH. MY. GOD!'

And I ran from the knees down into the toilet. And I locked the door behind me. I whipped the tweeds down in mid-run. Sat on the toilet. Not a *second* too soon: *Splutter-splutter-splutter!* 'Ooo-aahh!' *Brrrip-splutter-splutter!* 'Oh, Jesus!' *Splutter-splutter-splutter!*

It was like sulphuric acid!

'Eeeeeooooooow!' *Splutter-splutter-splutter!* I was *screaming*. My arse was red raw, hanging in *tatters*. 'Jesus, I'm going to need a hose-down!' *Splutter-splut-splut-splut . . . splut!*

'Oh my God . . . Ohhh . . . dearie me.'

I went to stand up. *Splutter-splutter-splutter!* Away again! *Splutter-splutter-splutter!* It was WORSE! 'Aaaaaagghhhh!' *Splutter-splutter-splutter!*

The next thing I hear is that my wife has just had a drink. *Brrrip!*

'*Open the door!*'

'Fuck off – don't be ridiculous!' *Splutter-splutter!*

'OPEN THE DOOR!'

'I *can't!* I'm shitting my *brains* out!'

'*Will you open this fucking door?!?*'

'I can't get off the *seat!!* Oh, break the fucking thing down! The wash-hand basin is on your right as you come in – throw the children into the bath!'

It was a nightmare! A *nightmare!*

When I came out it was *dark*. Everybody was asleep. I didn't want to go to bed, in case something *awful* happened, you know, in the bloody bed. I mean, can you imagine? So I paced the room, with very short steps, all night.

Don't go. Don't go to Ibiza, stay here.

We went out the following day. I had one of those vest things on, y'know, just a wee strap thing. Burned my bloody shoulders. Today, if you see me with no clothes on, I've got very freckly shoulders. That's what I ended up with – a very freckly look. But it was really deeply burnt.

You see, I'm from the north. We're not *supposed* to be in hot places. Our skin falls off round our ankles like fuckin' pyjama trousers! You can see us sitting on the beach, like baboons, picking each other's skin off.

And I got no relief. The room was hell. It was a horrible room, I couldn't stay in there. I couldn't lie down. I couldn't wear clothes – I was trying to get my T-shirt to sort of levitate above my skin, you know?

The only relief I got was when we'd go down and kneel in the swimming pool. With my head sticking out. Talking to people who swam past: 'Hullo.' I could hear them talking about me: 'I don't like him much . . . talking to people as they swim past. Nosy bastard if you ask me!'

And the hotel was full of British people with no skin. We really don't know how to *do* it, do we? We don't know how to sunbathe. The British – the English, the Scottish, the Welsh, the Irish. The Irish are the same as the Scottish: they should never be in hot places, the skin just falls off. You see these people in the morning: 'Don't *touch* me! Don't fuckin' TOUCH me!' Screaming sores, suppurating bodies. And you see the waiters, really confused, looking at this family with no skin, all of them screaming, 'DON'T TOUCH ME!' Honeymoon couples: 'DON'T TOUCH ME!'

And my son, the wee boy, on his fourth nose of the week. There's a wee pile of Nivea cream where his nose used to be!

Don't go. Don't go to Ibiza, stay here.

THE AUSTRALIAN SAFARI PARK

They've got a safari park in Brisbane. There's a big sign outside: 'ENGLISHMEN ON BICYCLES ADMITTED FREE'.

There's lions and tigers an' everythin'. And there's an Australian guy driving through in his car with his wee boy beside him.

'Oh, look, a lion!'

'Oh aye.'

'Oooh, look, there's another one!'

'Oh, aye, yeah, very good.'

And there's two lions over here, and one's licking the other one's bum.

So, the boy says, 'What's that lion doin', Daddy?'

He says, 'Oh, he's just eaten an Englishman and it's tryin' to get the taste out its mouth.'

THE C WORD

I often go to Canada, and especially Toronto. I've been there a lot of times since the Seventies. I'm quite big there.

And there's something that always haunts me when I'm in Toronto. The first girl who ever kissed me was called Gracie McLintock. She was five years old. So was I. Standing against an air-raid shelter in Glasgow. But a year later her family emigrated. I don't think it was anything to do with me kissing her. They emigrated to Canada, to Toronto.

And I've thought about her over the years, especially when I was getting big in Toronto. I thought, 'I wonder if she realises that I'm Billy Connolly?' We could meet in the street or something, and it would be nice; I would ask her how she's getting on, is she married, does she have children, what does she do, blahdy-blahdy-blah. But as the years went on it became more of a fantasy. Almost a kind of fetish. And these days it's ridiculous: I can see her running towards me in slow-motion, her breasts slowly bouncing, crying, 'Billy! Finish what you started!'

Anyway, as I said, I visit the place quite often.

I was in Toronto a few years ago, making a movie called *The Boondock Saints*, and I got five days off in the middle of it, which isn't really unusual. I'm very much a creature of habit – I do the same things most days – and every town that I play in I have a walk that I do.

I have one in London, but I'm not telling you where it is because you'll follow me. And you'll want a fucking selfie. Actually, I don't mind doing selfies. But please, if you ever meet me and you want a selfie – have your stuff ready. Don't make me stand there as you go through your fucking bag looking for your camera, because it looks as though I've asked you to do it.

Well, in Toronto, I had five days off so I did the walk five days in a row. And it's just a range of bookshops, music shops, clothes shops, cigar stores and it ends up at a coffee shop on a street called Dundas.

As I walked towards the coffee shop on the first day, there was a guy in the doorway – a sort of down-and-out homeless guy – and he held out a cup and said, 'Any change?' I said, 'Aye, I've got loads here,' so I put it all in the cup. 'Thanks, buddy.' 'No problem.' Then I went in, got a coffee and this magazine, which has two great crosswords in it.

I went back to my hotel to do the crosswords. My life is a ball of fire.

The second day, exactly the same: 'Thanks, buddy.' 'No problem.' Coffee. Magazine. Back to the hotel to do the crosswords.

Third day: 'Thanks, buddy.' 'No problem.' Coffee. Magazine. Back to the hotel to do the crosswords.

On the fourth day, I didn't wait for him to ask. I just put money in his cup. And he says, 'You don't *have* to give me money every time you see me!' I said, 'I'm quite aware of that. You little cunt.' I thought he had it coming. Fuck him.

It's not a word I usually use, especially on that side of the Atlantic, because it frightens the bejaysus out of them. Although they take 'motherfucker' like nothing happened. But being a Glaswegian I'm used to it. It doesn't really mean *anything*. You use it in all sorts of circumstances.

Like, when you're trying to remember a film star's name. People are giving you all kinds of suggestions and you say, 'No, no, not him. Some other cunt.'

I actually heard in Glasgow somebody say, 'Hey, who's that cunt with the Pope?'

And some people don't seem to realise that you don't need to be a complete cunt. You can break it up. 'What do you think of the Prime Minister?' 'Oh, seems a bit of a cunt to me.' And whoever it is, probably is. But just close your eyes and think of Donald Trump. Now there's a complete cunt.

During those presidential debates, I was just waiting for one of the other politicians to say, 'Mr Trump, do you think I think you've got hair?'

THE BRITISH NATIONAL ANTHEM

Britain is in a terrible state, according to some people, and I know why. Now, others have blamed all kinds of things – unemployment, the value of the pound and all sorts of other things – but I know the real explanation. It's because the national anthem is boring.

Don't get me wrong. I'm not arguing with the lyrics. Okay, I am. Overall, yes, I think the Queen should be saved, I think that's a great idea. And if anybody is going to save her, God is the very chap. Who am I to rock the boat?

But, come on, it's an appalling song. And it's racist – it's anti-Scottish. The fourth verse is all about Field Marshal Wade coming up to give us a belt in the mouth! And I don't like that. 'And like a torrent rush,/Rebellious Scots to crush' – oh, do you bloody think so? I don't see any rush to Hampden to crush anybody. I rest my case!

But look at the opening ceremony of any Olympic Games, when we're going round with the flag with the anthem playing.

'Daaaaaaah-daaaaaaah-daaaaaaah-daaaaaaah-daa-daa . . .'

We're being lapped! The Games hasn't even started yet and all of these emerging nations are running past us with their livelier anthems! 'We come from Gerovia, and we don't give a shit!' *Voom!* 'We've got a national debt of fifty-squillion pounds, da-da-da-da!' *Voom!*

'Go-oh-hod saaaaave ouurrr Queeeeeeeen . . .'

Is someone playing a recording at half speed? No, we're singing our fucking national anthem!

None of the other nations want us to win *anything*, because when *we* win it takes half an hour for the flag to get up the bloody pole!

'Goooooooood Saaaaaaaaaave . . .'

No wonder the likes of Daley Thompson were standing on the podium there scratching themselves and whistling. It's a long wait, they're seizing up!

So, I think it's high time for a change. And I think a refreshing change would be to use the theme from *The Archers*. *Dum-der-dum-der-dum-der-dum, Dum-der-dum-der-dah-dah* . . .

Can you imagine it? The Trooping of the Colour – the Queen sitting side-saddle on her horse, singing: 'Laa-laa-laa-laa-laa-ler-laa . . .' The trumpets could all join in – rumpty-tumpty-tumpyy-tum – and the public could be going, 'Rumpp-dee-diddley, rum-dee-diddley . . .'

That's got to be an improvement, hasn't it? Brighter, bouncier, better. It's *much* nicer.

And just think: all the immigrants can learn it on the bus

on their way in from Heathrow. They could jump off the bus and start singing it straight away: sorted!

ONLY IN DUBLIN

I find the Irish very funny, and I find Ireland very funny. Dublin especially.

For the Millennium, the Irish government decided to make this big silvery needle thing in Dublin, where Nelson's Pillar used to be in O'Connell Street in the centre. Why the fuck anyone would want a big silvery needle thing that size is a mystery. It was just a big, big needle. They ended up calling it 'The Spire'.

But there was something wrong. They couldn't get it right for a long, long time. It was in two bits, or several bits, and the top bit was proving extraordinarily hard to get right.

So, they get this crane from Europe – this fucking *massive* crane – and they were using that to try and sort out this top bit. But it wasn't getting any easier.

And for months, and months, and fucking months it went on. *Years* rolled on. The Millennium came and fucking went and still it wasn't ready.

And there was a beautiful shop down there called Clerys, which was the kind of Harrods of Dublin. They had big sort of barriers all around it so you couldn't see the place and there was still this big crane there, too.

Once it was finished, somebody on the radio came on and said, 'Phone up and give us your ideas about The Spire!' and some guy phoned in – and it could only happen in Dublin – and the presenter said, 'What do you think, sir?' And he sang: 'I can see Clerys now the crane has gone!'

That's why I love Ireland, and love Dublin, so much.

I was in the Kilkenny Shop recently – I like to go there for cups of tea – and a man with a cowboy hat came in. And at first I thought I knew him, because I'm getting quite old, and now when I see guys that I used to play with in bands and they've got the grey hair and all of that, it takes me a while to figure out who they are, because I think everybody stays the same, with the black hair and everything, you know? And this guy in the cowboy hat, he kind of winked over at me, so I wondered if I knew him.

But this could only happen in Ireland: first of all, he had a cup of tea with his friends, and then he came over, and he had a wee bag, the kind you would buy for a brooch or something, a wee paper bag, and a serviette. And he'd written on the serviette – you know when you write on a serviette it all tears and all that? – and he'd written:

Dear Billy,
You're brilliant. Welcome to Dublin.
Have a chocolate mouse.

And he'd given me a chocolate mouse! Now, there's nowhere else in the world that anybody would give you a chocolate mouse. And I was as happy as Larry. I was in my hotel room later on, watching David Letterman, eating my chocolate mouse in my bed.

On another occasion, I was going to the local television station to do *The Late Late Show* with Gay Byrne. That was an unusual show to do, you know – I mean, I liked doing it, but it's not often you get nuns in your audience.

Anyway, they sent a limousine to take me there, and when I came out and opened the door I was amazed because there was no one in it, but I thought, 'Well, this must be it,' so I got in. And the car radio was on, there was music playing, but when I slammed the door getting in, the driver suddenly sat up – he'd been lying flat out on the front seats having a kip with his cap over his eyes.

Then he leaned forward to turn the radio down and I said, 'No, no, keep it on, it's brilliant. In fact, can you turn it up a bit, please?' And it sounded like that Irish folky band Planxty, who I love. I thought it was them. Nice aggressive-sounding music. And it was rattling away there and I thought, 'Great, this'll do me.' So, we set off.

And as we were driving along, the record came to an end, and then the DJ waffled on about a competition or something the way they do. And he didn't bother to say who the record was by. So, I said to the driver, 'Was that Planxty?'

His answer will go to my grave with me. He said, 'I don't know. I don't normally work Friday nights.'

I was starting to get frightened. I was thinking, 'This guy thinks every Friday on the radio is exactly the fucking same!' Isn't that astonishing?

Then there was this other time, one morning, a woman in Dublin came up and said to me: 'Billy Connolly! You're the spitting image of yourself!' So, I said, 'Well, I'm pleasantly surprised, because I don't usually look like me until twelve or half-twelve!'

And only very recently, again in Dublin, I met another woman, a nice wee woman in a cardigan. I was sharing a table with her in a restaurant. The poor woman nearly fainted at first. I'd said, 'Is anybody sitting here?' and she'd looked up and gone, 'Agggh!' Because when you're famous you can give someone quite a fright.

Anyway, as we were sitting there, I said, 'Jeez, it's *cold* out there! It's *freezing*, isn't it? The sun's shining but it's bloody freezing!' And she says, very confidently, 'But it's going to be a *lovely* summer.' And I said, 'Oh, really?' She said, 'Yes. The dolphins are in Kerry!'

Now, I liked her. And I can trust that. When I'm in Ireland it makes sense.

TEA AND SCONES

Older Scottish women – women sixties onwards, pension age women – they all meet in the mornings. You only see them between ten and eleven in the morning. They're not there before or afterwards. They meet one another and they eat scones.

They wear lavender-coloured tweed clothes. I think they call it 'heather mixture'. '*Mmmm*, that's a lovely wee suit, *mmm*, oh, *heather mixture* goes with *everything*.' It's the Scottish version of beige. 'Oh, it's *luuvely*, that wee heather mixture, Morag, you really suit that, and it's a suit that's good for *any* occasion, you could mix with anybody in that . . .'

And nylons you can't see through. Heavy-duty jobs, y'know? Self-exploding cork-lined numbers.

And they wear the loveliest wee shoes. They're brogues: brown brogue high heels with laces. You *never* see them in shops. They're handed down from mother to daughter. 'And to ma daughter, Morag, I leave ma scone shoes – look after them . . .' You put these shoes on at ten in the morning and they fuck off for a scone by themselves! You put them on, and they go: '*SCOOOOONNNNE!!!!*'

And the Fair Isle Twin Set. It's a kind of plain colour with a wee wreath of flowers round it.

And the wee hat.

They all meet in these wee tea rooms, which happily are still there, and there's a lot of them in Edinburgh. And they *look* like scones! They're kind of *powdery*, you know? They've got that *sconey* look.

And when they *talk* about scone shops, they never say, 'Oh, they bake lovely scones!' They say, 'They *do* a lovely scone!' As if they only did the one. It's like Australia and the outback. They say, 'the bush'. I thought it was a desert with one fuckin' bush, you know? 'Ah, this must be the fuckin' bush they all talk about!' So: 'They do a *luuvely* scone!'

And the shops they shop at, these wee women, they have clothes in the window, all ruffled up so you don't know what they are. It's just a bunch of cloth. And a wee thing on it, a wee sticker, that says: 'Lovely On'. 'Just in: Lovely On!' And a bunch of cloth and it says: 'Two-Piece'. Two-piece *what*? Carpet? Scarf?

So, they meet. And they eat scones and they talk. There's

usually four of them. And they've all got Morris Minor Travellers, with the wood – it's a sort of Tudor estate car. And they talk away about things: 'Ooh, I *knoooow*!' And they eat. 'Ooh, I know . . .' – *munch* – 'Him? I can't *staaaaand* him!' – *munch* – 'He's a dirty bugger!' – *munch* – 'That Billy Connolly, he's a *diiiiirty* bugger!' – *munch* – 'More jam, Morag?' 'Thank you!' – *munch*.

Now, there's something in the tea, or the scone, or the jam, or the cream – I don't know where – it makes them *violent*, anyway. Because the whole thing always ends in a fight. They've all got their jackets off. They keep their hats on and they take the jackets off.

But it always ends up: 'PUT THAT PURSE AWAY!' *'NOOOOO!'* *'NOOOOOOO!'* 'DON'T. YOU. DARE!' And they do that rhythm: 'Don't – you – dare – do – that – again!' 'No!! – You – know – fine – it's – a – Tuesday – and – I – *always* – pay – on – a *Tuesday*.'

The waitress is standing there and they're saying: *'Don't* you *take* their *money*, dear! Don't you—' and she's going, 'Fucking *hell*! Come on!'

POTATOES OF THE NIGHT

I'm in this restaurant in Ireland, me and my daughter, Cara.

It was an incredibly simple thing, but it usually is an incredibly simple thing that makes me roar. It was one of those menus with nothing on it. You know those menus you get these days with no information? I don't know why they bother giving you the fucking thing.

It's got things like 'Soup of the Day'. So, you then have to ask what it is. 'What *is* the Soup of the Day?' Because you can't just say, 'I'll have Soup of the Day.' You know, a shot in the dark. Because it might be Octopus Arsehole soup! 'Soup of the Day' is nothing. Just get a pencil or pen and *write* what kind of fucking *soup* it *is*! Is that too much to ask?

And vegetables. 'Vegetables in Season'. That could be pumpkins or frozen peas or Japanese mushrooms, you've got *no* fucking *idea*! You see, you can't just say, 'I'll have the veggies in season.' It might be a great pile of shite! You don't know *what* you're going to get.

Fish. 'Catch of the Day'. What is it – a whale or a jellyfish or a tiddler or what? What are we talking here – some ugly fucking thing that lives at the bottom of the ocean you've never seen before that's got three arseholes and horns?

Or even worse, they'll send some limp-wristed lisping prick out to tell you 'The Specials'! What do you mean, '*specials*'? – there's fuck all *on* here! What about 'The Ordinaries'?

'Well, today's special is a fillet of monkfish on a bed of sautéed beetroot with balsamic vinegar—'

Fuck off! JUST. FUCK. OFF!

Write it down. Bring it out. In my country, this is called: 'A Menu'. You *give* it to me, I will *peruse* the aforesaid menu, and, when I'm *ready* for you, I'll *call*. You'll know me when I call. It'll be like: '*NOW!*' And you'll come and ask me and I'll tell you what I want, just like we used to do before.

Oh, there was another thing. About lobsters. It's got letters next to it like market prices or something: 'TFD'. Correct: 'Too Fucking Dear'!

That's when I burst out laughing. In this Irish restaurant.

The menu said: 'Soup of the Day. Veggies in Season. Catch of the Day. Blah blah blah. Lobster thing . . .' And *there* it was – only in Ireland – 'Potatoes of the Night'.

I just fucking *roared*! I nearly fell out of my chair.

'Potatoes of the Night'!

I thought, 'Maybe it's a *band*!' Maybe between the main course and the pudding. 'Ladies and gentlemen, put your hands together, give a big Galway welcome for . . . The Potatoes of the Night!'

And I was really looking forward to this. I said, 'Oh, Potatoes of the Night fer me!' I thought they'd bring them out one at a time: 'They're very *shy* creatures . . . no, keep the lights down, no sudden noises, no sudden movements – you'll scare the *shit* out of 'em . . .'

I was so disappointed. And I'm sure you will be when I tell you. 'Potatoes of the Night' was . . . how they were *doing* them that night. Mashed . . . boiled . . . baked . . .

Isn't it a *pisser*? Isn't that the *worst* news you ever heard?

'Potatoes of the Night'. I mean, you would expect Leonard Cohen to be singing about them! 'She gave me potatoes of the night . . .' I couldn't believe it. Because already in my mind I had it down. I mean, this was surely a *nocturnal* potato native to Ireland. Specialist farmers at four o'clock in the morning out in the fields, you know, miner's helmet with the light on it: '. . . There's one! Ah, that was a big cracker, ran down its hole just before I got a chance to grab it!'

The chips all scattered over your plate, running into dark corners: *'Fuckin' hell!'*

THE COOKBOOK

I was once up in Inverness, up in the north-east of Scotland. Culloden, the battlefield, is in Inverness, and I went up there, just to stand about. It's got an atmosphere that you just can't believe. You can still feel. We got murdered there, the Scots, just wiped out. They have a tourist centre, which has a café, and I saw to my delight: they have scones.

So, I had a wee scone to myself. And a scotch broth. I was dipping my scone in my broth, like a true Highland fuckwit.

While munching my scone I was reading a book I had bought next door. They sell wee hairy Highlanders and tartan and books, you know, those bullshit tourist 'artefacts'? *We* think that's the *culture*! We give it to each other, and it's the only country on earth I know that does it: 'Ah, here ye are, there's a wee hairy Highlander!' 'Oh, thanks very much!' They're supposed to be for the unwary and bewildered tourist, but *we* give them to one another.

Now, I like to cook, it's a great hobby of mine, and I've got *loads* of cookbooks. When I go on holiday I always get the cookbook from where I am, and I try things. But Scottish food's brilliant. That's not to say Scottish *restaurants* are brilliant. But Scottish *food* is.

So, I got this cookbook. It's brilliant. It's called *Lady Maclean's Cook Book*. There I was eating my scone, having a spoonful of soup, eating a scone, and reading the recipes. And I just *collapsed*.

Sometimes you just can't control yourself. I read one and

I laughed, but I had a mouthful of scone, so I laughed and coughed and kind of hiccupped, and half the scone was comin' doon my nose, and I was in distress. 'I-I'll clean meself up and the café wall an' stuff . . .'

This Lady Maclean had a wonderful restaurant at a place called Strachur. It's in Argyll.

Well, Argyll is now in Strathclyde, but I refuse to recognise all that. 'The new regions.' For instance, Clackmannanshire and Stirlingshire, and the bottom bit of Sutherlandshire, are now called 'Central'. They must have been up all fuckin' night thinking *that* one up, eh? Who *are* these bastards?

Lady Maclean had a place at Strachur in Argyle. A very good restaurant. She had her recipes, and she had recipes from her friends – sort of gentrified people, you know, Lady That and Lord The Other. They had all submitted recipes on their own writing paper, with their names and stuff on it, and handwritten.

Well, the Duchess of Argyll had submitted a recipe for venison something. 'Venison à la Inveraray-o-something'. But the important thing was, just below that, there was a wee afterthought in brackets, the way people do, and it said: '(An ideal way to get rid of that leftover venison.)'

Is this woman out of touch?! 'An ideal way to get rid of that leftover venison' – because that's *such* a fuckin' *problem*, I find, that leftover venison!

I was brought up in a housing estate just outside Glasgow – well, *in* Glasgow, but just *outside* civilisation – and they used to have these vans, you shopped at *vans*. All the shops were boarded up, it was like fucking Fort Apache. 'Whaddya want?' *Duck.* 'Cigarettes.' *Dive.* 'Here, now get the fuck oot of here!' The place was under siege.

And I was trying to imagine those people reading that recipe. 'Hey . . . Willie!' 'What's up?' 'Ah've got a recipe here that says we can get rid of that leftover venison.' 'Thank *FUCK* for that! Ah've had it up tae here! If Ah see another bit of venison Ah'll fuckin' lose control! Ah can't get the fridge door shut! Fuckin' deer's head hanging oot like that! Them big fucking antlers are spillin' all the yoghurts.'

So I had a *good* laugh.

It's a very good recipe, incidentally.

Then, I was whacking along through the book and I came to another one. I can't remember who this woman was. The Marchioness of Bridalbam or some-fucking-where. Lives up a tree in The Trossachs. And it was melon balls. In port or something. And as a wee addendum, it says: 'Insist on Afghan Melon'.

I was trying to picture the same wee woman going down to one of those old grocery vans. 'Wha? Wha ya wunt?' 'Is that an *Afghan* melon?' 'FUCK OFF! Ah'll tell ya what it is – it's the only melon we've ever fuckin' had!! Ah thought it was an *apple*, otherwise it wouldnae been here at all! There was no fuckin' *birth certificate* with it – d'ye wannit, or are ya gonnae get the fuck out the road?'

3.

Real Characters

'A mate of mine told me he's shagging his
girlfriend and her twin.
I said "How can you tell them apart?"
He said "Her brother's got a moustache."'

HARKINS OF THE SIXTIES

I'm a child of the Sixties. I'm 'damaged'. I'm a war baby as well. And in the Sixties I had all these weird friends. The language was different then, too. I wish most of you had been there. I guess some of you were there, but some of you weren't. It was amazing.

And if anybody tells you it changed nothing, they're liars. It made the world a wee bit more optimistic. Because I was there *before* the Sixties. I was there in the fucking *Forties*. I'm a very old man. And I remember. I remember the Forties and I remember the Fifties, and it was a shithouse. The world was beige and the music was fucking crap.

Five minutes mo-ore. Give me five minutes mo-ore. Only fiiiive minutes more, Let me stay, let me sta-ay in your arms . . .

It was like being stuck inside the fucking Eurovision Song Contest in a school uniform. That's what we were listening to.

And then 'Heartbreak Hotel' came and fucking saved us all. 'Weeeeell, since ma baby left me' – *bu-bum!* 'What the hell *is* that? That's for *me*!' 'I found a new place to dwell' – *bu-bum!* 'Fucking YES!' It was *amazing*.

And then the whole hippy thing and the hairy thing came along, and I was there as well. I was a teenager when they invented rock and roll. I was fucking blessed! I was the chosen one!

Oh, it was brilliant. And the whole hippy thing created optimism – a thing they knew fuck all about here in the western world in the years before that. Everyone was shuffling about in drab overcoats and hats. There was no such thing as a teenager then – they were invented in the Fifties.

But the Sixties was such a breakthrough. It was the biggest breakthrough since the Teddy Boy. You looked different from the soles of your feet to the top of your head, and scared the shit out of everybody. And parents got frightened. And I know what they were frightened of, because now I've got daughters, and they play my old records, and I can hear them in the other room listening to Bob Dylan, going, 'Everybody must get stoned!' 'Oh, for fuck's sake. I should have hidden that one.'

But I remember it with such joy. I'd just quit welding and become a banjo-playing folk singer kind of guy, all hairy and windswept and interesting. As I saw it. And at that time I had a lot of friends – actors and poets and writers and players and bits and pieces – and there was a guy called Harkins, who was a nutcase. We used to go to this pub where all the actors and poets and singers went, and he was the new barman in there. He said, 'I'm actually an actor.' As they do. And he made this sort of sucking noise with his lips. 'Oh really?' I said. 'Aye' – and he made the noise again. I thought, 'I don't think so. Not with that fucking thing he's got.'

But he took it seriously, or at least he gave you that impression. I remember, for example, during one week, whenever he served you he'd do this odd little hop and swivel with his hips when he went to get you a glass, then another little hop and swivel when he went to pour you a pint, and so on and so on. It looked really odd. So, I said, 'What's all this?' And he said, 'Oh, I'm doing a one-man play' – he was always doing 'one-man' plays and shows – 'and it's Oscar Wilde. Women had bustles on their dresses in those days, so when I'm playing the women I'm gonna do the bustle. I won't be wearing the clothes but I'll be doing the walk, y'know, that bustle thing?' He was always 'preparing' stuff like that while he was serving behind the bar.

Anyway, eventually he was fired from the pub – I don't know what for, being late, probably – and I didn't see him again for two or three months. And then he was in the pub again. 'Ah, Bill, how are you?' He was puffing on a joint all the time. I said, 'Where have you been, Harkins?' 'Oh, I was doing my one-man show in the Isle of Skye. It was fuckin' great, a great reception.' Every time he performed it was thousands of miles away, so nobody had any chance of seeing it. 'Oh yeah, my one-man show went down a storm, oh aye.' So I asked:

'Have you got a job?'

'Aye, it's a great job, I'm just down the road at the Western – it's a hospital just down the street.'

'Oh. What are you doing there?'

'I'm in the mortuary.'

He's working in the mortuary with all the dead guys and he's stoned all the time, you know, he was always out of his brain. This guy hadn't had a pupil in his eye for about nine months.

He was one of those stoners you'd meet who'd frighten the

life out of you. 'Ooh, Bill,' he'd say. 'A man gave me two yellow pills last Monday. Ooh, fucking amazing! Lost the power of ma legs for two days – fuckin' amazing!'

But he's somehow got this gig with all the deadies. And it's a huge hospital, and people just die there all the time – it's a busy place, the morgue. And part of his job was to take the dead guys out of there – on a wheelbarrow – and into the university, which is just around the corner.

So, I said, 'How are you enjoying the job?' 'Ah, it's fucking great.'

It was him who told me that dead people fart. I didn't know that. I've never personally heard them do this – because I've only been around dead people at funerals, I've not been down the morgues – but he told me that during the night you'd hear this sound: *Brrriiirppp!* He's sitting there, smoking a wee doubie. *Brrriiippp!* You see, they'd just died that day, and the air in your body still has to escape, out the arse, or it sometimes comes up out the other way, through the mouth, and some of them sort of sit up – can you imagine?

But he liked it. He said, 'Aw, it's a great laugh after a while.' He was a mental case.

The nurses would phone down: 'Is that you, Mr Harkins?' 'Sure, yeah, what do you want, darlin'?' '"Nurse", if you don't mind.' 'Oh, okay: Nurse, what is it?' 'I'm coming down to see number nineteen, can I come down just now?' You know, the corpses were all numbered. And he says, 'Er, look, it would be okay, but, listen, I'm just going out for a sandwich – how about in an hour's time, how would that suit you?' 'No problem, Mr Harkins.' 'Fine, Nurse.' *Click*. And he wasn't going out for a sandwich at all. He just ran out to all the dead guys and women and he started reorganising them!

He'd put them in poses. Some would be sitting up as though they were watching the telly, some would be leaning back on one arm, some would have their hand under their chin like they were pondering some thought or other, and some would be holding each other in a seemingly amorous embrace. So, an hour later, the nurse would come down, go inside, look around, and think: 'Fucking hell!' And she'd ask Harkins, 'What's going on here?' And he'd say, 'I dunno – they were like that when I came in this morning – they must have had a party last night!'

And his job, as I told you, was to take the ones who were going to be experimented on over to the university. He would take them in this rather beautiful wheelbarrow – it was a kind of Victorian thing with sides – and he's put the body in it with a tarpaulin over the top and away out into the street, Byres Road, and up to the right to the traffic lights – there was just a wee set of traffic lights – and turn right into University Avenue and up into the medical place.

Incidentally: don't give them your body. Keep your body to yourself. Because he told me stuff. He said there's testicles flying across the room, they're playing with bits and chucking them around, there's people going home looking for their bus fare only to find they've got a penis in their pocket: 'Oh for fuck's sake!'

So I meet him in the pub: 'Are you okay?'

'Aaaah, the fucking bastards fired me.'

'Well, what did you do?'

He said, 'Aw, they've got no fuckin' sense of humour over there.'

'Really?'

'Ah, all I did was make a fuckin' giant and they all lost their—'

'You did *what*?'

As it turned out, he had four men he had to take round to the medical place. And he thinks to himself, 'Well, I'm not making four fucking journeys!' So he's put the first guy in his wheelbarrow and he's pulled him up to the front so he's hanging over the edge, with his head dangling there. And he's got the next one on it, and his legs are down the bottom. So the head and the legs are about twelve feet apart. And then he gets the third guy on the left with his arm hanging over. And the fourth guy on the right with his arm hanging over. And he covers the middle with a tarpaulin. So it now looks like a huge big guy.

And then he's off, pushing the wheelbarrow, away up to the traffic lights, with this giant body with the head hanging and the arms hanging out. A guy in a lorry took one look and swerved off the road. There's people braking and crashing and screaming all over the place.

That's the way life is *supposed* to be, you know? You're not supposed to get up in the morning, go to work, come back, and sit and watch *Neighbours* and shite like that! Sixties people were different. They were characters. They had character.

ALOYSIUS MCGLUMPHER

There was a guy who worked for the Glasgow council, many years ago. He was put in charge of the maintenance of the city, and the sewers were part of his gig.

So, he's looking on the wall at the holiday rota system for all the sewage workers, and he says to one of his assistants:

'Who's this fella here, Aloysius McGlumpher?'

'Oh, he's a very good worker!'

'I see he never takes holidays.'

'Oh, no, he never does. He enjoys his work so much. He never takes holidays, he gives them away to the other guys.'

'Oh yeah?'

'Yeah. It's difficult enough to get him to go home at night. He's a very happy man.'

'I don't believe it.'

'It's true. I'll take you down there so you can meet him and see for yourself.'

'Sure, I'd like that.'

So away they go down to the sewers and they've got their wellies and the hard hats with the lights on. As they walk slowly through the sewers, in the distance they can hear: 'Sugar in the morning. Sugar in the evening. Sugar at suppertime.' This wee happy voice. And the assistant says, 'Aye. That's McGlumpher.' 'Well, let's go and meet him!'

They're paddling slowly away down there through all this stuff, with these terrible smells, and rats scuttling about and cockroaches crawling everywhere and all kinds of horrible things. And there's McGlumpher, singing happily to himself:

'Sugar in the morning. Sugar in the evening. Sugar at supper-time.'

So the new boss says, 'Hello, Mr McGlumpher, it's a delight to meet such a happy worker.'

'Oh, yes! I love it doon here! Oh, I wouldn't change it for the world!'

And the boss says, 'But, really, how can you like this disgusting place?'

And he says, '*Disgusting*? Disgusting nothing, sir! It's a very *interesting* place, I'll have you know.'

'Oh really? What's interesting about it?'

'Och, you wouldn't believe it. See that wee jobbie there?'

'Which one?'

'The one that's just come round the corner there – see it now? Wee beige number? Well, that belongs to a butcher three streets away there in Argyle Street.'

'How on earth do you know?'

'Well, you can see there's bits of sawdust on it and all that.'

The council boss is amazed by this. 'That's an incredible observation,' he says. And the guy says, 'Well, that's my hobby, I see all sorts down here.' Then he suddenly points excitedly: 'You see that one there? The one behind that one? See it? See it? *That* man runs a sweeties shop! You see the dolly mixtures and things? The wee Smarties in it? It's definitely from the sweetie shop up the road there!'

The boss is even more impressed. 'I really never thought a job like this could be so interesting! That's extraordinary!'

Then McGlumpher is off again, even more excitedly: 'Hey! Hey! Look there! Look, look – just behind that wee cardboard box, see it just coming doon there?' The boss goes: 'Yes, er, yes, I see it now, aye.' McGlumpher declares: *'That's* my wife's!'

The boss says, 'Well, how on earth do you know *that*?' He says, 'Easy – it's got my sandwiches tied to it!'

A CALL FROM GERRY RAFFERTY

Gerry Rafferty, the singer-songwriter, was an expert on the telephone. He used to make me scream.

He was a very complicated character, Gerry. Most people found him dark and kind of scary sometimes, but I remember him as a very funny person.

We were in a band together: The Humblebums. I was the frontman, doing the introductions and all of that, because Gerry hated that side of it; he didn't even like people looking at him. But he was very controlling of the musical side, because he really knew what he was doing with that.

He didn't share very well musically. Even when we recorded things, he would sometimes go back into the studio later on his own and change it – he'd take me off and put himself on! As a matter of fact, one of the most wounding things was when we played the Adam Smith Centre in Kirkcaldy. He was going to play a certain song – he announced it, I got all ready – and then he turned to me and said, 'I'm doing this one alone.' And I had to walk off. Ouch!

But he remained a dear friend, he really did. He came to my shows and we'd always have a right good laugh about old times. We were actually talking and texting on the phone right up to just before he died, and we'd be in tears of laughter. We laughed right up to the very end.

And I'll never forget the things we got up to before and after gigs. We had so much fun. And, as I say, using the phone was one of his specialities. He would phone people – total strangers – and have these hilarious conversations with them.

I'll tell you how it started: we were looking for 'Hitler' in a German phone book. And there are none!

We were at a place, Rosyth naval dockyard – the Royal Navy on the River Forth, just outside Edinburgh – underneath the Forth Bridge there. We were the entertainment. We turned up about seven o'clock, but we weren't on until about nine, so we tuned up and farted about. There were no dressing rooms; the man had said, 'Sorry, we've got no dressing rooms, just use the office.' So, we were in the office, fuckin' about, y'know, tuning up and singing wee Everly Brothers songs and all those things that you do while you're waiting.

Gerry goes over to the phone, and he's thumbing through the phone book, and I look at him, and the next thing is he's phoning his first one, Joseph Johnson, his first victim. Luckily the person lifts the phone, and he goes: 'Hullo?' And Gerry goes, 'How you doin'?' The person at the other end goes: 'Is that you Willie Ferguson?' Gerry says: 'Yes' – without missing a beat! – 'Certainly it's me.'

'Well, you *bastard*!'

'Aye, what's wrong with you?' he says.

'You said you'd be here tae sweep ma chimney at three o'clock this afternoon! We waited *all day*! I've had time off work!'

Gerry says, 'I'm sorry, Joseph. Can I tell you – you'll never believe this: new government regulations.'

I'm sitting there! This really happened!

'New government regulations.' Now the guy is bewildered. 'Fuck, *what?*'

'Took me by surprise myself. Tell me, do you have a safety net at home?'

'*What?*'

'I don't have one myself and the government has said we need a safety net. In case we fall off the roof, while we're doin' your chimney.'

'Oh aye? Well . . . I dunno . . . I've nae got a fuckin' safety net! What would *I* be doin' with a fuckin' safety net?'

'Well, have you got, like, blankets and sheets and that?'

'Er, aye, I've got a few of them.'

'Put them in the garden – we'll *make* a safety net. Do you have any scaffolding there?'

'*What??* What the fuck would I be doin' with *scaffolding*???'

'We need scaffolding. Safety measure by the government. It's a new regulation – I cannae leave the office without a guarantee of that. Er, could you get some furniture out the house? Maybe we could step up on it. A chair on top of a sideboard, we could get away with that and call it scaffolding, along with the sheets and blankets and that.'

'Er, aye, I guess I could do that.'

'But look, the other bit is: I can't come alone. I have to have four other people. That's the new regulation, right? I could do you at ten o'clock tomorrow morning, but I'll tell you what, the other regulation, the new one, is: you have to provide breakfast. Nothing much – fried egg, bacon, sausage, you know the kind of thing, potato scones, maybe a couple of mushrooms, a wee bit of black puddin' in there, all right, Mr Johnson? Five breakfasts, furniture, a few sheets and blankets – oh, have you any ropes, we'll need some ropes, aye, a washing line, that'll do – have it all ready. Five breakfasts, we'll be there at ten. No problem, okay? I'll be there with my men, you can trust me. All the best, Joe, see you later!'

'Aye.'

Bam.

So then Gerry's straight into the *Yellow Pages*: 'Now: Ferguson . . . Fucking Ferguson . . . Ferguson, Ferguson, Ferguson, where the fuck's Ferguson . . . *Ferguson, chimney sweep* – fuckin' got you!'

Dialling. *Brrr-Brrr.*

'Hullo?'

Gerry's off again: 'Aye! Is that you, Ferguson?'

'Aye.'

'Where the FUCK were you???'

'What are you talkin' aboot?'

'This is Joe Johnson! You promised three o'clock, I had a day off fuckin' work!!'

'Oh, er, ah, ma diary's full, I've got it up tae here, I cannae cope with it—'

'Well, look: I've asked for some time off tomorrow morning, can you be here at ten?'

'Er, aye, I-I—'

'You be here at ten, and I'll see you then!'

'Er, a-aye, fine.'

'Cheerio!'

Bam!

BILLY THE DRIVER

When I was performing in Belfast, I had this brilliant limo driver called Billy. A local guy, a Belfast man, and a real character.

And like all Irish men, he lied a lot. I don't mean that in a malicious way at all. But, over there, they'll tell you a lie to make you feel better, to soothe your journey a little. Like, if you're walking along, hiking along, and there's a farmer and his wife, and you shout out to them, 'How far to Dublin?' The farmer will shout back, 'Twelve miles,' but his wife will say, 'For Christ's sake, he's walking – tell him it's six!'

It's that kind of thing. It's a gentle, helpful kind of lying.

Billy's wife was wonderful. She looked like a hooker, actually. She chewed gum all the time, and she had jangly, sparkly clothes on, and very short skirts, red shoes, big red nails and big shiny lips like she'd been eating chips all night, and big charm bracelets that went *ching-ching* every time she moved. She was like in perpetual motion, her head and body was almost vibrating, she was always slightly moving.

I'd not seen anything like her since I was a child. The hookers in my hometown all did that. They'd always be slightly rocking and nodding while standing still: 'Hello, sailor!' And we used to run past them when we were wee boys and shout, 'Hey, missus, you left your engine running, ha ha ha!'

Billy said, 'My wife wants to come to your gig, would that be all okay?' And I said, 'Of course it would! Just see my manager there about the tickets, he'll sort them out for you, no problem at all. Any particular night? Just tell him and we'll sort it out for you.' Then he says, 'Er, she wants to come in the limo – how do you feel about that?' I said, 'No problem at all. Easy peasy poo!'

I thought she'd be in the front with him. But she got straight in the back. 'Hi Bill!' The smell of Estée Lauder; you cannae get it off you. But there she was, slightly moving all the time, chewing, jangling, all of that. And she was very funny and really nice. But she kept opening the limo windows on the way into Belfast and shouting, 'I'M IN HERE WITH BILLY CONNOLLY!' And she kept saying, 'Bill, Bill – *wave* to them, come on!' I'm cringing there going, 'Hullo.'

Billy used to make up old Irish sayings. And I would be on my knees laughing. I was supposed to believe this shit.

We were driving to the gig one night, and he says, 'You know, Billy, I'm amazed that you don't have a car yourself. You know, a nice car and a regular driver to take you around.' I said, 'Oh, I used to have that, but I gave all that up.' 'Why?' 'Because I like being by myself, you know, just take the B roads, stop and have a scone if I want to, and just have a nice life. And besides which, I was getting fed up with the driver.' And he says, 'Was he an eejit?'

Now, in actual fact, he was a nice bloke, my old driver, but to cut a long story short I just said, 'Yeah, a bit of an eejit.' So, he says, 'You know, we have an old saying here in Northern Ireland.' I said, 'Oh, really?' He took a wee while to reply, so

I knew he was making it up – I could hear the cogs going round. He said, 'Wherever you're going, never take an eejit with you. You can always pick one up when you get there.'

He was full of that sort of thing.

IVAN THE TERRIBLE

There is this circus that comes to Glasgow, and they had a wrestler as the main attraction: Ivan the Terrible from Russia. Everybody was terrified of him. He had two famous holds: the Half Pretzel and the Full Pretzel. The Half Pretzel broke your back and the Full Pretzel killed you. There was this trail of dead bodies all over Russia, and it had got to the stage where nobody there would fight him anymore. So, he joined the circus.

The circus arrived in Glasgow. Everybody knew it had come because there was elephant shit all over the High Street. The police were putting messages out saying: 'An elephant has shit in the High Street. Drivers are asked to treat it as a roundabout.'

One night, the ringmaster comes out: 'Ladies and gentlemen, all the way from Russia: *Ivan the Terrible!* I want a volunteer from the audience.'

Nothing. They're sitting there quaking in their seats.

'Five hundred pounds . . . ?'

'I'll do it!'

And this guy with a newspaper sticking out of his pocket, four foot nothing, six feet between the eyes, comes down.

'Now, you know what you're doing, sir?' asks the ringmaster.

'Aye!' says this wee guy. 'Who are you going to fight?' asks the ringmaster. 'I don't care!' replies the wee guy. 'It's Ivan the Terrible from the Steppes. Never been beaten. Two fam—'

'I DON'T CARE!'

The ringmaster says, 'Oh well, be it on your own head, sir.'

Then this big hairy thing comes out. The ground was shaking, and the fight began.

The little guy dived at Ivan's mass of hair and disappeared inside. Then this hairy arm came over and the crowd gasped – it was going to be the Half Pretzel for sure!

Then another hairy arm came over and the crowd gasped again – it was going to be the Full Pretzel!

They fell in a hairy ball on the floor and all of a sudden – WHAM! Ivan flew off, hit the pole in the centre of the tent, slid down unconscious.

The place went bananas!

The ringmaster got the wee fellow and asked him what his name was.

'Shuggy.'

'Well, hello, Mr Shuggy! Could you tell the audience how you managed that?'

'Well,' he says, 'I was nutting his belly button there, and I thought I wasnae doing too badly until I saw this arm come over, and I thought it was going to be the Half Pretzel. Then – *boof!* – the other arm came over, and there I was: lying on the floor, waiting for the lights to go out. And all of a sudden, right in front of ma' face, I see this huge willy! There's this willy staring me right in the face. So, I knew what to do. I sank my teeth right into it. And you know something? It's amazing the surge of strength you get when you bite your own willy!'

THE BRAVEST MAN AT THE BEACH

If I was touring Australia, when my kids were small, we'd get a place at Surfers Paradise on the Gold Coast, my wife and I and the children, and we'd have a two or three weeks' family holiday there. Then they'd go home, and I'd go to work. It was a nice arrangement.

One of my plans was to swim and get fit for my tour. There's a big outdoor pool there made from rocks and I was in there swimming up and down. But it was just me and a lot of children in there. It felt a bit odd.

Now, there's nothing odd about me – I've got no attraction to the priesthood or anything like that. And there was nothing odd about them – they were just having fun. But I could see people looking, thinking, 'What's that big hairy fella doing in there beside all those kids?'

So, I started to swim in the sea. And it was wonderful, and I was getting stronger every day and a bit braver every day. I don't like swimming, you see, but I was improving. My wife said, 'I was watching you yesterday, you're getting better all the time, aren't you?' I said, 'Oh, yeah, I'm getting good.'

With my hand on my heart, I swear this is true.

Sometimes I can be incredibly stupid. I said to my wife, 'I'm doing okay, but do you know what gets on my nerves? Those bloody car alarms! Every day when I'm swimming in there. Bloody car alarms! And they're all the *same*! They've all got exactly the same tone, so when all the guys get out, they don't know whose car's gone off!'

And my wife said, 'Billy – that's the shark alarm.'

I was reading the newspaper while I was staying at this place, and I saw the bravest man I've ever set eyes on in my life. He was this character from Newcastle, New South Wales. He'd been in the sea – I don't know what he was doing in there, but he was splashing around or something – and a shark came along.

It bites his thigh.

Now, in that position, my first instinct would be to put my head under the water and inhale deeply. I would like to be dead before this bastard's jaws come together, before the really painful bit comes. I don't know whether that's brave or cowardly, but that's what *I* would do.

Not him. He starts fighting with the shark: *Biff!* 'Ya bastard!' *Biff! Biff!* 'Get away from me, ya bastard!' *Biff! Biff!* But he can't get it loose, so he grabs it! He grabs it and he swims ashore!

When he gets to the shore, there's no one there. 'Ah, shit!' The shark's still biting into his thigh, and he's still punching it in a bid to make it stop. *Biff!* 'Ya bastard!' *Biff! Biff!* But there's nobody around to help. 'Ah, ya bastard!' So, he gets into his car – still with this fucking shark attached to him: *Biff!* 'Fucking *behave*!' And he drives until he gets to a beach where there's guards, lifeguards in their turrets, you know, all holding their stomachs in for eight hours a day.

He gets out the car, the shark still flapping away with its teeth in his thigh, and he runs towards them on the beach:

'Hey! Hey!' And they're all going: 'Fuck off – that's a *shark*!' And he's saying, 'I *know*!' But *they* can't get it off, either. So, they kill it. They cut its head off, and leave the body lying on the beach, with the head still stuck on his leg.

'Thanks, lads!'

Then he's away to the hospital in his car. And he shows up there, gets out, limps quite casually into the building, and they got the head off and stitched him up. And that was pretty much the end of it.

But I was left wondering how he would have got on if he'd had to go to an NHS hospital:

Limp, Limp, Limp.

'Yes? What seems to be the trouble? Are you sure you were first in line here? There's a man over there with a headache, it might've been him.'

'No, no, it's definitely me.'

'Hmmm, well, okay, then. Mother's maiden name . . . ?'

THE VASELINE SALESMAN

A Vaseline salesman came to town one day, and he had some free samples, which he gave out, and then went away again. He came back about a year later and went up to the first door.

He said, 'Excuse me, please. I'm the Vas—'

And the guy says immediately, 'Oh, I remember you! You're the Vaseline salesman, aren't you?'

He says, 'Aye, that's right.'

'Thank you very much for that wee sample – it came in very handy!'

'Oh, you used it?'

He says, 'Aye, I did, it was fantastic!'

The salesman says, 'To what purpose did you put it?'

He says, 'I used it for mechanical purposes. I was greasing my car, and I ran out of grease, so then I just remembered your wee sample – *pfft* – no problem, thanks very much!' He says, 'Just give us a couple of tins in case of emergencies.'

The salesman says, 'Great!'

And then he goes up to the next door: 'Excuse me, you might not remember me—' 'Ooh, aye, I remember you, you're the Vaseline salesman, aren't you?'

He says, 'Aye, that's right. Did you use my sample?'

'Certainly did!'

'To what purpose?'

'I used it for medical purposes.'

'Oh. How did you manage that?'

He says, 'Well, my boy was coming down that hill over there on his bike, fell off, skinned all his knee, and we hadn't any ointment in the house. Then I thought – Vaseline! Cleaned it up, a wee rub of the Vaseline – perfect! Hey, give us a couple of tins in case of emergencies.'

The salesman says, 'Aye, thanks!'

He goes up to the third door. It's always the *third* guy, isn't it? He's lurking behind the door. He's one of these guys who doesn't mind scratching his bum in public.

By the way – this *must* have happened to you. I reckon it's happened to everybody in the world at one point, and I hate it. You're on a busy street, hundreds of people around you . . . and your arse gets itchy. It never happens at home, does it? It never, ever, happens at home! Your arse just ambles merrily forward when it's at home, just being sort of arse-ish. But when you're out and about on a busy street – then, suddenly, your arse decides to get itchy.

And when I say 'itchy', I don't mean the cheeks. I mean *waaaaaaaay* in there! Right? It's so far up you could almost get at it better through the throat. And you think, 'Oh nooooo!' You're frightened to scratch it because there's hundreds of people watching you! So, you'll try anything else rather than ram your hand down there – like, you'll try walking really funny, trying to get the cheeks of your arse to rub together. But it doesn't work! I've found myself in dark doorways or elevators, just trying to be alone so I could finally have a scratch.

And even then, it's not easy to end the itch. You can get your hand down there at the back and have a wee scratch but all you're really doing is ramming your trousers up your arse.

As far as I'm concerned, the solution to the whole thing is: own up. When it happens to you, say in a proud and happy voice: 'MY GOD! MY ARSE IS INCREDIBLY ITCHY! I THINK I WILL SCRATCH IT!' And everybody will look away.

But to get back to this third guy.

He's behind the door, waiting for the Vaseline salesman. And the guy knocks on the door, and he can hear this noise inside the house: 'Will you shut yer damned mouth!' *Smack, slap!* 'Daddy, who is it?' 'Shut yer face!' *Smack, slap!* 'All of you, for God's sake, be quiet!' *Smack, slap!* All these kids making a hell of a noise. And he opens the door a little and sticks his head out, and there's all these wee heads behind him trying to look out as well – '*Get back! Get back in there!*'

The salesman's at the door:

'Er, hello, I-I'm the Vas—'

'I remember *you*! You're the Vaseline salesman, and thank you very much – best night I've had in my life!'

He says, 'Oh aye? Did you use my sample?'

He says, 'I certainly did!'

'To what purpose did you put it?'

'I used it for sexual purposes. What a night! You're a beauty!'

He says, 'How did you manage that?'

'I smeared it on the handle of the bedroom door and these buggers couldnae get in!'

A WEE SWEARIE IN GEORGE SQUARE

Now, as you know, swearing is a nasty. It's a real nasty. Everybody hates it and everybody does it, for some obscure reason.

I bet the Pope swears. Yeah, he swears in Latin – dead sneaky. And nobody's going to tell me that when the Moderator of the General Assembly of the Church of Scotland drops that big Bible he says 'Jings!' No way.

As I say, almost everybody swears. I certainly do. I used to get embarrassed by people swearing if I was out with a wee bit of stuff or sometimes even when I was with my wife. With anybody you like a lot, you'd be sitting with them on a bus and there's some eejit at the back, steaming, going, 'Fucking bastard – *mumble mumble* – fuckin' – *mumble mumble* – fuckin' . . .'

George Square is the place for the characters, for the great swearers and the great drunks. You've got all these rubber men waiting on buses, swaying away there, going, 'Aye – *hic* – yer bastard there . . . What's it all aboot, eh? . . . Am-Am I right, eh, pal, eh? . . .' They walk like puppets. Have you ever noticed the puppets on the telly – they always look as though they're steaming!

You see a wee man at the bus stop on George Square, walking with one leg – the other one dead – staggering around in a circle, wondering how he's knackered and not getting anywhere. He's got a fish supper in his left hand, it looks as if it weighs about two hundredweight, it's away down to his knee. He's trying to stub out the chip in his right hand. There's a bottle of beer in the left-hand jacket pocket, and a half bottle in the inside, so his jacket's all slanted down to the left. He can hardly walk, he still keeps walking in circles, and annoying everybody at the bus stop, asking them if they're all right. 'Alyaaaaaraaalllllraaayyytt? Eh? Aaaahyuuhraaaayyt? Eh? Eh? Wh-Why ahhhn't ye taaaaalllkin' tae me, pal? Duh-Duh ya think Ah-Ah'm a SHITE or sumthin'?' They have really delicate ways of putting things. 'Aye, y-yuz think Ah'm a sh-shite an-an Ah think yuz a POOF! Hi-High heels an-an yuz hair's dyed – yuz must be a poof!'

And he manages eventually to scramble on to the bus, slides up the stairs, and he's immediately sick over someone's wee dog: *Bleeuugghh!* 'Ah-Ah dun' remember eatin' THAT!'

Then he turns round and addresses the whole of the top deck of the bus: 'Shu-uuup!'

He manages to wobble his way along and find another drunk, so he sits down and talks to him. Well, they don't really *talk* to each other; they sit and swear at each other for a wee while. You know, to make it really convenient they drop all the other words and just swear: 'Yuhfuckin'bastard fuckin'fuckin'bastardyuh . . .'

Anyway, he looks at his watch and decides that it's time to be sick.

I saw an incident on the last bus to Drumchapel one night that will stay with me for as long as I live. There were two guys on that bus, both of them lunatics. One had been a boxer; every time the conductor rang a bell he got up and battered somebody, then when it rang again he'd sit back doon and fan himself. And next to him was this half-wit, steamin' out of his brain, the bunnet on backwards, being sick.

And there was a guy sitting directly in front of him with a duffle coat on, with the hood hanging over the back of the seat. Now, the one who's being sick, he's not being sick into the hood of the duffle coat, but the guy in front *thinks* he is, because he's hanging on to the hood thinking it's the back of the seat. And every time he bends down to be sick – '*Bleeuurgh!*' – he pulls on the hood and the guy in front shoots back in his seat. He's sitting there, feeling really grateful that he brought an umbrella.

But swearing: as I told you earlier, I swear, sure, but I'm sneaky about it when I want to be. I invented my own swear words that I can say in front of my weans – my 'childers', my 'offspring'. Because it's not nice to swear in front of your kids, because they take it to school and everybody knows it was you who started it.

So, I invented my own words. Bassa is a good one. That one comes in quite handy: 'Ah, ya *bassa*, get outta there!' And there's another very good one: 'getifu'. That one comes in very handy, especially if you string it with 'bassa': 'Getifu, ya bassa!' You can do it with complete confidence. 'Ah, ya bassa, getifu there!' It really sounds quite convincing.

It's not necessarily swearing if you invented the meaning for yourself. You can change the meaning every day if you like. It can mean: 'a lovely bunch of little pink daisies'. Like: 'Ah, look at the getifu ya bassa!' You see? It's entirely up to you.

There was a guy called Kenneth Tynan, who swore on television a long, long time ago. He said 'Fuck'. The country was up in arms, the newspapers were flabbergasted that somebody had dared to swear on the telly. Mary Whitehouse nearly fainted – mind you, I wouldnae be too cheery if *my* name rhymed with toilet. (Someone will be going: 'Whitehouse – Lavvy? It doesnae work!' 'No, it doesnae work with cludgie, either – I don't get it!') But I thought it was a good thing. I really did. Because it sort of opened the floodgates to everybody, and plays became more realistic after that.

The way they were before, they were all saying things like, 'Take *that*, you bounder!' 'You scoundrel, I'll box your ears!' 'Look away, Martha!' 'Yes, you gave Phillip everything, didn't you, Father? Well, you'll pay for it now!' 'Don't be a *fool*!' It was a load of nonsense, wasn't it?

But what Tynan did was to open the floodgates so that everybody could have a wee swear every now and again. And that's good.

But as I say, you have to draw the line somewhere. Like, *Jackanory*. I mean, can you imagine: 'Once a teddy bear found a little piece of chocolate. "Fuck, look at that!"' It doesnae work. It's not nice. Or you get Andy Pandy coming out his box: 'Where's that Looby Loo? *Corrrrr!* Get her intae this hamper! Fifteen years Ah've been in there wi-myself – Ah'm goin' BLIND!'

ISOBEL

McIntosh Hall was a wee dance hall – in a wee village up near Loch Lomond – where we would go every Friday. The women there were quite nice. The style back then was the very, very tight skirt, so they would walk from the knees down. I liked them all. But there was one very odd one called Isobel.

She would stand there – a 'wallflower girl' they used to call them in those days, standing against the wall all the time. And I thought she wasn't too clever. She had a very big face – I noticed that: 'God, her face is some fuckin' size, isnae it?' A big long face like a horse. And where all the rest had the tight skirt on, she had a big party frock. And she had these fucking wee socks on – it was like *What Ever Happened to Baby Jane?* – and too much lipstick, it made her look like she had huge great fucking lips. And rouge – I'd never seen rouge, that was before my time – she had big red rougey cheeks. It looked like someone had been throwing *plums* at the woman!

So I'm up on the dancefloor and they're all swapping partners and I'm not getting anywhere. 'Oh fuck it.' And then they had this country music section in the middle of the dancing. 'Now it's country time!' *Diddle-diddle-de-dee-diddle-diddle-dum . . .* 'and it's a Ladies' Choice!' *Diddle-diddle-dee-dummmedy-dummedy-dee . . .* Suddenly I felt a tap on my shoulder. 'Aaagh!' Isobel.

'Hullo,' I said, 'Oh, hullo, Isobel, how you doing?'

'Great. Would you like to dance?'

'Er, y-yeah, right, come on then.'

And it's the Gay Gordons, and the guys are all going at me: 'Wha-hay!' Me back at them: 'Ah, fuck you!'

In those days, when you'd been dancing, when you'd had her up on the floor for six numbers and she hadn't wanted to go back, you would slide two hands down over her bum, and get her hands and put them on your shoulders, ready for the slow number. And you'd start dancing, pulling her in close. It was called Fanny Dancing. It was fucking *great*!

She'd have her arms round your neck, going, '*Mmmmmm.*' And you'd be thinking, 'It won't be long now!' Her going, '*Mmmmmm.*' And you going, '*Yeessssss!*'

Well, Isobel did it to *me*!

'What the fuck are you *doin'*, Isobel?'

She says to me, 'Listen, Billy, I wonder if you can do me a favour?' 'Certainly, Isobel, what's the story?' She says, 'They put the lights out at ten o'clock here in the village, and I really hate walking up the road, up the hill to my house. It's very dark and dangerous. Would you see me up there?' I said, 'Certainly, no problem, Isobel.'

So, I take her. I'm just seeing her up the road, because I felt a wee bit sorry for her. It was a patronising thing. I don't *fancy* her. She's okay, she's all right – she certainly *feels* okay – but, you know, you don't want to make a fool of yourself with your pals.

We get to the top of the hill, and she says, 'Come in a wee minute in here.' And she's taking me into the graveyard.

'Isobel, behave yourself!'

'Come on in here, see this.'

'Wh-What is it?' I was brought up as a Catholic, I'm shitting myself – I think the place is full of fuckin' Protestant ghosts!

'Sit here,' she says, 'for a wee while.'

'Sure, Isobel.' We sat down. I thought, 'I'd better give her a kiss. She'd expect a kiss.' So, I turned her shoulders around, and said, 'Make your lips soft, Isobel.' And I couldn't see, because it was dark, but I puckered up and went in, and this . . . *thing* approached me! This void! This big shiny cave! She moves in – *pow!* She forced me backwards. Her mouth was all around my face. I'm breathing through my arse!

She's holding me down, ruffling my undergarments. She *violated* me! Bouncing up and down on me like I'm a fucking horse. Threw me away like a wet chamois when she was finished with me.

I drove home that night on my bike – standing up – my fly open, the wind blowing through my jeans. And my willy was glowing in the dark. It was like a *prawn*! I had to use Vaseline Intensive Care, Milk of Magnesia . . .

The following Friday I was back. Looking for Isobel.

THE DEATH OF ROBIN HOOD

Did you ever wonder what happened to Robin Hood? I used to wonder that a lot.

I used to lie awake at night, saying, 'I wonder what happened to Robin Hood?' I used to pound the pavements at four in the morning: 'Oh, Robin – what happened?'

You see, when I was a wee boy, I had several Robin Hood books, as most boys did. Kind aunties tend to give you Robin Hood books. And they were always the same. On the last page, Robin had just won that contest – that archery thing – and he was walking into the distance with Marian, with his arm over her, and the Merry Men were saying, 'Cheerio, Robin! All the best, Robin!'

'Yeah, cheerio, lads! Keep it goin', boys!'

'Keep in touch, Robin! Tell us all about it, know what I mean?'

'Hey, Robin, can we watch?'

'*No!*'

And they walk into the distance. And that's the end.

But I always wondered: what happened *after* that, to Robin – whatever became of the chap? Well, I'll tell you. Because I found out.

Robin didn't do too well at all. As a matter of fact, luck didn't shine on Robin. Things went from bad to worse. They got very poor, and ended up in furnished rooms in Nottingham, him and Marian.

And Robin got old like everybody else, and he had silver hair and a wee silver beard. And he was close to death, sitting up in bed, with his wee Lincoln Green pyjamas on, and the feather in his hat went: *wilt*. And for Robin it was all over.

And he said, 'Marian . . . Mar-i-an . . . MARIAN!'

And she came in. 'Er, what is it? What is it now – more Lucozade?'

'No, Marian . . . Marian, I fear I am close to death. Please fetch the Merry Men.'

She goes, 'Ah, aw right.' And away she went.

And then they came in:

'Hey, eh, how's it goin', pal, yer aw right, Robin? Where's the half bottle, eh?'

He says, 'Merry Men, I gathered you here because I'm close to death. Little John, you were always my very chum . . . please fetch my longbow.'

'Aye, aw right. Er, yer not goin' tae commit suicide or somethin', are ye?' So he gives him the bow.

'Thank you. And an arrow?'

'Jesus Christ, what am I, a message boy? Coh! There's yer arrow!'

'Thanks, Little John.'

He puts the arrow in the bow. And he knelt up in bed, with his wee scrawny legs shaking, and he says, 'Little John, please open the window.'

'Coh! Gawd Almighty! There ye go!'

And he points. He says, 'Wheresoever this arrow may land, there shall I be buried!'

Fliiiiiiiiiiiinng!

And they buried him on top of the wardrobe.

PAUL THE FURRIER

I had a friend called Paul. He was a wee, wide, broad man. He was a furrier; he made fur coats, him and his family, in Glasgow. And he'd been a boxer when he was young.

He loved boxing and would always talk about it. And I'll always remember, he said, 'A knockout punch moves eighteen inches, Billy, no further.' He said, 'All that John Wayne stuff, where you're winding them up and hurling your arms around all over the place – rubbish. One short sharp hit and it's over.'

Now, Paul had a big nose. And there was not a mark on it. Not a scar, not a blemish – nothing. And so, I used to think, 'Well, if you were a boxer, and there isn't a mark on *that* fucking nose, you must have been amazing!' I mean, you could have hit that thing blindfolded with your hands behind your back.

Anyway, we often used to meet for a drink in this pub in Stockwell Street in Glasgow. It was a very nice pub. It was called the Scotia Bar. It was one of the oldest pubs in Glasgow. Well, across the road was a place called The Egg Factory, and it was run by a guy called Egbert. Actually, his name was Bert, but we called him Egbert, of course, because he worked at The Egg Factory. And he was a prick. He thought he was funny: 'Blah blah blah blah' – always talking and talking, really loudly, always about himself and how great he was and how shite everybody else was. And we were all broke, we were hippy people, and we couldn't stand the sight of him.

He came swanning into the pub one night. I had my hat on – a big floppy hat with snakeskin round it – in a crass attempt to look like John Lennon. So, this prick comes wandering in, in his flash raincoat, and he's got a big glass jar with him – tied with string the way you tie a jar when you're going to fish for minnows – that's full of raw eggs. He's got it filled right to the brim. And he's come into the pub for a pint before he takes these eggs home to his wife, who bakes things.

And he passes me and Paul – we're standing there talking to each other by the bar – and as he passes he lifts my hat off my head and puts it on his. And I fucking *hate* that. I hate being touched in that sort of way – like when some-body grabs your beard and says, 'Oooh, your beard's long!' *Fuck you!* I just instantly say: 'DON'T FUCKING TOUCH ME!'

He's dumped his big jar of eggs in a wee safe place, whipped my hat, and he thinks he's Jack the Lad. He's going up and down the bar, singing, 'The Man from Laramie . . . a-yodel-odle-ee . . .' Generally being a complete prick as usual. So, I said, 'Look, give me my hat back.' He just laughs and ignores me. Me and Paul are standing there. Paul says to me, 'What a prick!' I said, 'I couldn't agree more!'

Well, after a while, Egbert's finally making his way back out, in his trench coat and his cowboy hat, and, as he's about to pass us again, he says this thing to Paul. I won't repeat it – that wouldn't do any of us any good – but suffice to say it was a shitty, anti-Semitic thing. And when he said it to Paul, there was this blur beside me – *whoosh* – and it was the eighteen inches.

BANG!

It was fucking brilliant.

Now, if you were to hit me on my right side, I'd go flying off to the left. And if you were to hit me on my left side, I'd go flying off to the right. But when the great guys hit you, the serious guys, you don't go anywhere. You just go straight down, like you're falling down a manhole. I tell you, Egbert folded up like an accordion. He fell so fast his hat stayed up where it was!

And I'd thought that Paul had short arms, because he had a big belly and his arms used to rest either side of it. They looked wee things. But boy could he hit!

So, Egbert was flat out on the floor. Utterly out to the world. And I got to do one of the things that I'd wanted to do all my life, just like in the movies. I got to pick up a pint and throw it in Egbert's face – *splash* – 'Wake up!'

Egbert's coming round, cursing and moaning. But he's no idea what happened. No idea at all. 'Wh-What happened?' 'Nothing. You were just leaving.' 'Wa-Was I?' And he gets up, looks at the clock and goes, 'Oh, fuck, is that the time? I'd better be away home!'

Well, he picked up his big jar of eggs, and there must have been a flaw in the glass or something, because the arse fell out of the jar. It was fucking wonderful!

There must have been ten dozen eggs in this thing. It was like *The Quatermass Experiment*. It hit the floor like a big yellow snot. It went: *Crack-splatttt!* All the drunks are stepping into it and sliding over on their arses: 'Wha's goin' on? Wha-the-fuuuuuuuuccckk!' This great yellow thing was slithering down the pub, carrying them all out with it.

THE DWARF ON THE BUS

My sister told me this – and she swears that it's true and I
hope it's true. If I tell it right, *you* will hope it's true.

My sister is a retired schoolteacher. And she supplies herself
to people who don't have teachers; she's a supply teacher.
When somebody is sick, or dead, she'll supply herself. And
a lot of her friends do this as well. And her friend told her
this story.

I was in New York, where I live, and she phoned me. The
phone's next to my bed, and I fell on to my bed. You know
that way you laugh – your legs won't work right? And I told
my wife, I said, 'Flo just told me the funniest story, I'm gonnae
tell my audience this! It's about a dwarf!'

And she said, 'Oh, Billy . . . You can't. You can't do that!' So,
I said, 'Why?' And she said, 'You can't . . . you can't say "dwarf".'
I said, 'Why the fuck not? I'm *talkin'* about a dwarf! Surely
you can say "dwarf" when it's a *dwarf* you're talkin' about?'

She says, 'They're "little people".' I said, 'But little people
aren't *dwarves*! There's a difference between a little person
and a dwarf: one of them's a fucking *dwarf*! And they both
know which one it fucking is! Don't give me that *shite*!'

So, I decided to tell it. And I'll tell it to you now.

My sister's friend was going to supply herself to a school
somewhere. She got on the Glasgow bus – oh, *please* be true!
– and she sat down, and it just happened to be the last seat.
The bus took off and trundled off into the day.

Four or five stops later, the bus stops, and a wee dwarf
woman comes on.

(I've now compounded the felony by calling her a *wee* dwarf. She wasn't a particularly *small* dwarf, she was just a dwarf-sized dwarf. There'll probably be all sorts of complaints now: 'Dear Mr Connolly, I read your otherwise excellent book. What a pity you descended to the dwarf story. I, personally, am a member of The Tall Dwarf Society – I'm six foot four – and *proud* to call myself a dwarf!')

Anyway, the wee woman got on the bus and discovered there's no seat. And so, she hung on to whatever was nearest – the seat or pole or whatever – and the bus took off.

There was a wee schoolgirl in a school uniform sitting over on the other side, who got up, probably urged along by her mother – 'Give the woman your seat, give that woman your seat' – and obviously wanted to be polite. She went over to the wee dwarf woman, and she said, 'Excuse me, would you like to have my seat?'

Whereupon the wee dwarf woman flew into a rage. She said, 'Oh *aye*? Because I'm a *dwarf*, you're offering me a *seat*? Simply because I'm a *dwarf*? Well, I have managed my whole *life* as a *dwarf*! It's not a *problem* to me! *Keep your seat!*'

The girl, cringing with embarrassment, went back to her seat. And the bus trundled on in silent embarrassment for a stop or three.

Then – oh, *please* be true! – a big Glasgow woman was getting off the bus. And, before she went up to the door, she went over to the wee dwarf woman. She bent down and tapped the dwarf woman on the head repeatedly with her finger. The dwarf woman looked up and the big woman said, 'I'm getting off the bus now. And I'm leaving my empty seat here.'

'Because I'm a *dwarf*?!'

'No! *Not* because you're a dwarf. Because you're another *human being*! I happen to be leaving the bus, my seat is vacant, I'm merely pointing it out to you that it exists.

'As a matter of fact, I thought you were extremely *rude* to that wee girl, and you owe her an apology!

'And what's more . . . when you go home tonight, I hope *Snow White kicks yer arse*!!!!'

THE HITMAN

There were two guys on a golf course in Glasgow. They're just having a relaxing old time playing a game of golf. There's no one else around.

And one of them has got a smart black attaché case with him. So, the other one says, 'Hey, what's with the case? What's that all about? What's in it?'

And the other one says, 'It's my tools, isn't it?'

'*Tools*, eh?'

'Aye. I'm a hitman.'

The other guy is completely unconvinced. 'Ahh, piss off!'

But his mate is adamant. 'I'm telling you! Do you want to see?' 'Sure!'

The guy puts his case down. He clicks it open, lifts the lid, picks up these different bits of shiny black equipment, screws them all together – *click-click-click* – and there in his hands, sure enough, is a professional sniper rifle.

'Jesus!' says the other guy admiringly. 'That's a cracker, isn't it?' He's given it to inspect. 'Do you mind if I look through the sights?'

'No,' says his mate, 'carry on, be my guest.'

He holds the gun out in front of him and squints through the sights. 'God! That's amazing the things you can see through this, isn't it? Hey, I can see my own house! Well, look at that. My own house. God, I can even see into the bedroom win— You bastard! You *bastard*! That's that swine from next door! With my *wife*! And they're . . . They're taking their . . . You *bastard*!'

And he lowers the rifle, looks at his mate, and says: 'How much do you charge?'

The guy says, 'A thousand pounds a bullet – that's my price.'

So, the other one thinks for a second and then says, 'Okay . . . I'll have two. You zap her right between the eyes and zap him right in the willy!'

'Okay, sure.'

The hitman picks up the rifle, gets into position, looks through the sights, and gets himself ready. He finds the house, finds the bedroom window, and he looks inside. He can see them. And then, with his finger on the trigger, he starts moving the rifle slowly up and down, up and down, up and down, up and down, up and down, up and down . . .

And his agitated mate is standing next to him, saying: 'Come on! Come on! Hurry up!'

He says: 'Take it easy, ferchrissakes – I'm trying to save you a grand!'

THE LOONY ON THE BUS

I'll tell you the best loony I ever saw: George Square in Glasgow.

I lived way out in this housing estate called Drumchapel. The one with the vans, y'know? There were no pubs out there. There are now. But, when I lived there, there were no pubs or discos or entertainment or anything like that. As a matter of fact, there were no discos anywhere – they hadn't been fucking invented yet.

There were dance halls, where you went dancin' with people. You got to touch them and everythin', it was fab. You'd been broke all week but on Fridays we'd get paid, and we'd put the Old Spice on and come into town. It was like *Seven Brides for Seven Brothers*.

You couldn't take women home, because they lived the other way – fuckin' *miles* that way to go home – but there were special buses at midnight or one o'clock in the morning, and we'd all gather there.

There were an awful lot of drunk guys, and waifs and strays and scoundrels, footpads and vagabonds. You'd be sitting on the bus and they'd come on, with their drunken attempts at singing: '*Oh-ohh-yehh-ehhhh* . . .' Four coats on. All with only the top button done up. The helmet all buckled up. Four pairs of troosers, all with the fly open. A big dark cave. You could see somethin' jiggling around in there. You didnae know where to look. Once you've seen it, you can't . . .

It's like seeing a woman's knickers – like when you're in an airport and those seats that go back and the knees come

154

up. Airport seats are designed to embarrass you. They're that Kentucky Fried Furniture stuff. They've got farting chairs. That vinyl – *pfffttt!* But you feel, as soon as you make the noise, you want to say, 'Excuse me,' but if you say that you're admitting you did something, so you're better off to go and move your arse around – *pfffttt-pfffttttttt!*

Sometimes women sit down and their knees come up. *Zhooom!* You're on it like a *flash.* Now, I'm not . . . Well, I *am* a dirty person, but there's just something that makes you go: *Zhooom!* And have a look.

You know when you see a deer running away from you and its white tail goes *fiz-fiz-fiz?* Or a rabbit's tail comes up: *flash!* Well, that wee white diamond of knicker . . . It has that same animal attraction. 'Oh God, it's a woman's knickers, I'd better look away!' But something drags your head to it. Your eye's coming out your ear trying to get a fuckin' look at it!

Oh, I was talking about these loonies on the bus.

These guys come on, and there's one seat beside you: Oh, fuck, no!

'D'ya wanna sweetie?'

'No, thank you, no!'

'Take a fuckin' sweetie!!'

'Ah. I'll, er, have it after.'

'You'll have it *now!* Eat it! Fuckin' *now!*'

'Okay, okay, take it easy!'

Gulp.

'That's been up ma bum! *Ha-ha-ha-ha!*'

AT HOME WITH HARKINS

I have to tell you another wee story about my friend Harkins. There are many stories about him but here is just one more of them. It's from when he was still working behind the bar.

I went into the pub one day with two other actor friends. Harkins loved them and we were all drinking away, being very 'actorish' and generally getting on like a house on fire. Towards the end of lunchtime, he said, 'Do you boys want to come up to my flat later? It's the Scottish Cup Final this afternoon on the telly. I've got a lovely wee telly and you can come up and watch it, we'll get some beer, get pissed, have a laugh.' 'Aye,' we all said, 'sure.'

So, we went up to his flat. It was the most awful flat you've ever seen in your life. It had an overpowering smell of cat's piss. Harkins didn't have a cat, but he always had his window open on the roof, so every cat in Glasgow used to come in, piss in his house, and go off again. I'd say, 'Why do you leave the window open?' He'd say, 'To try and get the smell of cat's piss out.' There was litter and shit all over the floor, half-eaten bits of food lying about and milk bottles with things growing in them and all that kind of stuff. Weird, weird shit.

His 'lovely wee telly' turned out to be this horrible little ancient thing, with a black and white eight-inch screen that we'd all have to sit close together on the couch and squint at to even see. And it had all kinds of interference on it: it had a sort of twitchy black goalpost floating up and down the screen all the time, with phantom snow falling down, and every so often the picture looked like it was being hijacked by aliens. It was a nightmare.

But we started drinking anyway and we were slowly getting pissed, and then he asked, 'Any of you boys hungry? Do you want anything to eat?' We all looked around at all the shit everywhere and shouted, 'Oh no, no, no, ah, we're *so* full, three big breakfasts us, we couldn't wedge in another After Eight here, so no, no, no food, thanks!' But he says, 'Nonsense!'

Off he goes into the kitchen. There's a lot of crashing and banging going on out there, with smoke coming out through the door. We're sitting on the couch looking at each other nervously. And eventually he comes back out: 'Here you are, lads!'

He's got a fried egg on a spatula, dripping with hot fat, and he's holding it out and offering it to us, holding it under our noses. And then he thrusts it at John, who was the most delicate and campy-looking one: 'John?' And John looks down at his left side, and then down at his right side, and sort of sniffs, and says, 'I don't appear to have a plate.'

And the answer Harkins gave him will go with me to my grave. He said, 'Oh, don't be so fuckin' *bourgeois*!'

In the peculiar head of Harkins, it was bourgeois to want a plate. He seemed to have convinced himself that the working class routinely ate fried eggs in their bare hands.

But I loved Harkins, he was a lovely guy.

His face always had wee cuts and scratches all over it. You know those guys who are always drunk and fall down and bump into things on their way home? That was Harkins. He once came in with a bandage on his hand. I said, 'What happened to you?' 'Aw, I was just walking home last night and some bastard stood on ma fingers!'

CHRISTMAS DINNER

My wife, Pamela, was invited to a Christmas dinner in a huge house in Yorkshire. A big castle, you know, an enormous house, with hugely rich people. One of those houses where, when you go in the gate, you've still got half an hour to go to get to the house. It's like they're living in a huge park bigger than the Kelvingrove. Rivers, lakes, fuckin' deer running about – herds of five hundred: 'Moo!' or whatever fuckin' noise they make (spot the naturalist!).

You get to the house and there's white gravel – you know those shiny pebbles? – none of that gravelly crap you used to fall off your bike on and you'd lose half a stone. None of that flint pish. This is your shiny round white fellas here. You're crunching through, you look in your rearview mirror and there's two people run out from behind the rhododendron bush and rake your tracks.

Like, serious dough. We're not talking Bishopbriggs here. We're talking *super* toffs. We're not talking Spam here, we're talking *venison*.

Now, I get out the car, go up to the house. I was met at the door: 'Aou, hillo, har are you?' One of the boys, one of the younger guys in the family, goes: 'Ay *know* you. Ay know your feece.'

I said, 'Well, that's nice.'

'Ay do. Ay *do*. Ay know your feece. Ay don't know h'where. Ay don't know h'where from. Ay'll get it. It'll come to me. It's on the tip of my tongue. But Ay *do* know you. Yes, Ay do. Ay *do* know you!'

I said, 'Do you think we could go in?'

'Of course. Of course. How silly of me . . . Ay do *know* you, you know.'

So, he shows me to my room. We have to dress for dinner, the bow-tie and all. It's Christmas dinner, but it's Chinese food. I thought, 'Oh, *now* you're whistling Dixie, this is *brilliant!*' Because I *hate* Christmas dinner. I hate all that turkey, I just wannae go to sleep, I wannae die. But this, I thought, 'This'll do me!' Y'know, 'Let's get intae this!'

But the extras were English. There were Yorkshire puddings, and bits and pieces you could add. I thought, 'Oh, *now* you're talkin'!'

'Ay know you.'

'I know. You fuckin' know me. Right, ye *know* me!'

He's on the other side of the table and he's beginning to *irritate* me, this guy.

'Ay *do*!'

'I KNOW – you told me outside!'

But the man of the house was a *wonderful* guy. What I discovered on that occasion is that the upper class – the *serious* upper class, you know, ignore that *suburban* fuckin' mob – the big shots, the proper fucking *big* shots: they're all *nuts*. They're a great laugh. The working class – they're all fucking nuts as well. And *they're* a great laugh.

It's just the *middle* that sucks. You know? It's the V-neck pullovers and that fucking Volvo crowd that fuck the whole thing up. It's *climbers*.

I'll give you an example. When I lived in Drymen, I used to drink in a wee pub in the centre of Drymen – The Clachan, that wee white pub in the square – and in Drymen you had some serious money in those days, like Sir Hugh Fraser and all those people – he owned *Harrods* for Christ's sake! The bit I lived in was big houses and it was known as 'Millionaires' Row' by the locals. And then you had the sort of Bungalow Land, with all those wee type of houses – fair enough – and then over here you had council houses, for the real Drymen guys, who did various jobs but originally would have been farm labourers.

What I found, when I was there in the pub, was that the rich and the successful and the 'Millionaires' Row' kind of people mixed very easily with the council house people. You're all standing there, laughing, you've got a lot in common, 'Blah-blah-blah,' and then the V-neck pullover Volvo mob were all saying, 'What are *they* talkin' to *them* fer? They should be talkin' to *us* – we're *nearly* toffs, we're *nearly* toffs! Why are they talking to *them*? There's no arse in their trousers, there's no fuckin' arse in their trousers! Hugh Fraser and fucking Connolly all talking to *them* – the fuckin' *scrubbers*! And here's *us* – here's us with the fuckin' *accent* and everything – not a fuckin' word, not a kindly look!'

One day, a great and dear friend of mine, Davie Haggerty, who lived in a council house, was standing there with the rich guys – the seriously millionairey guys – and we're all drinking pints. One of the V-neck pullover crowd comes mincing over, and he says, 'D'you know? It's astonishing, the value of houses round here, isn't it?'

We're all going, 'Aye . . . aye . . . aye.' Everybody's losing the will to live. Wishing he would just fuck off, right?

'Yehhsss,' he said, 'I reckon, in the nine months I've lived here, my house must have gone up by, h'what, twelve thousand pounds?'

He's waiting for a fucking round of applause. And so, he picks on Davey, who lives in a council house. He says, 'What do you think *you* would get if you sold *your* house?'

Davey says, 'About sixty days.'

So, I'm in this posh place and the guy who owns the place, he's giving us all a drink – and I still drank in those days – and it was called 'Snake Eye'. I think that was the name of it. It was green and it was hot. I don't know what was in it, but it was his own recipe. We all got it in a bowl and I got well into it. I thought it was well tasty.

And I got *so* pissed.

Like everybody did. But I felt I was sober. Until I needed to go to the toilet. I went to get up and my *legs* were pissed! I thought, 'What's goin' on?' Because my head was sober, but my legs were giving it that! We were getting drunk from the feet up. I thought, 'This is *weird*!' I couldn't get out of my chair.

'Ay know you, Ay *do*, Ay *know* you . . .' I wanted to punch this bastard, but I couldn't make it round the table to get him.

There's a woman, two places away, an older woman, who wants to be a bishop in the Church of England. They don't even allow female priests yet and she's upset about the whole thing. And my wife – she's been there for two or three days, so she's getting into it. And this woman's saying: 'It's *ghastly*! The whole thing's a *ghastly* nightmare! It's just *ghastly*!' And every time she says '*ghastly*' she punches the table and all the cutlery somersaults. 'It's *ghaaaastly!*' But now and again she punches the soup, so we've all got the occasional noodle and diced carrot in the hair.

Having vegetables in your hair is a great leveller, I think.

And I'm getting into it: 'I couldnae agree more!'

'The whole thing's a *ghaaaastly* nightmare!'

'Hyre! Hyre! Fuckin' terrible!'

'Ay *know* you.'

'I *know* you fuckin' know me! *I'm eating Christmas dinner in yer house! Can we take that as read?* You fuckin' *know* me! I know you – you know me! Isn't it *fuckin' terrific?*'

Meanwhile I'm getting wolfed into this Snake Eye, hoping they've got it on draught in the kitchen here.

The guy next to me is an uncle of these guys and he's the brother of the guy who made the Snake Eye. He hasn't spoken to me yet, so I thought, well, maybe he doesn't like me. And I thought he wasn't very well, because he's making weird noises – '*menemen . . . menemunmunamum . . . menemiee . . .*'

'It's a *ghaaaastly* nightmare!'

'Ay *know* you! Ay *do!* Ay *know* you! Ay *do!*'

Oh, and there was another guy. An odd guy. I didn't like him that much. He said, 'Don't you like The Goodies? Aren't they *good?* Aren't The Goodies *good?*' And I sit there saying, 'Well, *I* think they suck!' And he told me a whole episode. A WHOLE EPISODE. 'Oh, it was *wonderful!* They arrive on a *bicycle*, and the three of them get off the bike and they *fall* down a *hole!* Ha-ha-haah-haah!' I'd fucking lost the will to live.

'*Oh, the whole thing's ghaaaastly!*'

It's fucking *raining* chicken soup.

'*Menem . . . nemenemnana . . . mmmnnngg . . . nemena . . . mnnnna . . .*'

And then I got it, what he was doing. Because I've *done* that. He's obviously got an itch, right in the centre of his head. And you can't get to it from any orifice, so you have to make the bit next to it vibrate.

Now, he suddenly goes quiet. And he just turned to me – he didn't say, 'Excuse me,' or 'Billy, we haven't been introduced,' nothing like that. He asked me the best question I've ever been asked. He said, 'Isn't Norway a strange shape?'

I'm trying to remember what shape Norway is. I said, 'Isn't it kind of a long and skinny country, stuck to the side of Sweden?'

'Exactly, exactly . . . Ay skied the entire length of Norway once. Ay was much younger, of course, and Ay skied the entire length, north to south, the entire length of the country.'

I said, 'Er, that's very impressive.'

He said, 'Here's a question for you: if you were to take Norway, and stand it up on its southern-most point, and allow it to fall forward, in a southerly direction, where would its northern-most point land?'

I said, 'This is, like, a *hypothetical* question, right? I don't have to run oot and get a JCB or anything?'

'Of course, of course.'

'. . . France. It would be France, I would say.'

'*Morocco!*'

He'd *measured* it before coming to dinner! I thought, 'That's *brilliant*! I think I *like* you.'

And in the middle of all of this: 'Ay *know* you! Ay know *where* Ay *know* you from!'

I said, 'Where am I from?'

'ETON! Ay know you from ETON!'

But he was right. I didn't *go* to Eton, but I'd *played* there in a band, and he had seen me. He said, 'Yes! You're the Hum-Humble Chaps or something!'

I said, 'Humblebums.'

'*That's* it! Ay *saw* you, Ay *know* you! Told you Ay know you!'

I thought, well, bugger me! 'Did you enjoy the concert?'

'Aou, it was wonderful!'

I said, 'Well, what do you do now?'

He said, 'Toboggan.'

And *this* is what I'm getting at!

I thought, well, it was *snowing* outside. It's Christmastime. I thought, well, maybe he thought I was saying, 'What were you doing before I got here?' Could've been out with his sledge, you know. So, I said, 'No, I meant, what do you do for a living?'

He said, 'Toboggan.'

I said, '*Toboggan?*'

'Yes, toboggan.' As if it was the most normal thing on earth. And the others said, 'He's a jolly *good* tobogganist. He keeps his toboggan *lovely*.'

And *that's* the difference!

It isn't money. That's the difference between them and us. *They* think it's all right to be a tobogganist!

You tell your father *that's* what *you* want to be! 'I wanna

164

be a tobogganist.' 'Get off tae fuckin' *work*! Get off yer lazy arse! Lyin' aboot!'

Go to the dole in Govan or Possil or anywhere. Maryhill. Go to the dole, and when they say, 'Occupation?' say, 'Tobogganist.'

'*WHAT?*'

'To-bog-gan-ist.'

'. . . Er, hang on a minute, I'll, er, have to see Mr MacLafferty about that.'

He goes over to the supervisor: 'He says he's a tobogganist.' 'Who? Has he got it *with* him? Has he got a *toboggan*? Has he got a woolly hat an' that?' 'No – it's fuckin' *June*.' 'Oh, aye . . . I suppose that must be why he's signin' on, maybe? . . . *Tobogganist*, y'say?' 'Aye.' 'Fuck me! . . . Maybe . . . maybe he's got a speech impediment or something.' 'Aye . . . that'll be it.'

'Write doon: "Tobacconist".'

4.

Accidents & Adventures

'Never trust a man who, when left alone in a
room with a tea cosy, doesn't try it on.'

THE WORST GIG

I've had some shit nights in my life. Did I ever tell you about the dead guy? A dead guy in the audience can really fuck the night up.

I had this friend called Les Smith, who was a splendid guitarist and singer. He had parents who were brilliant as well – they had a little country band and they sometimes played together, but mostly at that time he was just a solo guy.

Well, his mother had phoned and asked me to do a charity gig with them – which they were going to do together – and would I come and play my autoharp? She liked the way I played it.

An autoharp is like a zither. You play it high, up on your shoulder, and play Appalachian hillbilly music. As a matter of fact, there may be some of you who've said, 'I wish I'd learned an instrument back then, I'd be good by now.' *This* is the one for you. It's the only instrument you can play as soon as you've got it home from the shop. As long as it's in tune.

It's got thirty-six strings and twelve bars, each bar's a chord, some have got different numbers of bars – fifteen, twelve . . .

well, you know what numbers are, so I won't go through them all – so you can accompany yourself that night.

Now, *I* can play jigs and reels and tunes. And that takes a wee bit longer.

So, I agreed to do the gig.

She said it was at a hospice. I didn't even know what a hospice was – I thought she had a speech impediment. But we all turned up at a hospital in Glasgow, and they directed us to the hospice. We were in a big room with nothing in it, just us. And floorboards, highly polished. It looked like a ballroom.

I said to Les, 'Where are the people gonnae sit? There's no chairs or anything. Do they lie on the floor or somethin'?' He said, 'I dunno.' But we didn't have to wait long to find out.

There was a door over in the corner and a bed got pushed in. Well, that happened twenty-four times.

There were two semi-circles of beds. Then the wheelchairs came in. The big exotic ones that looked like the Forth Bridge, for guys in traction. Twenty-four of them.

Then the self-propelled wheelchairs, driven by moaning-faced whinge-bags: 'Ah didnae wanna come here, Ah wanted tae watch *Coronation Street!*' 'Who are they anyway – The Smiths? Ah never fuckin' heard of them!' 'Aw, look at the big *hairy* one with the *harp*! That's a *nancy boy* if ever Ah saw one! Away, ya big fuckin' *jessie*!'

How does a puncture sound, you cheeky prick! Don't let the hair fool you – I'm not a hippy, I like violence. Shut the fuck up!

We got ready. I said to Les, 'I don't think there'll be much applause in here tonight – most of the hands are under the covers.' But it went surprisingly well. We started with: 'Keep on the sunny side/Always on the sunny side . . .' And we got a kind of muffled applause at the end.

Now, people seldom believe me when I tell them that the guy died when I was singing 'Bury Me Beneath the Willow'. But it's true.

'Oh bury me beneath the willow, under the weepin' willow tree . . . When she sees that I am sleepin', maybe then she'll think of me . . .'

I got to there, and Mrs Smith leaned over and she said, 'Take an instrumental break, Bill.'

I said, 'Certainly.' *Chiiiiing-Ching-Ching-Chiiing-Ching-Ching-Ka-Ching-Ching-Brrrrrriiinnng-Chiiing-Ching-Ching* . . .

And a guy over in one of the big wheelchairs, with a yellow tartan blanket over him, went: '*Aaaahhuuuuuhhh*'.

I said, 'That's the stuff – join in!'

Chiiiing-Ching-Ching . . .

'*Uuuuuuuggghhhhhh!*'

'You're doin' well!'

'*Uuuuuuaagggggghhhhhh!*'

And then his tone changed:

'Uuuu*aaaaaaaa*hhhhhh! Uu*aaaaaayyyy*eeerrrr! Uhhhhh . . .'

'. . . Holy shit!'

I backed over, and Les was standing there with his guitar. He said, 'What's wrong?'

I said, 'That guy just fuckin' *died*! I was singin' with him and he bought the farm right in front of me!'

'Fuck off!'

I said, 'I'm *tellin'* you!'

'Where is he?'

I said, 'He's the one with the yellow blanket.'

He said, 'I'm going to look.'

I said, 'Please yerself!'

Chiiiiing-ching-ching-ching . . .

'. . . Je-sus . . .'

He said, 'He's *dead!*'

I said, 'I just fuckin' *told* you that!'

Well, they just left the guy there. Nobody pulled the blankets up. Nobody did the magic eye-closing hand gesture. Nobody put pennies . . . They just left him there!

Because that's what they do in the real world. They just leave you. It's only in Hollywood they pull the blankets up over your face. And I've had proof of this before. I was in Baffin Island – to my deep disappointment – which is just to the left of Greenland, there, at the top of Canada. I was with the Inuit people making one of those travel films, and they'd offered to take me out on a twelve-dog sled.

Now, if you ever get the offer to go out on one of those sleds, pulled by twelve huskies, say: 'No, thank you.' And I'll tell you why. Those dogs fart. Like farting was invented the day before yesterday. And they all do it at the same time: *Pppbbrrrrriiittt!*

Holy Jesus!

Pppbbrrrrriiittt!

Lumps of dog shit in it.

Pppbbrrrrriiittt!

Now, you know it's bad enough when your *own* dog farts

in the house? '*Oh!* God *Almighty*!! Fluffy, *behave* yerself!!!!'
Well, they don't even *have* a house! They just lie out in the
snow 24/7. They throw them bits of frozen walrus and seal,
which they lick until it thaws and then they eat it and they
have a kip. It's a fuckin' nightmare.

So, I'm sitting on the sled. They'd made me a suit of seal-
skin – a shealshkin shuit from Shashkatchewan – and I'm
sitting up at the front like an Inuit. The big Inuit guy stands
at the back. He's got a whip and he goes: '*Tsssssssssshhhhhh!*'
Because he can't do the whip crack, he has to do that noise
with his mouth: '*Tsssssssssshhhhhh!*'

He says: 'Ka-tyakakka! Tyatta Akayakka!'

I said, 'Oh, *come on!*'

He said, 'What?'

I said, 'Whatever happened to "*Mush!*"'

Every Eskimo movie I ever saw they go, 'MUSH!' He says,
'Ah, that's a Hollywood word.' He said, '*We* say: Ka-tyakakka!
Tyatta Akayakka!' He said, 'Roughly translated, it means:
"That's enough of the fartin', lads, let's get some runnin' doon!"'
I can't tell you how disappointed I was.

So, anyway . . .

The gig at the hospice ended and we went home. We went
home to the Smiths' house, because they were putting me up
for the night. Mrs Smith was at a wee table, making some
toast. Lovely woman. You don't *need* to be lovely to make
toast, but she was. And it doesn't do it any harm at all.

I wandered over and I said to her, 'That was a terrible
shame tonight, wasn't it?' And she said, 'What?' I said, 'That
guy.' '*What* guy?' I said, 'Come on!' She said, 'No, really.' I said,

'The guy who died at our gig.' She put the knife down. She said, 'Billy Connolly, I'm going to tell you something, and I would like you to remember it: Your sense of humour is going to get you in trouble!'

I said, 'He *died*!' She said, 'Don't make it any worse for yourself!' I said, 'Ask Les! He'll tell you – your son!' She goes: 'Leslie!' Full title – deep shit. He came wandering up. She says, 'According to your friend here' – no title, deep shit – 'someone died in the audience tonight.' He said, 'That's right.' She said, 'Oh. I see. Two of you against your wee mother! You must be so proud of yerselves!' He said, 'Mother, it's *true*!'

She said, 'Don't make it worse. Look, I'm going to phone that hospice in the morning, and I want you two standing here!' We said, 'Fair enough!'

So, in the morning, we're standing there. She phones the hospice. 'Hullo, is that the hospice?' 'Aye, this is the hospice here, can I help you?' She said, 'I'm Mrs Smith, I was performing last night with a country band called The Smiths.' He said, 'I remember you well – you were brilliant!' She said, 'Oh, I'm glad you enjoyed it.' She said, 'Well, you'll remember, one of the band was a big tall fellow, he played the autoharp, he had long hair—' He said, 'Oh, aye – the poof!' She goes, 'Oh for goodness sake! We don't like that kind of talk round here! Stop it!' He goes, 'Aye, all right.'

She said, 'He insinuates that somebody died in the audience last night – is this true?' He said, 'Well, actually, I'm not at liberty to divulge that kind of information. But a guy did die, right enough.'

She says, 'Oh my God, that's terrible!' He says, 'Not really

– that's what they're here for. Well . . . they're here to spend the rest of their lives, but it comes to the same thing anyway, d'you know what I mean? As a matter of fact, we lost another one today. A particularly sad one. It was a suicide.'

She says, 'Oh, for God's sake! What means did he use to take his life? Did he save up his drugs and take them at once? I believe they do that sometimes.' He says, 'Well, actually, I'm not at liberty to divulge the method he used. But he jumped out the window. And plummeted to his death on the stairs below.'

She says, 'Oh, for God's sa— Wait a minute! We were there last night – as far as I can remember you're in a *bungalow*! You're on the ground floor! What's all this plummeting to your death on the stairs below??'

He says, 'You have to remember, Mrs Smith: old people are very *brittle*.'

BUNGEE JUMPING NAKED

I find being naked very funny. And I found the thought of being naked while bungee jumping very, very funny. So, I decided to bungee jump naked.

I was in New Zealand. I make travel films – we call them the world tours – and I always dance naked in them.

I did it first in Scotland. In these films, I go out during the day and look at stuff, and then in the evening I go on stage and be funny about the stuff I've seen, then we cut between the two. And in Scotland they have this thing, a bit like

Stonehenge, it's on the island of Orkney and it's just stones, a ring of standing stones. It's actually called the Ring of Brodgar. I was looking at it and I didn't know what to say, apart from, 'Ooh, it's a big stone!' And: 'Ooh, there's another one!' So I was trying to work out what it was for, but the notice on it just said something like: 'It was thought that perhaps they were used for worship, or perhaps for something else . . .' It was obvious they don't know, they didn't really have a clue, and so they should have just put: 'We've no idea what this is. Try and leave it like you found it.'

So, being a hippy, I thought I would give it all that 'mystic' stuff, and so I took off my clothes and danced around it, doing a big sort of magical fairy dance. It just seemed the right thing to do at the time. And the funny thing is that somebody has told me that since I did that, since it was shown on TV, the local people have started doing it, getting their mates to film it on their wee cameras and phones or whatever. So maybe in fifty years or so, some other documentary maker will be there, saying earnestly: 'This is a quaint but mysterious custom, probably going back thousands of years . . .'

But anyway, after that, in every subsequent travel film I made, I also did a wee naked dance.

I did one in England at Piccadilly Circus. It was obviously very crowded with buses and taxis and cars moving around and lots and lots of people, but the only complaint we got was from this drunk guy, who said: 'You're – hic – offending the children!' He was puking all over the place at the time.

You see, it's only if you're in bad shape that it's funny. If you're in good shape, it's just showing off. I have the physique of an over-ripe banana. I'm all squidgy. I'm always going to send for those things to get abs, but I never seem to get around to it. So, running around naked is okay when it's me.

When I was filming in New Zealand, I knew that they had invented the bungee and that the highest bungee jump in the world is there. The Nevis bungee near Queenstown – it's from a cable car into a gorge. It costs about two hundred dollars, but if you do it naked it's free.

So, it seemed sensible to bungee jump naked. I mean, if you don't do it naked, all the money can fly out of your pockets, so that's hardly appealing. Maybe you have to be Scottish to understand that. I mean, I remember when I first came to America, and there were homeless guys there saying, 'Spare change?' And I went: '"*Spare* change"? I don't get the concept!'

But it's an extraordinary experience, bungee jumping naked. There are certain forces working there as you do it, certain forces working on you, that certainly have a dramatic effect. And when you reach the bottom part, and start to go back up, you usually feel two lumps on the back of your neck.

But I'm glad I did it. I saved about two hundred dollars.

SHAMPOO

Things used to be quite simple. Like buying a shampoo, for example. Do you remember, you used to be able to go into a shop: 'Excuse me, can I have a shampoo?' And the person would give you one. 'Thank you very much.'

You go to Boots the Chemist now and there's about five *lanes* of shampoo! Six deep, all different colours, things you'd never heard of in your life. Jojoba! What happened to *soap*?

'Jojoba!' I said, 'what's Jojoba?' In Glasgow, that's the month before November! I said, 'What's Jojoba all of a sudden?' She says, 'It's a Mexican bean.' I thought, 'Great. You'll have farting hair!'

Fucking Jojoba! Henna? Henera? Avocado and walnut? *Egg and mushroom* shampoo? When I was a boy that would've been straight into the frying pan! 'Egg and mushroom? That'll do me!' 'Where's my shampoo, by the way? You say your father's away to work with it on his sandwiches?'

And the women who work there. Jesus! They're so *smug*. 'Oh, sir, when did you last buy a shampoo? It's *much* more complex than that.'

'What's so complex about it?'

'Well, sir, for instance, what *kind* of hair is it for?'

'Pubic hair.'

'*What?*'

'Find that in yer fancy labels! It might be under Short and Curly.'

People don't like you to talk about pubic hair. Now, talking about your *willy* is becoming socially acceptable. You can say it on talk shows now and everybody goes 'Ha-ha-ha! "Willy" – ha-ha-ha! Ha, he said "Willy"! I think *I'll* say it, too: willy-willy-willy!'

But, you see, pubic hair is fascinating. Mine is particularly fascinating, because it's definitely now going grey at a rapid rate. And every day is a wee adventure. It's getting really *distinguished.* In a certain light now you would swear my willy was Stewart Granger. Distinguished, you know? I've got to really kind of like it. It's very *pleasant*, I find, pubic hair.

And isn't it extraordinary – your pubic hair is always shiny and full of life. It's always in great condition. It's never dull and lifeless. And you wouldn't squander your conditioner on it, would you? You give it a quick rub with the old soap and then: *phhiiissshhhh.* 'That'll do *you*. It's not cheap this stuff!' There's a lesson for us all, there. Don't squander your money on hair conditioners. Wear your underpants on your head! Don't you think? I think it's fabulous, oh yeah, I'm all for it.

I don't mind it going grey, but I thought, 'Oh Jesus, I hope it doesnae go *bald*!' Wouldn't it be *awful* if it receded and it all went away? A wee willy like a Southern Fried Chicken. I couldn't *bear* that, to be an old man lying on my bed, with my wee bald willy lying on my thigh – like the last chicken in the supermarket, you know? The one everybody picked up and squeezed and threw back.

Do you know what's always intrigued me? The way pubic hair only grows to a certain length, and then stops. How does it *know*? It's one of the great unanswered questions. The same as: How does the guy who drives the snowplough get to his work in the morning? Or what did the guy *think* he was trying to do when he accidentally discovered how to milk a cow?

These are the things that keep me awake at night.

I think it would be brilliant, you know, if your pubic hair just kept on growing. Right out the legs of your troosers. Wouldn't it be fab and groovy? Like those big hairy après-ski boots. You could *brush* it – a hundred strokes a night. 'One . . . two . . . three . . . four . . .' A great swooping mass. You could *backcomb* it.

Heavy metal pubic hair! Your willy would look like Robert Plant!

You could do all sorts of things. Punks could put lacquer on it and have *huge* Mohicans. Country and western singers could plait it. Willy Nelson!

BREAKFAST IN BED

I like toast. Tea and honey – no milk – and toast and butter and Vegemite, which is like Marmite. In England they have Marmite. In Scotland they're not keen on Marmite, but if you fight they get some in the hotels.

'That's all I want,' I say, 'and I like it at nine o'clock, and that's me sorted. No problem, nothing else – no fruit, no porridge, no cereal, no bacon and eggs and all that. It gives me heartburn and I don't like it.'

The following day: *ding-dong*. Three seconds to nine. Oh, that's fine.

'There you are, thank you, just leave it there.'

'Can I—'

'Just. Leave. The. Fucking. Thing. There! And get out!'

Och, he's hovering about the fucking place.

'C-Can I do that? Can I get this? Can I—'

'Do *nothing*! Fucking *vanish*! There's one too many people in here! Get out!'

So, he's left me with my bread and all, and I'm as happy as a clam. It's nine in the morning, breakfast telly is on – you know, the usual shite – and so I start to watch that, and endure those presenters, those 'Honest, I'm not bald' guys!

The whole thing's going like a fair. And I'm munching away, and I've got the butter and the Vegemite – which is brown, like Marmite.

Spread-Spread-Spread. Munch-Munch-Munch.

Then I do another one. Ladling on the old Veggie brown gear. It's better than Marmite. It's thicker. You know Marmite's that wee bit runny? This is a stage denser, and not so shiny, and thicker. Killer Diller. You won't meet an Australian who doesn't love it.

Whoopi Goldberg *hates* it. She was in Australia and she said, 'Have you tasted Vegemite?' And I said, 'Yeah, I love it.' She says, 'Ugh, how can you say that? It's like licking a cat's ass!' I said, 'Who did your research?'

So I'm lying in bed watching the telly. *Munch-Munch* . . . Oh *fuck!* I dropped the toast.

SPLAT!

It never lands bread-side up! Right on the sheet.

I went, 'Oh *fuck!*' Tried rubbing it – I'm only making it worse. 'Ah, fuck it!'

I finished and I'm getting ready to go.

Ding-dong!

I opened the door.

'Can I help you? Is there anything I can do? Can I carry your bag?'

I said, 'Aye, if you can just get my thing there and give it

me here.' So, he goes over and suddenly stops. He's seen it.
Big brown stain on the sheet.

'What's wrong with you?'

'O-Oh, er, n-nothing at all, sir.'

I said, pointing: 'It's *that*, isn't it? You're embarrassed about
that, aren't you?'

'N-No-No, sir, I-I haven't seen anything!'

So I said, 'Watch this.'

And I bent over and licked it.

The poor guy nearly fainted!

THE OLD WOMAN ON THE BUS

I was on a bus, years ago, I was with my cousin John. Very
crazy person. And he was sitting on my right. And I was
sitting on this bus in a place called Clydebank.

Now, the bus at the terminal was late at taking off, so to
make up time the guy's going like a bat out of hell. And it's
a double-decker bus. It was one of the most awful things I
ever saw in my life. And yet . . . funny.

Awful, at the time.

Afterwards, fucking hysterical.

Do you know that weird shit? If you go camping and you
get washed out, and it's misery, and you come home, you're
telling your friends, and you're pishing yourself laughing?

And Glasgow's like that. And New York and Liverpool might
be the only other towns like that. Where you'll say, 'Oh, you
should've been here yesterday! Tam was trying to fix the

puncture, and he had the thing up and that shitty jack, he's pushing it up – it's a jack for a Mini, this thing's a 1953 Riley! – he's pushing it up like that – it weighs more than the building he lives in! – he's fixing the puncture and the fucking car came flyin' doon, right on top of his hand, and his fucking *pinkie* flew off, *ha-ha-ha-ha-ha-ha-ha!!!'*

What?

'Aye! Oh, what a *laugh*! I had to take it up to the hospital! Nearly pished meself laughin'!'

What?

Well, you know that thing? Well, *that* happened.

John and I were sitting there. For those of you who don't know, there's a double-decker bus with a door at the back with a big pole in the middle, and if you were standing on the platform where that was, holding on, there's another wee bar here at the back so you can stand like balancing between the two if it's going a bit fast.

We've struggled up this hill. Turned right. And now there's a long gradient going down, and there's a fork at the bottom.

So, we've taken off from the top and we are *flying*. Trying to make up time, I suppose.

That's when I heard a noise, and a woman came down the stairs. An old woman. An older woman. I don't know *how* old. But the kind of woman you would say, 'Look at that old woman!' She came down the stairs – and it's a kind of spiral thing – this poor wee woman with a wee shopping bag – there was nothing in it as far as I could see. She makes a dash across the platform. This bus is fucking flying. She makes it to the platform. She's got a hold of the wee pole at the back.

And she's looking at us and she's going, 'Isn't it hellish, son?'

I say, 'I know, they're goin' too fast! Aye, the bastards, they're drivin' terrible!'

Well, the guy came to the fork in the road. And he's talking to his conductor while glancing back down the bus. Then he looks forward again and suddenly cries out: 'Ooooh, *fer fuck's sake!*'

He whacks it round to the right. The thing's on two wheels. *Screeeeeeeccccccch!* 'Jesus!'

And I looked up. And she was GONE!

Now, when I say she was 'gone', she was *gone from the bus*. She was still there, but she was about two feet outside, at the same height she had been on the platform. Looking kind of bewildered. But now her hair's flying back, and so is her shopping bag, like a wee flag.

She's flying at seventy miles an hour. And getting steadily lower. And eventually . . . she reached the ground. And took off!

So now she's *running* at seventy miles an hour!

And she was like, real old! She was an old lady. Running like the fucking clappers!

And her crotch was about a foot off the ground!

And there was a big hedge, at the fork, and she shot up the left fork, and we shot up the right fork, and I never saw her again!

And I've often wondered about her. You know . . . Where did she run to? Is she running still?

THE BICYCLE

I hope I can get away with this. It's a beauty.

This man, he says, 'How's the wife?'

The other one says, 'Ah, she's deid.'

He says, 'Wha?'

The other one says, 'Deid. In the ground. I murdered her. I'll show you if you want.'

He says, 'Aye, yeah, show me.'

So they away up to his tenement building, through the close – that's the entrance to the tenement – and sure enough there's a big mound of earth. But there's a bum sticking out of it.

He says, 'Is that her?'

He says, 'Aye.'

He says, 'What did you leave her bum sticking out for?'

He says, 'I need somewhere to park ma bike!'

BOB AND EDNA

I was watching the telly and playing my banjo. As I do from time to time; I play louder when it's boring and quieter when it's not so boring. And my wife came in, and she said, 'Aren't you getting ready yet?'

'What?'

'We're going out.'

'I didn't know we were going out.'

'You've known for ages!'

'Where are we going?'

'For dinner.'

'Who with?'

'Bob and Edna!'

'I hate them!'

'No you don't!'

'I fucking *do*!'

'Then why did you invite them?'

'I *didn't* fucking invite them!'

'You *did*!'

'When?'

'Eight years ago.'

'WHAT?'

'When you met them. In Barbados. You said: "If you're ever in Los Angeles, we must have dinner!" Well, they're here!'

'That's not an *invitation*! Translated it means: "You're a boring piece of shit and I'm off! I've had enough of you!"'

'No it isn't. It's on. It's on tonight.'

'Oh, for *fuck's* sake! When do we have to leave?'

'Quarter to eight.'

'Oh, shit! What time is it now?'

'Six.'

'Fuck, I'm not getting ready yet. You go up and get ready first. And I'll leave you room to manoeuvre up there.'

You sound kind of *kind*, you know, when you say that? 'I'll give you some room.' And up she goes – she falls for it right away. And I get more time sitting around.

Now, in our bathroom, her side is a *mountain* of products. And she's a beautiful woman, you know – she *starts* beautiful, and then she takes it somewhere else, you know? It's not like me, where you try to knock a couple of years off with your fuckin' toothbrush. But this mountain of products on her side: bottles and bottles of stuff. 'Primrose Oil Earlobe Rub' – what the fuck? And there's tools: there's pliers and tweezers, and things that can turn your eyelids inside out, prodders and plonkers and brushes, and scissors with balls on them, scissors with fuckin' spoons on them, there's palettes of colour for daubings and scratchings and rubbings, and brushes of every fucking size, eyelashes and moustache brushes, and lip liner pencils and pens, and fucking big balls of cotton wool, and wee balls of different colours of cotton wool, cotton wool on big wooden sticks, cotton wool on wee fuckin' matchstick things, stuff for putting on your nails and stuff to get the stuff off again . . .

A fuckin' *mountain* of stuff!

Over on my side: there's a glass with a fucking toothbrush in it.

If you go to a man's side of the bedroom, you'll find a wee pile of stuff: dirty socks, underpants and last night's trousers. But if you go to the woman's side, you'll find a wee tiny pile of dirty stuff: the wee knickers and the wee tights there, a wee bra on the chair maybe. And then a big pile of *clean* clothes: because that's the 'trying on' stuff.

'. . . No . . . Er, No . . . No . . . Hmmm . . . No . . . Um . . . No . . . No, No, No . . .'

But she comes in and starts getting ready. And then it's about time for me to go up – it's about ten minutes before we leave – so I go upstairs and I just change all my clothes right away. I'm not going to wash; playing the banjo doesn't make you dirty. I stand behind her, doing my hair – wind-swept and interesting is my usual choice, a bit of studied carelessness – and in the middle of it, the *silence* comes.

'What? What? *What?*'

I'm behind her, you see, so I can't see her face.

'What? WHAT?'

I have to talk to her in the mirror, which is really infuri-ating, talking to somebody in a mirror.

'*WHAT???*'

You see, when you're married, you say the same things to each other every day, and it's not boring, it's nice. It's *comfortable*.

It's like people who don't understand California, they always say, 'Oh, they're *phonies*! "Have a nice day!" They don't mean a fuckin' bit of it!' And *of course* they don't. But what would you rather have, somebody saying 'Have a nice day' and not mean it, or 'Fuck off' and mean it? The choice is yours.

But anyway. It's like when you get up in the morning. I have five kids – they're adults now, they're scattered about, fucked off with my money and left me – but you'd get up in the morning and you'd go, 'Mornin'.' 'Aye, Mornin'.' 'Mornin'.' 'Yeah, Mornin'.' And you're not really saying 'Good Morning, I hope the day goes your way' kinda thing. You're just estab-lishing where everybody is in the room – in case they gang up on you, you know? Because as you get older, you lose your appearance. You take on the appearance of a fucking ATM machine as far as I can see. And it doesn't operate with buttons. It's sound-operated. And it operates with that Australian diphthong thing: 'Daaaa*aad*?' 'Dad' is like: 'Have you seen my keys?' 'Daaaa*aad*?' means 'MONEY!'

Pam and I say the same things all the time to each other. I'd be doing my hair, and the silence comes – 'What? What? WHAT???' – and she *always* says:

'Is *that* what you're wearing?'

Translated, it means: 'Where did you find that? I threw it out a month ago!'

Did you ever buy a house with a woman? You're a man, and you make stupid decisions, like: buying a house you'd like to live in. Oh, how *stupid* can you get? 'Oh, look, he's picked a house he wants to live in! Oh for fuck's sake – when will they ever learn??'

Women don't see that. *They* see this thing they call 'potential'. They see this *other* fuckin' house. You don't realise that until you've moved into the one you wanted to live in! And these guys in overalls arrive and start knocking down walls. 'What the fuck? Who are *you*? Get out of my fuckin' house! What are you doing to the wall?' 'Oh, this wall has to come down because if the kitchen's going to go out there, this has to be a supporting wall, this has to do that, the roof has to—' 'What the FUCK are you talkin' about?? Where is *she*? Hey, hey, where are you??'

So, you say, 'Why didn't we just keep *looking*? Till we saw a house that looks the way *this* one's *going* to fuckin' look?' But they don't get it.

It's the *potential*. Fucking *potential*.

And then one day you find them looking at *you*. 'Wh-What are you looking at?' They don't see *you* anymore. They see this prick with no memory and a lot of money!

HECKLERS

I hate hecklers. As I always say to them: 'I'll give you a little hint: when your light goes off and mine comes on, it's my turn, okay? So shut the fuck up!' But there's always some fuckwit who doesn't seem to understand that simple concept. They need shutting up. And I shut them up.

But a while ago, on some radio programme, I heard one story about a heckler that turned my blood to ice. This guy said he was in a London comedy club and a complete novice got up – it must have been an open mic night – and the novice is up there on stage and he's trying his best. He says, 'My wife's away on holiday to, um, to Jamaica – oh, no, no, I'm not supposed to tell you that, I'm sorry. I'm just supposed to say that my wife's – oh, and it isn't Jamaica anyway, it's Barbados, I think . . . or is it the Bahamas? – But anyway, I'm supposed to say, "My wife's away on holiday," and you're supposed to say, "Where to?" And I say, "Jamaica" – but it isn't Jamaica, is it? Where on earth was it? Er, Barbados, no, Bahamas, no, um . . .'

And a voice came from the darkness. It might even have been the Devil. And it said:

'You're not funny and nobody likes you. You should have remembered that from school.'

Isn't that a bastard? That's a dagger straight through the heart. The poor guy.

But sometimes you'll get a heckler who at least has a sense of humour. You go to a place like Glasgow or Liverpool and you'll find a fair few of those there. Mario Lanza, the famous

American tenor, encountered one when he played the Glasgow Empire.

He was a big favourite in Glasgow, Mario Lanza, back in the Fifties. And he was giving it all that: *'Guarda il mare mare com'è bello! Spira tanto sentiment-o-o-o . . .'* But some guy in the gallery kept shouting out: 'Hey! Mario! Mario! Hey Mario! *Mario!* Hey *Mario!'*

So eventually he goes: 'What? Whadda you want?'

And this guy shouts: 'Give us "Softly, Softly"!'

Mario says: *'What?'*

The guy shouts: 'Sing "Softly, Softly"! It's ma favourite!'

Mario shrugs his shoulders and says: 'I dunno "Softly, Softly"!' And he clears his throat and goes back to his song: *'Come il tuo soave accento, che me desto fa sognar. Senti come illeve salle, dai giardini odor d'aranci-i-i-I . . .'*

And it starts again: 'Hey! Hey Mario! *Mario!* Hey Mario! *Mario!'*

So Mario – who is really rattled by now – breaks off again. 'Whaddaya want???'

'My mother's very ill.'

'Eh?'

'My mother's very ill. It's her favourite, too – "Softly, Softly". Would you please sing "Softly, Softly"?'

'I dunno "Softly, Softly"!'

And once again he tries to get on with his act: *'Un perfumo non v'è uguale per chi palpita d'amore. E tu dicro parto addio-o-o-o . . .'*

But the guy just won't shut up: 'Hey! Hey Mario! *Mario!* Hey Mario! *Mario!'*

'WHAT? WHADDYA WANT NOW?'

'Mario, *please*: "Softly, Softly"!'

Mario is red in the face and twitching, he looks like he's going to have a nervous breakdown. He says, 'For the last time: *I DUNNO "SOFTLY, SOFTLY"!!!*'

So, the guy thinks for a bit and then shouts out: 'Okay – show us your cock then!'

I never had a heckler as bad as that. But I had one who was almost as bad. I'll tell you about him: the worst heckler I ever had. He was in Dundee University Folk Club.

I used to be a folk singer, and, as I've said, I played the banjo. Now, the banjo is a nice instrument, it's kind of complicated, but some of the songs associated with it leave a bit to be desired. They're usually about chicken pie, and cuckoos, and things like that. But I love it. I don't give a fuck.

But I was trying to entertain people in this place in Dundee, and I was going down pretty badly. It was a bad night. There was a jukebox at the back of the room, which was supposed to be switched off, but some prick kept switching it on, so in the middle of my 'Chicken Pie' I got '*A-wop-bop-a-loo-bop-a-lop-bam-boom!*' And a dog had wandered in and had a piss, and then left again – he didn't even stay out of mild curiosity.

Then I started doing a song called 'There's a Rabbit in the Log'. It's a great song. It's about a rabbit stuck in a hole in a log and it can't get out. It's full of suspense. 'Got a rabbit in a log and I ain't got my dog' – *a-ruccu-rucca-rucca-tong-tong* . . .

And this prick in the audience shouts out: 'Needle of Death'.

He had this very flat, very nasal, and very irritating way of saying it: 'Needle of Death'.

I said, 'I'm sorry?'

'Sing "Needle of Death".'

I said, '"Needle of Death"? That's a song about heroin addiction!' I said: 'Have you noticed this is a fucking banjo? Banjos don't do heroin addiction. It's a good song. Bert Jansch – great guy, great writer. But the minute I heard it I didn't learn it because I knew I wouldn't be singing it. Because I'm a banjo player, right? So that's it. Okay? Finished. Don't ask for it again. Anyway, you'll like *this* song, it's about a chicken: "There's a chicken on the limb and I've got my eye on him—"'

'NEEDLE of DEATH!'

I said, 'I told you I don't *know* the fucking thing! Why do you keep asking? I told you I don't know the fucking *words*, I told you I don't know the fucking *chords* – how the fuck can I possibly sing it?! *Don't ask again!*'

So I started playing again: *Dunk-a-lunka-dunk-dunk-dunk-dunk* . . .

'NEEDLE – OF – DEATH!!!'

I stopped. Took off my banjo. Pointed at him: 'Stay where you are.'

I stepped down from the stage, I went up the aisle, along the row, asking people, 'Was it *you*? No. Was it *you*? No. Who did you say? The fat prick with the moustache? Thanks.' So I went up to him and said: 'Are you the guy who keeps asking for "Needle of Death"?' He said, 'Yeah.' So, I hit him. *Boof!* I gave him the Order of the Fat Lip. It was the biggest mistake I ever made.

He was the treasurer. I didn't get a fucking penny.

HAEMORRHOIDS

The Queen was visiting a Scottish military hospital. She's going round the beds there with this big sergeant-major. He's strutting around, you know, doing the number.

And there's a fella lying face down on a bed. So she says, 'What's wrong with that poor fellow there?'

'Haemorrhoids, Ma'am!' barks the sergeant-major. 'Chronic haemorrhoids!'

'Oh, that sounds *dreadful*, doesn't it? What treatment is he receiving?'

'Wire brush and Dettol, Ma'am!'

'For God's sake! The poor man's arse must glow in the dark!'

And the poor guy's going: 'Oh . . . Ooohh, nooo . . . I-I can hear voices . . . They must be coming again . . .' And the Queen goes away over, and she says, 'Hello, soldier. Have you any ambition left in life at all?' He says, 'Oh, *yes*, Ma'am! To get rid of this disgusting affliction and get back to doing my duty for you and the country, Ma'am!' 'Oh, how noble!' She motions to the sergeant-major: 'Give this man a medal, will you?' So, it's pinned on the back of his pyjamas there. 'All the best!' 'Cheerio!'

She then goes up to the next bed, and there's a guy lying

on his back on the bed. 'Oh . . . Ooohhh . . . nooooo . . .' He's got a thing covering his crotch, you know. And the Queen asks, 'What's wrong with that man there?'

'Venereal disease, Ma'am!' barks the sergeant-major. 'Self-inflicted injury!'

'Oh . . . yes. I read about it in a book once. Mmm. What treatment does *he* receive?'

'Wire brush and Dettol, Ma'am!'

'Oh, my goodness! The poor man's willy must be in tatters!'

She goes over. 'Hello, soldier. Have *you* any ambition left in life?' He says, 'Yes, Ma'am! To get rid of this disgusting disorder and get right back and do my duty for you and the country, Ma'am!'

'Oh, how excellent! Another medal, here, thank you very much!' And it's pinned on him.

Now the third guy, he's sitting up in bed. He's taking great interest in the proceedings. He looks as if there's nothing much wrong with him.

And the Queen goes over and says, 'What's wrong with *you*, soldier?'

He can only croak. He says, 'Laryngitis, Ma'am.'

She says, 'Oh, that's terrible, that. *I've* had that before, it's *awful*, isn't it?' He croaks: 'Yes, Ma'am!'

'And what treatment are you receiving?'

'Wire brush and Dettol, Ma'am!'

'Oh, for God's sake, what's happening in here??'

So, she says to him, 'Have *you* any ambition left in life?' And he says, 'Yes, Ma'am – to get the wire brush and Dettol before those two filthy bastards over there!'

A PEE AND A FART

I'm going to tell you a story about a man in Scotland who was in terrible trouble. He was in acute discomfort. He needed to pee exceedingly badly.

And I don't mean: 'Oh . . . God almighty . . .' kind of thing. I was thinking more along the lines of: 'OOHH-OOEEE-AGHH!'

He was coming down streets backwards at an angle of forty-five degrees, holding on to his private parts, his eyes rolling in the back of his head.

'OOOHH-OOOWW!'

Crashing into folk, scattering their shopping.

'Watch where ya bloody goin' man!'

'OOOEEEEOOOHHHAAAHHH!'

Careering across busy streets.

Screeeeechh!

'Hey, ya bloody nutcase!'

'OOOOOOOOHHHH!'

He cared not a jot. He went rocketing down Buchanan Street in Glasgow. His legs were just a blur. Comes right into Argyle Street, sparks coming from his heels:

'OOOAAAAEEEHHHH!'

When out of the corner of his eye, he saw a little public convenience. He shot across the road like a man possessed—

VOOM!

And into the door of the public toilet.

There were two guys already in there, having a pee:

'There wuz a guy just shot intae the door like a man possessed, did ya see that?'

'Aye, right enough, Ah saw him ma self.'

He saw the porcelain thing you pee against, and in one bound he was there.

Ziiiiiiiiiiiiip!

Out with the willy.

And he proceeded to pee. But . . . it didn't go: *peeeeeeee*. As a pee should. As is a pee's wont.

Although, I must say, a pee doesn't actually make a noise like that. I wish it did! Wouldn't it be great at a football match: *Peeeeee-eeh-eeh-eeh-eh!*

You know, you could have good fun messing about with sounds like that, putting sounds where there aren't any and changing sounds where there are sounds. Like, can you imagine, if you farted one day, and instead of going – *brruuutchhh!* – what if it went – *faaaaartttt!* in your own voice. And they'd go, 'Oh, who farted then?' 'It wasnae me!' 'Ah, don't gimme that, I'd know your voice anywhere!'

It's good all of this talking about farting, isn't it? Because it's such a strange thing.

The vindaloo produces farts that sound like a duck being chased around a small bathroom, followed by depth charges and gunfire. It's the most dangerous of them all: *Puch-puch-puch-puch-puch-puch-pkkkkkaaaaaaaaoooowwwwww!*

But not only is it the noise. The noise embarrasses everybody, nobody's bigger than that noise. I don't care if it's Hitler. *Brrrttchh!* If you fart you get embarrassed. But not only is the noise embarrassing. It's also followed by this horrific *smell!* 'Wow! Jeez! Hooooo!' It really is *awful*, isn't it? How'd we get lumbered with that? Whose idea was it? That's bad design as well! I mean, if God had wanted us to fart He should've given us a bloody *chimney* or something like that! Then we'd all know who it was, and at least it could be given a colour. *Boooopph!* 'There it goes!'

I mean, I must admit, I've got a cheek even talking about it, because, personally, I don't fart. Because I'm a showbiz personality and *we* don't fart. And Royalty do not fart. It's a fact of life. Have you heard the Queen farting? There's no mistake – she doesn't do it! Have you ever heard anyone on stage fart? Sir John Gielgud? No! There's no mistake.

I'll tell you why. Because *we* go for an operation at Harley Street. It's called a Fartectomy. They open you up and they find this wee gland. *Phaaarp!* That's the one. *'And you'll never fart again!'*

For some reason, when you fart, you lose credibility. I don't understand that. Really, no matter what you say, when you fart nobody believes you. You can discover the answer to the riddle of the universe – just don't fart when you're telling anybody!

'You know, darling, I think if I sold the car, and got my money out the building society, and perhaps borrowed a little from my father, we would have enough for the deposit on a little house in the country and we could get married. You know I love you desperately . . .'

Brrrruuuuuutttttch!

'Ooh, you dirty filthy *liar*!! If you really loved me you wouldn't *fart* all over the place!!!'

Now, the last thing on earth that guy wanted to do was

fart at that moment. You don't *choose* to fart, *it* chooses *you*! It's passed out by the bloody rectum and everybody blames you. And I'm speaking as a man of some authority because I did used to fart, a long time ago. When I was a welder I suppose I must have farted, not that I can remember ever doing it.

I farted on my first date. You can imagine what *that* was like.

I met her in Partick Burgh Hall. That's my hometown, Partick. She was the only one left. And I took her home and she gave me a kiss. I thought, 'Oh, yes, this'll do me!'

'Can I see you tomorrow night? We could go tae the pictures, maybe?'

She said, 'Yeah, sure.'

The following night I'm getting ready. Tie and hankie to match – Killer Connolly strikes again! – and the paper collars out of Woolworths, you know, six in a packet and you ruin five of them trying to get them on? Then you get the one eventually sort-of neat. And the bum-freezer jacket. I had a Crombie jacket – a right killer, that was beautiful when I was sixteen. With the huge cufflinks – big rubies with eagles standing on them – that were thirty bob a pair, so you looked as if you owned South Africa. And the winkle-pickers, in a shoebox like a coffin, all bashed up at the front and turned up, so you looked like Aladdin.

Brutal Perry Como haircut. My hair all scolded by the barber. And I'd shaved round the acne. No mean task. I usually looked like a butcher's window after a shave. My father thought I'd been slashed. 'What happened to ya, son?' Shave round the acne and get the Old Spice on there.

What a state to get into!

So Killer Connolly is waiting at the chemist. Well, we used to wait at the chemist. I'm waiting there for Big Olive. They called her Big Olive. She was only the same height as me but the rest of them were all bloody midgets. Then I'd feel the ground shaking and I knew Olive was coming. Here she comes, the shadow over the sun. She was that big – her shadow weighed four and a half stone.

'Hello, Olive. Right, let's go tae the pictures. There's a good one on at the Rosie.' So we go to this picture house in Partick.

'Two, please, back balcony.'

'You're all right tonight, Olive. Sit doon there, Olive!'

Coat off.

'Are you okay? D'you want sweets? Chocolates?'

'Ah don't eat them.'

That's good. I've got two bob left – if she'd said yes I would've just have gone home.

It's Dana Andrews in *My Foolish Heart*. I thought, 'Oh aye, it's bound to be a wee smoochie. Back here, I think there's a good chance of a *feel* here!' I'd never had one before.

That's when it happened. I felt it in the middle of my stomach. 'Oohh, nooohhh!' It was building up like Hurricane Hilda.

Oh. My. God! It's gonnae be a *monster*! It's gonnae be lift-off at Cape Kennedy here! What in the name of Christ am I gonnae do? I know: I'll press ma left cheek doon and I'll stretch the right one away and across and ma bum'll be open . . . So when I fart it'll go: *whhhhhhh*. And then before the smell comes, I'll say, 'D'you smell something, Olive?'

Because she'll never think it was me if I brought the subject up!

Because you know yourself that the noise of a fart is caused by the expelled air rushing through your closed bum. See, your bum's always closed in case you drown in the bath. Well, you don't really drown, you fill up – they'd have to get a crane to pull you up. So, the air rushes through your closed bum, which opens and closes – imagine the sound of clacking castanets – so you're not really farting, your arse is just applauding.

But I thought, 'Ah, nae, she'll see me sitting all weird like that! She'll know it was me . . .' Plan B: get the hell out of here!

'Excuse me, Olive, I've gonnae get some cigarettes here.'

'I've got some ci—'

I said, 'No, it's okay – I smoke purple Tibetan ones. They sell 'em doon the stairs.'

So, I'm out along the row now, keeping my bum tightly closed, and meanwhile your bum's passing all the faces cheek to nose – very precarious. I get to the bathroom and lock myself in and finally let it go: *Pfffffftttttttttttttttt!!!!!* It's bouncing off the walls like a balloon with the air coming out!

It's a terrible thing to go through. Surely after all these years we can fart in front of each other?

But remember the fella I told you about who was peeing?

'OOOOAAAAHHHHH!'

Him.

Well, I told you that he proceeded to pee but it didn't go

'pee', right? As a pee should. It went: *Pssswiiiiiiiiiiiisssssshhhh-swiiiiitchh-swiiiiitchhhh!*

And the other guys in there, these poor guys, they're getting side-sprayed something rotten:

'Watch where ya spraying, ya bloody maniac! Ya bloody pervert, it's in ma hair an' everythin'! Damn crazy bugger! A hundred and forty quid fer a suit and you come an' piss all over it!'

'I'm awful sorry about that. Something's wrong with ma willy! It never happened before, I can assure ye!'

'You wanna get a hold of yerself, yer crazy bampot, ye! It's a sad day when decent folk can't come in a public place without guys peeing all over 'em!'

'I'm terrible sorry aboot that. Never happened before. It's just gone all funny!'

'You wanna see a *doctor* about that before comin' in here!'

He says, 'Aye, I'll do that. I'll take your advice. Thank you very much, I'll go tae see ma doctor.' And he managed to get out of there. Which in Glasgow it's some kind of minor miracle.

So, he's away home. He gets changed and cleaned up, and then he's away to see his doctor.

He says, 'Eh, Doctor, eh, it's aboot ma . . . thingamabob . . . Can't remember the right name of it offhand. D'ye know, I believe it's a "venus" or somethin' like that?'

Doctor says: 'Aye, somethin' like that. Well, what's the problem?'

'Well, when Ah go tae go tae do a, er, toilet, eh, tae do a urinification there, it goes like a big fountain, like that!'

'Well, that's very strange. You'd better get it oot and give us a look. Just put it on the table there, that'll be just the job.'

'Ohhhhh.'

Plonk.

'Eeooohh.'

And he's embarrassed because the table's quite high.

And the doctor's got a huge magnifying glass.

Tut-tut-tut-tut-tut! 'Never in my entire career, twenty-six years, have I seen anything like that! . . . I don't suppose ye play *darts*, d'ye?'

'Nae, Doctor, I'm a dominoes man, meself.'

'Hmmmm, just a thought. I thought, perhaps, y'know, you'd been carryin' them around in yer trooser pocket . . . I've never seen anything remotely like this! It's riddled with *holes*! Here – have a look fer yerself!'

'. . . Oh . . . so it is . . . look at that! Sure is a hell of a size to this, Doctor, isn't it! What am I gonnae do?'

'I'll tell you exactly what yer gonnae do,' he said. 'Just go and see this fella here, he'll sort you out and nae bother at all.'

'Well, thanks very much. Is he a specialist or somethin'?'

'Nae, nae, he's a clarinet player – he'll show you how tae hold it!'

THE JOBBIE WHEECHER

We're always being told these days that everything has to be recycled. Apparently, it's the law. I was wondering where all the jobbies on a jumbo jet go – how and where do *they* get recycled? A guy who was quite knowledgeable about these things – or thought he was – said to me, 'It all goes into a big tank, and when it gets to the destination they change it for an empty one and they get rid of it all some place.' No they don't.

I know, because I was watching this science programme on TV just after he told me that, and this guy came on and he'd invented a thing called a Jobbie Wheecher. Now, 'wheecher' is a Scottish word for something that goes 'whoosh' – in Scotland it goes 'wheech' – and he'd invented this thing.

It was like a ladle, a kind of spoon thing, with a spring on it, and you stretch it back and keep it really taut. It's in the bowl there. So you come in, do a wee jobbie, shut the lid: *wheech*! Done. Bowl empty, jobbie outward bound.

They do it over the sea. It's now called 'organic redistribu-tion'. Natural recycling.

They don't do it over towns for very obvious reasons – you know, there could be a guy there directing the traffic, and one minute he's waving people on and the next minute – *splat!* – a jobbie hits him on the side of the face. It's kind of antisocial, isn't it?

They don't do it over mountains, either, again for fairly obvious reasons: because you get these nice outdoor types, with the woolly hats and the knee-length trousers, always climbing up stuff: 'I love to go a-wandering along the moun-tain path—' *Splat!* 'Oh my goodness – the eagles are some size up here!'

So organic redistribution dumps it into the sea. The basic

process is: *wheech – shooo – splash!* Well, actually, it wouldn't go 'splash' from that height, it would go *thumsch!* Anyway, it all gradually makes its way back to the surface, and then it's all sort of swaying and rocking around there on the water. And along comes a fishie: swimmetty-swim, hungritty-hungry. 'Jesus, I'm starving!' Then it spots something: 'Ahoy there!' Munchetty-crunchetty. Happy fishie – backstroke.

Then along comes a fisherman. Rowitty-boat. Spots the fishie: 'A-ha!' Net, fling, catches the fishie, into the boat – rowitty-home. Up to the market, he sells the fishie. You come along, you buy the fishie. Munchetty-crunchetty.

Then you go in an aeroplane. 'Hmmm, I need to go to the toilet.' Into the toilet, do a wee jobbie, close the lid – *wheech!*

And that's organic redistribution.

SCUBA-DIVING

I was on holiday once in Barbados and they were teaching scuba-diving. And I said, 'That'll do me.' I always fancied a bit of that – you know, Jacques Cousteau and all that?

So, I went down and learned it. The instructor took us all under for a wee look, and I thought, 'Christ, this is *it*! This is a new direction in my life! Communing with inner space! At one with nature!'

I felt so at *home* under there. I picked up the terms so quickly: 'fish'; 'stone'; 'seaweed'. That's the first sign you're a natural. The guy was saying: 'You're fuckin' amazing, you! Where did you learn that stuff?'

And I loved it and I thought, 'When I go home, I'm going to go up Fulham Palace Road to that shop, and I'm going to get all the gear, the full kit – the big helmet that you can talk in, and spears and guns, 'cause I'm going to fuckin' kill everything!' That's the British way, isn't it? 'My God, is that a nightingale?' 'I dunno, let's have a closer look' – BANG! – 'Aye, you were right enough!'

But before I had a chance to acquire all of that stuff, I went out to get some videos. I was with my eldest daughter and I said, 'Let's go and get a few movies for the weekend.' *Viva Zapata!* – yet again – *Brief Encounter*, maybe even a wee bit of Norman Wisdom now and again – I like that one where he's a wee policeman – because I like to do that Sunday afternoon thing, watching old movies. Anyway, we're in the video shop, and my daughter says, 'Let's get that one – *Jaws*.' I said, 'Sure.' I'd honestly never seen it. It was the worst move I ever made. It's all about a shark that plays the cello – I don't know if you've seen it. A fucking weird shark if you ask me.

But it *ruined* my new hobby. We went back to Barbados, I put all the gear on, and every time I put my head underwater: *dun dun dun dun dun dun dun dun* . . . 'What the hell? There's some bugger playing a cello here!' I kept telling myself: '*Conquer* it, Billy, *conquer* it! Get on top of it! GO!' And away I went. But my heart wasn't in it.

The thing I used to love was doing that sort of fluttery thing with my legs, you know? Fluttering through the big, big shoals of tiny fish, the millions that you'd swim straight through, fluttering your legs. It's like travelling through a big silvery tunnel. I developed a French accent like Jacques Cousteau.

But I couldn't do it anymore. I was halfway through and suddenly they all changed direction. They went: *Shooooo!* 'Fuck!' I thought. 'What do they know? What do they know?' I was looking everywhere. 'What have the bastards heard?' I was flying around, burping and farting. And I can tell you: when you fart in a wetsuit, you come out the water like a Polaris missile!

Completely ruined it for me.

So, I went back to snorkelling. But I get scared in case something's climbing down that pipe. You never know. You have to watch when you're away in these foreign places, they're full of *things*. In Nigeria, there's things that crawl up your bum. Snails – up the bum. And they don't come out. They live up there. Whole families of them. They have noisy parties and there's not a thing you can do about them.

But I tried snorkelling again. I'm looking up every now and again to check that the beach is still there, you know? You can't be too careful – sometimes the tide turns you round, you look up and think: 'Aggghhh!' You think you're halfway to fucking Venezuela! I can only do two lengths in the baths!

I don't know why I go into the sea at all. I panic in the fucking swimming baths.

You see, in these places, you don't need to go far out to see incredible things. I was just enjoying myself looking at all the wee fish, when something suggested to me that I should turn around. I don't know how or why, but some heavenly voice said: 'Turn round.' 'What?' 'Go on: turn round.' 'Eh?' *'Go on: turn round!'* So eventually I turned round.

My heart stopped. Not five feet behind me was a black fin. I thought, 'Oh fuck.'

I took off like a motorboat. I thrashed the water to a foam. In one huge long fart I was going through the water like a torpedo. As I got nearer the shore I was throwing children behind me. Well, we're talking *survival* here! We're not talking paddling, we're talking survival!

It was like that Scottish film crew in the Serengeti Plain. They were filming the lions there, two guys, and the lions are giving it the roar: '*Raw-ruu-raaah-ruuu-roar!*' And one lion is eating a zebra. One of the cameramen takes his boots off and changes into a pair of Nike running shoes. The other cameraman says: 'You'll never outrun a lion in them.' He says, 'Fuck the lion – as long as I outrun you I'm okay!'

So, I'm flying through the water, throwing these children behind me. I carved a trench right up the beach. My fingers were bleeding. And on I went, right up the steps and on to the street. I nearly got run over by a bus on the main road! *Screech!* 'What are you doin', ya crazy fucker?'

I turned round, and that's when I noticed – it was my own flipper.

ASKING FOR DIRECTIONS

There are certain things that you have to know about when you're asking for directions. There are three lies that you must keep your eyes open for.

The first lie is: 'It's easy.'

No, it isn't. If you say, 'How do I get to blah-blah-blah?' And they say, 'Oh, it's easy!' No, it fucking *isn't*. It's very, very difficult.

The second lie to look out for is: 'You can't miss it.'

Yes, you can! You can miss it so many times that you never, ever, find it in your whole life. You may set off to find it, not find it, and then just go on with your life and give up fucking looking for it altogether. It can be a life-changing event.

Now, the other one to look for, the third lie, is a dodgy one. It's when they say: 'And as soon as you're past the roundabout, turn right.' And you say, 'That's your left hand you're holding out there.' Then they just say: 'Well, anyway . . . Do that.'

These are the things to look for.

And you really have to look out for them these days, especially, because all of the routes seem to change on a weekly basis. It's completely bewildering.

Let me give you an example. I was on tour in the UK. We left Blackpool after a lovely gig at the Opera House, and then went to Liverpool.

Now, at that time, Liverpool was getting ready for its year as Capital of Culture, so it was ripping the place up. It looked as though they'd rolled it up and sold it to Zambia. There were roundabouts where there hadn't been roundabouts before. You know those roundabouts that workmen just 'make'? They're just like oil drums joined with planks of wood. It was like that, all over the place. It was all very confusing.

So, I'm trundling along, in that awful way when you're flying through the one-way system, feeling increasingly tense, and at last I saw a sign: Town Centre. 'Oh, great!' *Whooosh.* We pull off into a wee housing estate and there's a man selling cakes and doughnuts and shit from the back of this van. And he recognises me: 'Oh, hello, Bill, how are you doing?' I said: 'Hello, man, I'm lost!'

Now, I can't remember whether it was the Prince's Hotel, Queen's Square, or the Queen's Hotel, Princes Square, but something along those lines. So, I said, 'Look, I'm really stuck here, I've been on this fucking one-way system, I'm going off my fucking head! I'm completely lost, I'm starving and I've been going round and round and round!' I said, 'If you could just point to roughly where this hotel is, I'd be really grateful.'

Now this man, he said: 'Bill, it's easy.' I went: 'Uh-oh!' He said, 'You can't fuckin' miss it!' My head went: 'Ding-ding!' He said, 'Go on the one-way system—'

I said, 'I've just *come off* the one-way system! It's *impenetrable!*'

He says: 'Bill, trust me. Go on the one-way, go left, as soon as you leave here. It'll whisk you round to the right, down past the – do you know the Liver Building? – it'll whisk you up to the right, up a hill. At the top of the hill there's a roundabout. On the roundabout there's a big sign. Follow the signs to the Tunnel. But don't go *in* the Tunnel. And when you think you should be turning right, turn left.'

'Thanks very much,' I said.

'You can't miss it,' he said.

'I'm sure you're fuckin' right,' I said with a heavy sigh.

And off we went. We were hopelessly lost again within seconds.

We came down a street – one of these streets you hardly see anymore, a city centre street where it's a kind of dell. You come into the street and it plunges downhill, then at the bottom of the hill you find the railway bridge goes across at right angles, so the street goes under through a tunnel, and if you go down into the tunnel, you're just whisked wherever the tunnel wants to take you. They'll be no turning round here if you make that decision.

So, we're halfway down, and I say: 'Stop, stop!'

There's a building on the corner – it looked like a bank or an insurance company, with big pillars – and there were three big girls coming out. Big fat lasses – not obese, but no strangers to a fucking Mars bar, if you know what I mean. I think they'd been on The Mars Bar Diet, but they'd been doing it wrong: they were *eating* the Mars bar, whereas you're supposed to stick it up your arse and get a Rottweiler to chase you home. These were girls with slow metabolisms and fucking fast appetites. Nice big well-fed lasses.

I said, 'Hello, ladies.'

'Ah, Bill!' They recognised me. 'How are you doing?'

I said, 'Look, I'm lost here.' I told them where I was trying to go, the hotel.

Then one of them said it. I swear, and I have a witness, my manager was there, he was my witness. She said: 'I don't think you can get there from here.'

I thought, '*What?* Have I slipped into a parallel universe or something? I'm going to have to be airlifted into the gig! *I can't get there from here?*' Jesus Christ all-bloody mighty! So I said, 'Oh, well, I'll just try and find it, y'know?'

And off we drove into the heart of Liverpool, whereupon I saw a taxi rank. So, I said to my manager, 'Stop here, we'll get a taxi, we'll give them a few bob, and say "Take us there," and we'll follow them,' so that's what we did.

Watch out for this kind of nonsense. The phantom roundabouts, the one-way systems, the ripped-up roads, the sheer chaos of it all. They're doing it to every town now! They're fucking the whole world up! You cannae work your telly, your phone's fucked, you can't call for help – *brrr-brrr* – some prick in Calcutta: 'What's the problem?' 'Get the fuck out of my life!'

AEROPLANE TOILETS

Flying interests me, because it terrifies me. I thought if I flew more, it would get okay, y'know, the less horrible it would become. But it doesn't, it gets worse. And I know, because I'm an international jet-setter.

I don't even like the concept of flying in aeroplanes. There's something basically wrong with it. We don't belong up there. I agree with John Lee Hooker. He said, 'If God wanted us to fly, he'd buy the tickets.'

And they lie to you all the time. All that shit about 'in the highly unlikely event . . .' They talk to you like you're mentally ill. They get these people on the plane who suddenly start behaving like they're doing children's TV. They go in this singy-songy voice: 'This is your safety belt' – they're smiling at you like it's a cute wee duckling or something. Then they start telling you the instructions – the instructions are already printed on it! We're not idiots! 'This bit goes into this bit . . .' Oh fuck off!

They're basically lying to us. 'In a sudden loss of pressure, oxygen masks will fall down as if by magic, and you'll be able to breathe, and it'll all be jolly, and if you secure your safety belt you'll be very, very safe with your lovely nice seat belt on . . .' When were you ever listening to the news on television, and it said, 'Today, a jumbo jet smacked into a mountain in Peru. Luckily, all the passengers were wearing safety belts!' You're sitting there with your fucking life jacket on, heading upside down towards the fucking Atlantic Ocean. 'I'm all right. I've observed all of the safety procedures.' Fuck off!

If they were to tell you the truth, then they'd have to say: 'Ladies and gentlemen, in the highly unlikely event of loss of power on all four engines, then, in all probability, we'll be going towards the ground like a fucking dart. You won't be screaming – you'll be trying to get the seat in front of you out of your mouth. We would be obliged if you would wear your life jacket on the way down. This will do you no good at all, but when archaeologists find you in two hundred years' time, they'll think there was a river here.'

I get well stewed when I'm going to fly, because I cannot handle it. I need to get a bit pissed. And then it's up there and you've had a wee sleep, and you wake up, and you're dying to pee – because of the drinking – so you think, 'I'd better have a pee.' And always, *always*, I need to pee just as they've served the meal to the three of you. 'Er, excuse me, please.' 'Oh, ferchrissakes!' They're all standing out in the aisle, holding their trays above their heads. And you leave your tray in his seat, so he can't go back in.

So, I away up to the lavvy, on the plane. Now, aeroplane toilets were made to frighten you. I'm sure the guys who designed planes said, 'Oh, we'll have a right laugh with the lavvy!' There's no safety belt – you're just sitting there hanging on to the sink: 'Oh, please, don't crash, I don't want to be found with my trousers around my ankles!' It's claustrophobic in there, because most of them are a sort of triangular shape with no windows. There's no reason why they shouldn't have a window. It's not as if anyone can see in, you know? Unless you've got the most determined pervert in the world out there!

Once you're done and you're just about to leave, you think, 'Oh no, wait a minute: I'd better flush this.' Now, this is where the designers had another good laugh. They tucked the thing you flush it with away in a wee corner and you cannae find it. And then you see in the underside of the lid: 'TO FLUSH CLOSE LID'. No problem. Closed. Right, that'll do.

But then you wonder. And you lift the lid back up. And sure enough: it's away.

You should always make sure, because there's nothing worse in the world, is there, than the indomitable jobbie? National Rail specialise in that one. You know: in the toilet, shut the door, look down – 'Oh, for crying out loud!'

There's the wee jobbie. A wee beige jobbie.

You flush and flush with all your might – *doo-doo-doo-doodle-a-doo*: it's back. Sometimes it actually goes under the bend bit as well. It *hides*. And just as you start taking your trousers down: *Bing!* It's back! There's no way you're going to bare your bum above this beige jobby that belongs to somebody else!

You try battering it to death with paper towels. '*Go awaaaaaayyyy!!!*' And you can't leave. You're *stuck* in there with this bloody thing!

If you've *got* to leave, you walk out the door and somebody's coming in: 'Er, by the way, *that's* not mine!'

SEXY BANDAGES

There are unsexy bandages and sexy bandages. Most of them are unsexy. But a few of them are sexy. A sling is one of the latter. A sling is a sexy bandage.

I'm sure you haven't thought about that recently yourself, but if you ask any man how he felt when another boy walked into the playground at school wearing a sling, I bet he remembers thinking to himself, 'Oh, I wish *I* had one of them! If I had one of them, Agnes MacDonald's knickers would *fly* off!' It just happens to be a sexy bandage.

As a matter of fact, it happens to be the second sexiest bandage there is.

The *un*sexiest bandage is the top-of-the-head bandage tied under the chin. You couldn't get laid in a brothel with a note from your doctor when you wear one of those.

I saw a guy in Belfast with one of them on. He was walking up the road, up the centre of the pavement, doing the 'Couldn't Give A Fuck' walk. Now, if you had one of those bandages on, *you* wouldn't be doing the 'Couldn't Give A Fuck' walk.

You'd be walking close to the wall, in case whatever happened to you happened again.

I was being driven down the road that time in Belfast, and I said to my driver, Billy: 'Look at that prick!' His answer stays with me. He said, 'It looks like he was talking when he should have been listening.'

But I've said that the sling is the second most sexy bandage of them all. Well, the sexiest bandage is only worn by Clint Eastwood and other people who play the lead in western movies. You'll have seen them, after they've been in a great fracas. They'll be sitting up in bed stripped to the waist, their skin shining, their muscles glowing with sweat, talking to the leading lady, whose legs are already going, because he's wearing The Bandage. It goes over one shoulder, around the top of the left arm, under the left arm and across the chest and then under the right arm. Leaving one of those arms free for fucking about with the leading lady's body.

Now *that's* a sexy bandage.

Bearing that in mind, I'd like to tell you now about what I thought was going to be my very own sexy-bandage moment.

I was on an airstrip in Mozambique, standing in front of one of those single-engine aeroplanes. One of those Buddy Holly pieces of shit. The ones that sound like: '*Eeeeeeeeee*'. I hate them.

I was there for Comic Relief. Me and another comedian. The people of Mozambique were suffering from starvation and terror attacks, so we sent two comedians. And we were waiting for the pilot to take us into the interior.

Now, whenever you see one of these single-engine pieces

of shit, they've got terrible habits – like suddenly going silent before making a noise again: *'Eeeeeeeee . . . Eeeeeeeee'. 'Don't fucking do that again!'* But my least favourite is when they very briefly shut up and you feel this lurch downwards. That's what's known as the Atheism Test.

Whenever you see any of these aeroplanes, or maybe several of them together, look around you and you'll see The Bore. You'll recognise him. He has a blazer, cavalry twills, and suede shoes, and he usually has a moustache, and there's a badge on the blazer and it's on the tie as well. That's The Bore. And he'll be saying, 'That's *real* flying! Oh yes, real seat-of-the-pants flying! Up and away into the wide blue yonder. *Real* flying!' And I'd like to say: 'Fuck off!'

'Real flying' is sitting up at the front in a jumbo jet, being spoon-fed caviar by a woman with huge tits, who whispers in your ear that your air miles entitle you to a complimentary blow job! If that's not *real* flying I don't know what is.

Now, for some reason, when you're doing these charity things in Africa, the people who fly you around tend to be fat American born-again Christians. I don't know why that should be, I only know it is thus. So, we're standing waiting and they showed up: two guys in shorts, flip-flops and T-shirts. One of them says, 'Hi, I'm Chuck, I'm the pilot!' I said, 'Fuck off, Chuck.' I said, 'Did they sell men's clothes in the same shop?' He said, 'What?' I said, 'Go and get lace-up shoes, long trousers, a short-sleeved shirt with epaulettes and a breast pocket with a packet of Rothman's showing through, hairy arms, a stainless-steel Rolex, a moustache and a hat with an eagle on it. Is that too much to ask?'

Well, we managed to get round it, and he had us all belted up in the back seat. Then he said, 'Before we go, I think I'll have a word with the Man Upstairs.' I said, 'Oh fuck!' He bows down and says, 'Oh Lord, look after these pilgrims, they know not what they do. They are simple souls, Lord, lead them on their way.' And I'm whispering: 'Put the Bible down. Have a look through the manual.'

So now he's ready. 'Everybody okay?' 'Aye, we're fine.' Then he starts all the pressing and clicking of buttons and starts speaking in that weird language to whoever it is he's connected to. Then that horrible engine starts up, with that horrible noise, and we're eventually up in the air:

Eeeeeeeeeeeeeeeeeeeeeeeeeee!

'Everybody okay?' 'Yeah.' 'Okay. Just be careful.'

And we're sitting at the back saying to each other, 'Just be careful? How are we supposed to do that?'

So, I tapped him on the shoulder and said, 'Excuse me.' He said, 'Yeah?' I said, 'You were talking to us a second ago, I'm sure you remember. You were urging us to be careful. Could you tell me of what we're supposed to be careful?' He goes, 'Well, for the last two weeks we've been flying over here and the bandits have been shooting up at us. Just be careful.'

I thought, 'There's some prick down there pointing his rifle up here.' I imagined the bullet flying straight through the plane, straight through my shoulder, and all of us plummeting downwards. We'd land in the bush.

Then I thought, 'I might be on the news. I might have The Bandage!'

I'm practising my speech: 'It's not about me. It's about the children.' And then I thought, 'Wait a minute. I'm directly above the guy, and he's got a rifle, and I'm in a sitting position. He's not going to hit me anywhere near my shoulder. He's going to shoot me up the arse! Or in the willy!'

And that's a different kind of bandage altogether. You don't get on the news with an arse bandage. It's like a big nappy.

'It's not about me—'

'Get the fuck off the air! There's people here with shoulder bandages desperate to get on!'

DANGEROUS DRIVING

I need to issue a warning in the name of health and safety. Because apparently, you've been driving like fucking maniacs.

Now, eating and drinking while driving is a stupid thing to do. I'm sure you realise that. And texting while driving isn't the most clever thing you've ever done. Masturbating while driving is certainly a worry. And smoking while driving can be desperately dangerous.

Smoking is dangerous enough in itself. I would still smoke today if my wife hadn't nagged the fucking face off me. I loved a smoke. I used to go to sleep at night thinking about my first smoke in the morning. That's how much I loved it. Even though everybody knows that when you light up a cigarette God takes an hour off your life and gives it to Keith Richards.

I used to smoke non-filtered cigarettes. Proper cigarettes. Fags. But the non-filtered cigarette has one desperate failing.

It sticks to your face sometimes – not all the time, maybe every six packs you'll get one that sticks. Now, when I say it sticks to your mouth, I don't mean it has a slight tackiness. I mean it's welded to your face. You can cajole and coax it, but nothing happens. The only thing that's going to get it off is a good healthy tug. Ooof! And if you say the word 'Ooof!' when you do it, that helps as well. 'Ooof!'

You get one of two results. Either the cigarette will burst, so there'll be shag all over your face, and what's left will be unlightable, or you'll pull a chunk off your lip, and it's really painful and it bleeds.

Well, I was driving down the M1. I had an old Jaguar that I'd bought from a hire company who saw me coming. When you got to seventy it made a weird rumbling noise and things would fly past the window, like mirrors and things like that. It was a heap of shit, but I loved it. I had the radio blaring ZZ Top, and I'm giving it plenty, smoking. I was as happy as a clam, and you know how happy clams are – they're the happiest things in the sea.

But then it happened. The cigarette had stuck to my lip.

There was a car in front of me, a car behind me, and a van to my left. I was in a wee coffin space, doing about eighty. I decided to go for the 'Ooof!'

'Ooof!'

Neither of the two things I've described to you happened. A third thing that had never happened before happened. 'Ooof!' My fingers slid along the cigarette and lifted the lip bit off the end.

So now part of the cigarette had been dropped on to my

crotch. Smoke started to drift up. I thought, 'Oh shit!' I was waving one of my arms up and down trying to beat it out. And there were people driving the other way up the motorway going: 'Look at that prick – he thinks he's on a horse!'

Now, imagine that swirly imagery, accompanied by harp music, that you used to get on the telly to signify a sudden change of scene. Because that's what's happening.

We're now in a pub in Glasgow, the Scotia Bar, where I used to play my banjo. It was always full of great players, great guitarists and mandolinists and violinists and autoharpists and accordionists, as well as writers and poets and playwrights and directors and producers. A fine cross-section of Glasgow's unemployed at the time.

We were over on the left of the pub. In the middle were the guys from the fish market, giving the place its certain ambience, and at the other end was a motorcycle outfit called the Blue Angels, who looked like mass murderers, but they were actually rather nice guys. One of them only had half an arm. It was missing from his elbow down; well, it would hardly be missing from the elbow up. And I swear this is true: tattooed round the stump was: 'To be continued'.

So that describes what the pub was like. It was a fucking madhouse.

And into this one day wandered a guy called Gordon, with his vertical-stripe velvet coat, his shoes that turned up at the front, his Brylcreemed hair, his Ascot tie and his violin. And a weird look about his face. I became instantly friendly with him.

Gordon only had one eye – he'd lost the other one in a motoring accident in Spain – but that's not when we discovered it, that came later. We found that out one day when it was somebody's birthday in the pub. 'Happy Birthday!' – *chink-chink* – 'Happy Birthday! All the best!' – *chink-chink* – 'Yeah, Happy Birthday to you!' – *chink-chink*. And Gordon went: 'Yeah, Happy Birthday!' and he lifted his glass and chink-chinked it with his glass eye. We were amazed: 'Did you see that? He chinked the glass off his fucking *eye*!'

He was a crazy bloke. He drank Guinness, and when he needed to pee, he'd take his eye out and put it in the foam, because there were a lot of thieves in the pub. We called them 'mine sweepers', because they'd go up and grab somebody else's glass, saying, 'That's mine!' Well, they'd try it with Gordon's – 'That's mine!' – and then they'd see this eye floating in the foam: 'Aaaggghhh!'

Well, I was walking through the pub one day, and he came in the door with his arm in a sling. I said, 'What happened to you?' He said, 'You'll never believe it. I was driving up Sauchiehall Street, I was scratching my good eye, and I ran into the back of a bus.' He'd thought because his artificial eye was expensive he could see through it!

SAT NAV

I was on tour, and we had a Range Rover that had its own GPS system, with this posh fucking woman's voice in it. This stuck-up, upper-middle-class fucking bitch!

She kept saying things like, 'Turn left soon.' What's *that* supposed to mean? 'Soon'? What – in a fortnight? Tomorrow?

A quarter of an hour? What do you mean, 'Soon'? Five minutes?

And another thing she said: 'In a third of a mile . . .' Do *you* know what a third of a mile looks like? I don't have a fucking clue what a third of a mile looks like. Stupid fucking bitch!

Do you know another thing she said? She didn't call a roundabout a 'roundabout'. She called it a 'traffic circle'. 'At the traffic circle'? What the fuck? Where did *you* come from? A fucking 'traffic circle'? It sounds like a country dance: 'We're all in the traffic circle now, *diddly-i-pum-pum*, Form into a traffic circle, Take your partner by the hand, *diddly-i-pum-pum* . . .' Fucking 'traffic circle'!

And then, if you don't do what she tells you, she goes in a huff! Really. Like, she'll say, 'Take the second exit at the next traffic circle.' So you'll come up to the roundabout, and you don't know whether to count the first one, because it isn't an exit, it's just one way coming that way – you can't exit that way, you'd kill yourself, you'd have a head-on collision with somebody. So, you look beyond it and think, 'Well, *this* must be the first exit, because I can't exit in the other one.' Wrong! She has *counted* that one, the stupid bitch, because *she's* not driving, *she* can't crash, she doesn't give a fuck what happens to *you*! *She's* in the fucking black box. Safe as fucking houses.

It's the same as when aeroplanes crash into the sea, and they're searching for the black box. And they always find it, and it's in mint condition and you've got to say: 'Why don't they make aeroplanes out of the same fucking stuff?'

Anyway, I take what she says at her word – the second exit, although one of them isn't really an exit, it's an 'ins-it', except she has counted it as an exit, and I'm completely wrong. So, it's the middle of the night, and we've ended up in an industrial estate. We've driven into hell.

'*Help! Help! Help!*' And I'm shouting at the box: 'Where *are* you, you fucking bitch? Where are *you*? Where are *we*?'

Not a sound. She's giving us the silent treatment.

Finally, by sheer chance, we manage to get back on to the original roundabout. And then she comes back on. 'At the second exit . . . maybe you'll do as you're told this time.'

THE CAT

This happened while they were making the movie *Rob Roy*. I wasn't in it, but I was up in Scotland at the time, taking a few days off just relaxing and fishing. Liam Neeson – who *was* in it – is a friend of mine, and he got in touch with the hotel where I was staying, and he said, 'Tell Bill to come over for dinner.'

So, we met and had dinner. He's a lovely big man, Liam Neeson, and he was telling me about making the movie. And, God bless him, he told me this thing as a *sad* story, but I'm afraid I was pissing myself laughing pretty much all the way through.

Apparently, on this one particular day, they're up on the mountains, being eaten alive by midges, getting ready to start filming. They're waiting for the armourer – the guy in charge of all the guns and gunpowder and bombs and all the other weapons – and they couldn't start filming until he's there, for safety reasons.

Everybody hates the armourers anyway, because they never let you play with their stuff. They're very possessive, and they're always checking the safety of the guns, taking them back off you for another look, and generally fussing about. They're constantly saying, 'Don't do this, don't do that, watch yourself there, be careful holding that', and all of that kind of stuff. It's their job, but it can get quite irritating.

The armourer on this movie was actually lost somewhere in the middle of the Highlands, desperately trying to find the rest of the film company. He's in his van, studying this map he's got balanced on his knee, muttering 'Holy shit' as he stares at all the Gaelic names, and he can't figure out where the hell he is. And time's passing and he's getting increasingly anxious about the whole thing.

So, he's driving faster and faster out of panic. He knows everybody is waiting for him to arrive. But he's in his wee van, with all the guns and bombs and swords and daggers and stuff bouncing around in the back, and he's getting pretty reckless. And at a certain point he's passing through this strange wee village in a glen. You know those villages where there's just two rows of houses on either side of the street, called something like Auchternucht'uchty? Somebody should've bought another vowel years ago. You know, when you say the name of the village and people say 'Bless you!'

Well, he's driving along in his van through this village, and suddenly a cat runs straight across the road. He goes, 'Oh,

Jesus!' There's a screech of brakes and then two dull thuds – he's hit it with both sets of wheels. 'Oh fuck! Oh shit!'

He gets out the van and goes and has a look, and the cat's in the gutter, twitching. 'Oh *shit!*' So, he goes back to his van, reaches into the passenger seat and opens his toolbox, takes out a hammer, then walks back over to the cat, whispers 'Sorry, pal,' and goes *BANG!* It's stone dead.

But just as he's picking the poor wee lifeless thing up, suddenly a woman comes running out of one of the nearby cottages, her apron still on and her hands all covered in flour – she's been making scones all day – and she shouts: 'What the hell's going on here? You just killed my cat!' He says, 'I'm sorry, missus, I'm so, so sorry, but I just ran over it in my van, I couldn't help it. It was in absolute agony, I just had to put it out of its misery.' And she shouts: 'No it *wasn't*! That's a *lie*! You *animal*! You *psychopath*!' She's raging. And she turns her head and shouts: *'Archie! Archie!'*

And the man next door is a policeman. He comes out, halfway through his dinner, sausage roll in his hand: 'What's the fucking trouble here?' She says, 'Archie, this . . . animal, this . . . this . . . maniac, just got out of his car and killed my cat for no reason at all!'

He says, 'You bastard! What's the story here?'

And the armoury man says, 'Constable, I'm working on the film *Rob Roy*, and I was just going up to meet them. I was driving through the village here, and the cat ran straight in front of me! I slammed on the brakes, but I was too late – *bang*! It went under the front and back wheels, it was in terrible agony, and I hit it with a hammer. I'm awful sorry!'

The policeman sighed. 'Aye, I can understand that. Well, let's go down and we'll see the skid mark and all that. Let's see what the story is here.'

So, they walk down. 'Aye, well, I can see your skid mark right enough, hmmm, and there's blood on the front wheel there, yes, hmmm.' And then they go to inspect the rear wheel. And it's got those rubber mudguards at the back, so the policeman pulls one up and looks underneath it.

And there, in the wheel arch, is a dead cat.

Poor fucking Tiddles. He'd just been lying in the gutter, dozing away in the sunshine, dreaming happily about chasing mice and all that. And the next thing he knows: *bang!*

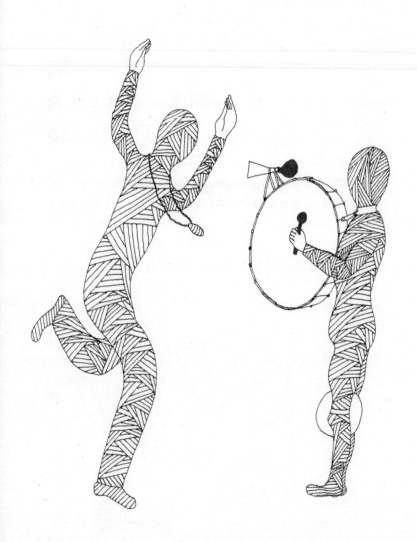

5.
Sex, Drugs & Folk Music

'Apparently, women need to feel loved to have sex. And men need to have sex to feel loved. So, the basic act of continuing the species requires a lie from one of you.'

THE CIGAR

I used to have a house in Aberdeenshire, three and a half hours from Glasgow. One day I had an errand to do in Glasgow – I forget what the errand was – and I knew I was going to have a three-and-a-half-hour drive to Glasgow.

But it was a Saturday, so I thought, 'Oh, great, I'll be able to hear the football on the car radio.' Then I thought: 'I know what I'll do – I'll drive into Aberdeen, I'll get a huge cigar, and I'll smoke it during the games as I go. I'll be driving down there and I wouldn't call the Queen my granny.' That's an old expression from when I worked on the Clyde, by the way – 'I wouldn't call the Queen my granny' – it means 'I don't see anybody above me and I'm as happy as a clam.' That sort of feeling. I imagined this scenario: driving along, the radio on, a nice cigar on the go, keeping the windows open just enough to let enough smoke out and enough air in. That's what I call a holiday!

So, I drove into Aberdeen to get myself a cigar. I came down Union Street and I turned into Market Square. Now, I didn't *know* it was called Market Square at the time. That will become obvious as this story goes on. And on.

Right in front of me was a toyshop, and in front of that was a huge armoured car – you know, those cars that deliver money to banks and pick up money from banks, with the bars on the windows and all that. Well, the only parking space was right behind it, on a double yellow line. I thought, 'Fuck it. If *he* can do it, so can I. I *am* Billy Connolly – there must be the *occasional* benefit.'

I pulled up behind him and I went to get out and go to the cigar store, when my car was suddenly completely surrounded by Aberdeen supporters on their way to their match – they'd spotted me and wanted autographs, there were fifty or sixty guys. So, I put the window down and I was signing away there, mostly on money – five, tens, twenties – because working men seldom carry autograph books.

And I'm signing, signing, signing, signing.

'Can you put it to "Alistair Montgomery N. Dimpner?"'

'No. If you want your name on it, go and stand over in the other corner and do your own fucking autographs.'

Signing, signing, signing, signing.

Eventually they all disappeared and I went to get my cigar. Now, the cigar store was just a little kiosk against the wall of House of Fraser in Market Square. It isn't there anymore, it's been shut down thanks to the efforts of those fucking 'no-smoking' zealots, who should mind their own business.

God, they get on my fucking nerves! 'Do you know that could kill you?' 'Yes. So could boredom – it just takes longer!' They've even taught their children to do it: 'Do you know that could kill you?' 'Do you know *I* could kill *you*?'

Do you know who they remind me of? The brown bread/ white bread brigade. Absolute pains in the arse. You're just about to bite into a lovely big white bread sandwich and some spotty wee idiot comes along and says, 'Do you know they put bleach in that and it poisons you?' 'Aye – and it's fuckin' *delicious!*' And I also like to say to them, 'I hate brown bread – you never know when it's toasted!' But instead I ask them: 'You eat brown bread your whole life. I eat white bread my whole life. How much longer are you going to live than me? A fortnight? Ten days? Don't say twenty years – you know that's crap. We're talking a fortnight – tops. But it isn't a fortnight when you're eighteen, shagging everything that walks in front of you. No, it's a fortnight when you're in an old folks' home, pissing in your troosers, being fed out of a blender! And the nurse who's feeding you is going: "Aw, you're looking awful sad! There's such an awful sad expression on your face. Is that because all your friends are dead? Aw, they were the white bread crowd. But don't you worry – *you've* got another two weeks to go!"'

Anyway. I got my cigar. And I went back to my car and I took off. I was going back up Union Street, heading for the Queen Victoria statue, when I heard the siren: *woo!-woo!* I looked in the mirror and there's a police car behind me and I thought, 'Oh shit.'

And this amplified voice says: 'Will the driver of the red Range Rover pull into the first street on the left! The driver of the red Range Rover pull into the first street on the left!' I looked back, and the voice said: 'Aye. *You!*'

I drove into this wee street and I stopped. I thought, 'I know what I'll do – I'll leap out of the car like a gazelle just to show them how sober I am.' So, that's what I did. And I met a policeman standing there. He must have parked and sprinted straight up to my car. And he reached out and grabbed my cuff and put his fingers in and did a wee twisting thing that tightened my jacket around my sleeve. It's the thing policemen do when they don't have handcuffs with them.

I said, 'What the fuck? What's going on here?' 'Everything will be explained, Mr Connolly, just come with me.' So we go back to the squad car and he sat me in the back between two cops. And they were fucking about with the radio and they couldn't get it to work. There was an awful lot of crackling going on, with them saying: 'Hallo? . . . Hallo? Hallo? . . . Hallo? . . . Hallo? Hallo? . . . *Hallo?* . . . Hallo? Hallo? . . .'

And eventually, this woman's voice goes: 'Hallo, Inspector McCorkindale here.' You could tell by her voice that she was ugly, it was really strange. 'Who am I speaking to?' One of the coppers goes: 'Constable McBumpherty here.' That wasn't his name, I just made it up. She says, 'Have you got the driver of the Range Rover?' He says, 'We have indeed! And it might surprise you to know it's Billy Connolly!'

Well, there was a wee confab at the other end of the line. You could faintly hear them saying: 'He says it's Billy Connolly – *mumble mumble* – comedian – *mumble mumble* – D'you think it's the same guy? – *mumble mumble* – you'd better ask him . . .' So she speaks to the coppers again: 'Is that Billy Connolly the comedian?' I'm desperate to shout out: 'No, it's Billy Connolly the donkey shagger!'

And as all of this was going on, it dawned on me. I said: 'Oh – I know what this must be about! It's because I parked behind that van. Look, it was a stupid thing to do and I won't be doing that again, I'm very sorry.' But she says:

'No. It's not about that – although you shouldn't have done that. Were you parked in Market Square?'

'I've no idea. I was parked next to the cigar shop at the House of Fraser.'

'That's Market Square.'

'In that case, yes, I was.'

'What were you doing there?'

'I was buying a cigar.'

There was another wee confab. You could just about hear them mumbling, 'Buying a cigar . . . *mumble mumble*— . . . Well, that's what he said – *mumble mumble* – Cigar . . .' Then she came back and said:

'What else were you doing?'

'Nothing. I just drove away.'

'Weren't you talking to some people?'

'Oh, yeah, I was doing autographs for some Aberdeen supporters.'

Another confab. '*Mumble mumble* – autographs . . . football supporters – *mumble mumble* – Aberdeen, he says . . . yes . . . *mumble mumble* – autographs . . .'

She's back again talking to me: 'And what were you signing these autographs on, Mr Connolly?'

'Money. Fives, tens, twenties. Working men seldom have autograph books, ha-ha, er, ha . . .'

There was a stony silence. I was starting to get pretty anxious. So eventually I said, 'Can you tell me what this is all about?' Then she comes back and says:

'Well, I'm sure it's okay for me to tell you. I'm sure you're completely innocent here. We were watching you on closed circuit television. And, when you were signing autographs, you happened to be talking to three of the biggest drug dealers in Aberdeen. And all we could see was money changing hands.'

So, I said, 'Well, you can search my car, I've nothing to do with drugs.'

She said, 'Ah, no, I understand, that's fine, you can go on your way, Mr Connolly.' But then she added: 'I'd appreciate it if you didn't mention this to anybody.'

I said: 'My lips are sealed!'

SMOKING THE BIBLE

We smoked a Bible once, Gerry Rafferty and me. Well, it was the Sixties, you know?

In those days you would play the folk clubs and the fee would be x-amount of money, plus accommodation, which usually meant a couch or the floor or something. That's where you ended up.

On this particular occasion, we'd just played a gig in some remote corner of the Highlands up near John O'Groats. It was the usual arrangement – we'd been given a room to share for the night. So, we were in this guy's house and we were all drunk. And I had some hashish – goodness knows how it got in my pocket! It was Pakistani black hashish – you'd be ducking under low bridges with this stuff; it was very strong.

I got it out towards the end of the night and said, 'Anybody got any papers?' Or 'skins' as we used to say – us cooler guys – but nobody had any. I said, 'Well, I saw a movie once, a prison movie, and they were smoking the Bible.' You know, in an emergency, using a page of the Bible, you can get a reasonable cigarette paper from that.

So, the guy who owned the house was up in his bed, drunk. And I said, 'I'll go up and ask him if he's got a Bible.'

I was kind of drunk as well. I went up into the room, and he was sitting up reading, this guy, pissed – I'll always remember, he was reading a book of war planes, one of those long books with the silhouettes, *How to Spot War Planes*, that was his chosen reading – and he was sitting there saying, 'Yes, what's the problem?'

And I said, 'You wouldn't happen to have a Bible, would you?'

He said, 'Yes, yeah, I've got a Bible. Do you want it?'

I said, 'I just want a couple of pages.'

And he said, 'Yes, yes, certainly. Any particular pages?'

I said, 'No, no, any will do.'

Riiiiiiiiip!

He hands them over. 'There you are.'

And it was Revelation.

LIGHTS. CAMERA. CAUTION.

I'm a huge film star. You probably know that. But you have to hurry to my movies, because I usually die in the first fucking fifteen minutes. I'm the only guy I know who died in a fucking Muppet movie. I'm never in the sequel.

I like making them, but it can be a test to your patience when you're working on a movie, simply because there's so much waiting around doing nothing. And then when you *do* get to do something, there's often someone lurking around who can really get on your nerves.

I'll give you an example. When I was making *Boondock Saints* in Toronto, I had one particular scene to do and I was desperate to do it. I was really looking forward to it.

I was playing an assassin in the movie. I had a long black coat on and a leather waistcoat down to my thighs, and on the waistcoat I had six 9mm pistols – four Glocks and two Berettas. I had to blow the shit out of this building. Halfway between me and the building was Willem Dafoe as a gay detective doing a fantasy dance. And there was a car behind me that was to be blown up by special effects. I've got a cap on, sunglasses and a cigar that I'm biting on.

The director was talking to me and he said, 'Here's what I want you to do. I want you to take out the first two guns, empty them shooting at the house while you're smiling and chewing on your cigar. *Ba-boom-boom-boom-boom!* When they're empty, just throw them away – you don't give a shit about them. Then take the next two, and do the same: *Ba-boom-boom-boom-boom-boom!* And throw those guns to hell. Now, with the last two, cross your arms and grab the two and spin, and when you've spun all the way round, whip them out and empty them at the house, and then throw them away. Do you think you could do that?'

I said, 'I was fucking *born* to do it!'

So he goes away to the camera guys to talk to them, and I'm standing there, mumbling to myself, going over my moves: 'Okay, first two guns, shoot, throw away, next two, same again, last two, spin, take out, shoot, throw away. Shout "Motherfucker!"' See, I was adding bits already.

And suddenly I heard this wee voice: 'Mr Connolly?' I looked around. 'Mr Connolly?' I still couldn't see anybody. 'Mr Connolly?' I said, 'Where the fuck are you?' 'Over here.' And it was the armourer – the guy in charge of all the weapons on set – and he was poking his head around the side of the fender of the car. He was on his hands and knees there, looking very anxious.

I whispered: 'What are you doing here? We're about to start!' He whispered back, 'I realise that, Mr Connolly, but I heard the director talking to you, and he was telling you to throw the guns away. Well, they're in beautiful condition, and they're very expensive. Do you think, instead of *throwing* them away, you could *hand* them to me?'

I said, 'Rearrange these words into a popular phrase or saying: "Yourself". "Fuck". "Go".'

THE SCROTUM

Isn't the scrotum hideous? No wonder they stuck it away in a fuckin' corner. It'd frighten the horses, wouldn't it? I think it's a design fault.

You know, in the body shop, when human beings were being designed, there must have been a scene like this:

'God!'

'Yes, what's the problem?'

'We seem tae have an awful lot of elbow skin left here. What'll we do with it?'

'Ah dunno. Er . . . make wee bags. Make wee pursey bag

things. We'll put their balls in 'em. I was gonnae have them carry them around in their hand. We may as well put them in a bag.'

Bad idea. The scrotum. Right from the start, a really bad idea. I don't know why it shouldn't be in a wee velvet box or something. It's a fucking *horrible* thing! It's like a wee hairy walnut. And sometimes it looks like a brain. And sometimes it fuckin' *acts* like one!

Even the name is horrible. 'Scrotum'. They must have been up all night thinking that one up, eh? 'What'll we call the hangy-downy bit?' 'Hmm, dunno . . . "Scrotum" should do it.' That's definitely a Scrabble word, isn't it? That's what it was invented for. 'Where did you learn *that* one, Dorothy?'

Women's words are nice. 'Vagina'. That's a nice word. You can imagine that on the back of a Weetabix packet: 'Ten days in Vagina could be yours!' It sounds like a lovely place. It bloody is, too! But not men's words. 'A fortnight in Penis could be—' 'Oh fuck off! I'm nae going there!' It sounds like the really shabby end of Cyprus, doesn't it?

And 'Scrotum' sounds like something that lives in a swamp and bites your leg. 'I saw it in the pictures, there wuz this man, an' he wuz pushing this boat through this swamp, an' his wife pulled him back intae the boat an' his legs were all covered in *scrotums*! She had tae burn them off with a fag, it wuz fuckin' awful!'

I'd never had a good look at it before, my own scrotum. But I was at yoga. It was a terrible experience. I don't have the same kind of body as other people. You know, all of that 'Just lean forward . . .'

And I tell you, if you're going to go to yoga, prepare yourself for this: 'Just open your legs, now I don't want you to force yourself, that's fine, just about there, and *fall* forward, don't *push* forward, just let your body fall, and let the weight of your body take your hands down like this, that's right, just relax, you'll find yourself getting lower, you'll find a strain at the back of your knees and the base of your back, don't worry about it, it's fine, that's right, let the weight carry you . . .'

Then it happens: the fart.

Pfffffffftttttttt!

I'm telling the truth!

'Now, lean over to the right, push down your leg, again, don't force it, let the weight of the top half of your body just—'

Pfffffffffffffftttttttttttt!

It's a fuckin' *nightmare*! You don't know where to look, you know?

Pffffffffffffffffftttttttttttt!

And other people are farting, too, and you don't want to go, 'Oh, come on! Behave yourself!!'

It's an extraordinary practice, but you all pretend nobody farted! It's weird, the *air* changes: 'Pick it up just as far as you can, that's right—'

Pffffffffffffffffffffftttttttttt!

Because these organs have never been *tested* like this before!

'Put your leg there, put your elbow there, now twist round—'

Pffffffffffffffffffffffftttttttttttt!

There's air in there that's been in there since *nineteen-forty-seven*!

Pffffffffffffffffffffffffffffffffffffffffftttttttttt!

It's a nightmare!

And when I had to go on tour, I said to the guy, 'I'm going on tour,' he said, 'Well, take the book and the cassette, and do it while you're away.'

So, I did. I was in my bedroom, in an empty house, you know, in my wee knickers, doing the thing. There's heaters blasting all around. And I fell backwards. And I was in a knot. I was all fucked up. My bum hit the floor, my legs came fucking whooshing up, I thought: 'Shit – I'm gonnae go out the window!' There was a bay window behind me. I thought, 'Fuck, I'm gonnae go out the window feet first! And they'll find me in the garden!' I can just see the headline: 'SHOCK HORROR SEX MURDER AT CONNOLLY HOUSE!'

And I opened my eyes, and I couldn't believe it. My scrotum was there in front of my face! My legs had shot over my head! I was in fucking agony as well.

There it was, my whole *business* upside down. My willy's coming down and my scrotum was over it – I thought it was an alien! 'What the *fuck?*' I thought it had come down the chimney, shot up my arse, and knocked me over!

But, you know, when a man turns fifty, the weirdest and most disappointing thing happens. Your doctor loses interest in your testicles. And takes an overwhelming interest in your arsehole. It's the strangest thing. Because the chances of testicular cancer recede as you get older, and the chances of prostate cancer increase.

Isn't life a fucking bowl of cherries?

SEXIE SADIE AND LOVELY RAQUEL

I was on this tour, and when we came down from Scotland and we first went into England, in the north of England, somewhere on the M6, we stopped at a transport café. Now, of course, I don't know how well *you* know transport cafés, but let me tell you something: I was shocked and stunned. Shocked and stunned.

They sell magazines there – bad boy magazines. Magazines you would've got arrested for five years ago in Soho, they sell now in transport cafés, besides *The Beano* and *Bunty*.

Beano, Bunty, Bare Arse Monthly.

You can get anything you like. *Leather Skateboarder.* Anything.

Well, my driver, in a moment of weakness, mistook it for *Bunty* and bought one. I was shocked and stunned. There's a part, about two-thirds of the way through, where people send in Polaroid snaps of their own ladies in 'those' positions. You know. (I don't know why they *point* at it all the time – I've known where it is for ages!)

Un-be-liev-able. Shocked and stunned and not a little amazed.

So purely for reference and research purposes, I looked through the rest of the magazine. Pretty duff, I thought.

I went to the back and I came to the adverts. Have you *seen* the things you can buy? The sort of things that people must be *doing* to one another??

There's a thing: you tie it securely around the willy, and you then tie it around your leg, and then secure it again – and

243

then you go jogging. So, if you see a jogger in the street, go: 'There you go, ya *dirty* bugger, you! Get the children indoors! Ya *pervert!!'* (That's part of my anti-fitness campaign.) You see them leaning against walls, sweating – if you see a jogger who looks like that, like he's just had a coronary, leave him alone, he's quite happy there.

And there's other things. Electric things. They whizz and whirr and jiggle up and doon. 'Aids' they call them. 'Aids perfect for every part of the body.' *Buuuuuuuuzzzzzzzzzzz.* Can you imagine it? The lady in bed, going:

'Darling, come to bed!'

'Ah, I won't be a minute, I'm just changing the batteries here!'

'*What?* What's *that*?'

'Oh, you'll like it!'

Judder-judder-judder . . .

'What the—'

Judder-judder-judder . . .

'You'll *like* this – come on, don't be a spoilsport, everybody's intae it!'

'Keep it away from me!!'

'Aw, *come on* – it cost me a *fortune!*'

'Get it AWAY!'

Shocked and stunned.

But then it came to my favourite bit. Well . . . I was *still* shocked and stunned, but I couldn't believe my eyes this time.

There they were. There were two of them. Inflatable ladies.

'Sexie Sadie and Lovely Raquel.'

You could buy the basic one: it's just an inflatable woman and you sort of just got on with it. But if you're prepared to splash out a few more quid, they get more and more exotic. I wonder if you get a John Bull repair kit with it, in case you blow its arse off. Anyway. There's the basic model, but then, if you *do* splash out, you get all these exotic bits, like: 'electric moving parts'.

And if you splash out another few quid: it *talks* to you! It's a wee cassette you get. I wonder what it says. 'At the third stroke . . .' I had all these fantasies, you know, about all these women, trying to imagine what it would be like. Maybe there's a poor guy in bed with it and somebody comes to the door: 'Oh *ferchrissakes*!' Stabbing her to death: *Ppp-heeeeee-wwwwwwww!* 'Oh, come in now, yeah!'

And what about the electrical moving parts? Well, you blow it up first – 'I'm in the mood for love, simply because you're near me . . . Ah, you're here, darling!' – then do you start the moving parts first and then get your timing right? (Do you remember when you were a kid and there were skipping ropes and you were waiting for your turn to jump?) Or do you get on, get comfy, and *then* start it?

Then there's the fear of it bursting. *Pheeeeeeeeww!* '*Talk* to me! Sadie! Come on!' Or even worse than it bursting, imagine if it burst and then flew around the room: 'Sadie! You're *peeved* at me, I can tell!' With all the electric parts falling down, and she's away out the window: 'Oh NOOOOOOO!!!! Ferchrissakes – shoot it down before the neighbours see it!!!' *Boom! Boom! Eeeeeeeuuuunnnnnn-tisssshhhhh!*

What about the irate customer, going back to the shop, with the Sexie Sadie slumped over their arm?

'That's a load of bloody rubbish, that!'

'Well, what seems to be the trouble, sir?'

'It went down on me!'

'If I'd known that I would have charged you another fiver, sir!'

'That's nae what I mean! Ah just gave it a wee love bite and it farted and flew out the window!!'

A HOLLYWOOD SEX SCENE

I had to pretend I was giving one to a girl in a movie. She was kneeling on the bed, and I was behind her, giving it: *woof-woof!* You get my drift?

It was a movie called *The Big Man*, with Liam Neeson. And he was next door, his character. We were in a shabby hotel, and I'm doing the business in this room and he's in the next room, looking out the window. The theory is that I'm to be bashing away and he hears it. And it's his girlfriend that I'm doing it to. And he comes running through and belts me one.

That's the scene.

So, I'm doing it, and it's murder, because you're doing all this fucking nonsense and there's forty people in the room, reading the paper, eating chips, looking out the window . . . And it's fucking roasting and all of that.

And the director came over and said, '*Mmmm*, that's *excellent*, that's *excellent*, we've got *wonderful* footage, Billy!' We'd been doing it for about three hours. 'We've got *wonderful*, *wonderful* footage!' He said, 'We're just going to go with one or two more takes – could you be more . . . *verbal*? More *vocal*?'

I said, 'Well, there's nothing in the script.'

He said, 'No, no, no, no. Just . . . you know . . . sexually motivated noises: *Oooh-Aaaah! Ooh, yes, ooooh!* And maybe: *Fuuuuck!* Fuck's good, yeah!'

So, I'm trying my sexually motivated noises: '*Ooh-ooh-oh-oh! Aaah-aa-aa-aaahh!*' And she's going: 'YES! YES!' I said, 'I don't remember fuckin' *asking* you anything!'

I'm not much of a vocal guy in bed anyway, in my real life, my sexual life. I don't shout out. I've got nothing to say. I'm just quietly fucking grateful, really. Anyway, I have hardly any voice left after the three hours of pleading.

So, I'm giving it the '*Ooh-yeah-Ooh-yeah-Aah-Aah-Ooh*'. And she's going: 'YES! YES!' And he's next door, looking all cool. Because he's the handsome one. I'm the fucking idiot in the movie. He's looking out the window, the light's out in his room – it's only lit by streetlights, that kind of effect. He's got the big cheekbones and all that, the rain's running down the window, it looks like tears. All that shit. Saying nothing. The director's saying, 'Just *think* up the lens. *Think* up the lens of the camera. The public will *feel* it, they'll *feel* it coming off the screen, they'll feel they *know* you!'

The audience feels fuck all! They're just eating stuff! *Crunch-Crunch-Crunch!* 'Why isn't he sayin' anythin'? He's never said anythin'! Why's he starin' at people fer?'

And the director's going to me: '*Mmmm*, that's good, that's good, but you're going "Ooh-Aah!" as if it's *hurting* you. Do noises as if you're *enjoying* it. "*Ahhoooooooo! Ahhhheeeeeee! Oooooof! Ooooooooof!*" Copy *her* noises. If she goes "Yes!" you go, "Fuckin' hold THIS!!" Just like they do in blue movies. X-rated, Triple X – you must have seen them!'

But the fact is I haven't. I'm not into that. You know, watching Triple X fucking stuff. That's for wankers. That's why *Playboy*'s got shiny paper. For people who fucking *drool*.

Years ago, there was a fiddler in Edinburgh. 'Big Alan' somebody. He was a big hairy bugger. He used to live in a place called Portobello, outside Edinburgh, and we'd all go up to his house on a Friday or a Saturday night. Loads of booze and a bit of dope, and we'd all get out of our faces. Completely trousered. He'd make cakes and biscuits with hashish, and invite neighbours in – wee fat women and all that. I used to love that, watching them getting stoned – 'Heeeee-Heeeee-Heeeee!' Bombed out of their faces. And then he'd put on X-rated movies.

Now, I don't know if you can do this – maybe video's good now, you can do it – but it was film. He had a projector, and he would show the films backwards. And when you're out of your face, it is the funniest thing you'll ever see in your life. Pornography backwards. People going instead of coming. It's very weird. The willy becomes a sort of hoover – *Voom-Voom-Voom!* People jump off each other and into their trousers. And the whole thing ends with everybody fully dressed around the coffee table talking.

CUDDLING

You know that 'cuddle' thing that women have got? 'Let's just cuddle!' 'Oh . . . okay'.

I've never, ever, been in a pub where the guy says, 'Listen, I'm only having the one – the wife's promised me a cuddle!'

'Jesus Christ, I've been working in Saudi Arabia for six weeks. Do you know what I need? A good *cuddle*!'

Now, I'm not against cuddling, but it doesn't belong in bed. In bed a cuddle's fucked. It's not the place for cuddling. It's a place for sleeping, or, if you're going to get about it, fucking *do* it.

I'll tell you what's wrong with it. Your knees get in fine, you know. You're always behind, the guy is always the one at the back, while the 'cuddle-ee', the one who suggested it, is at the front, because they're the one who gets cuddled – the one at the back gets fuck all. He's the 'cuddle-er'. And your knees are tucked in, and her bum is in there at your crotch, and her wee body comes up around your chest. And one of your arms is fine, it goes over and around her, but the other one is a real problem. You can sort of bend it, rest your head on it and drape your wrist over your face, or tuck it under you, but no position is comfortable.

The only one that's comfortable is to put it *under* her, lying straight out. But after a while it goes *grey* and you can't feel anything in it anymore.

And you can't get your head in the right position because her hair goes up your mouth and up your nose. So, you have to strain your neck to hold your head back.

And then she says, 'See? It's *nice*, isn't it!'

You're thinking, 'I wonder what's on TV?' And eventually you think, 'I may as well make a move and see what happens.' So, you get your free arm, the one that still works, and start moving it, fingers flexed, and you touch her . . . And she goes, '*Don't* – you'll *spoil* it!'

It *always* ends in tears!

It always ends with the woman suddenly jerking her bum away, saying, 'Oh for goodness *sake!*' And you say, 'Oh, I'm *sorry* it finds you *attractive!* It's not something I can *control* here!'

SEX AND DRUGS AND VOMIT

I have always had a problem with sex. I've always had a problem in that department. In as much as I've always tried to be, like, a funny guy, and it would get in my way.

Women would laugh and laugh all night, and I didn't know how to make the quantum leap from laughing to getting into bed. They would say, 'Oh, you are so *funny!* You are my best friend!' 'I don't want to be your *friend!* I've got plenty of friends! I want a *slut!*'

Because sex is a very, very important thing. Not only in our lives but in everybody's lives, in the whole world. You wonder why religious extremists commit suicide? It's because of sex! It's because they're fuckless! They've never been laid, and they've only got one book.

Holy sweet Jesus! One book and no sex! What kind of leisure life is that? What they need is a fire-breathing whore. Bombers full of them. Parachute them in. Problem solved. And the next bomber full of books. Parachute books down on them. I guarantee you, the whole thing's solved.

My own sexual demands are very, very simple. I like the missionary position: standing in a cook pot with a safari suit, looking towards Africa. It's nothing much to ask, is it?

Well, I was with a folk singer girl in Glasgow. As I said, I used to be a folkie with my banjo and all that. And she was a guitar player, a singer. You know those folkies – the long hair with the nose sticking through like a carrot through the curtains? Well, she lived in one of those fabulous Glasgow tenements, and we are up there – I'd managed to get back there – and we were playing the banjo and having a laugh. Then there's a knock at the door and this policeman came in.

I whispered, 'What the fuck's this?'

She whispered back, 'He's a neighbour. I think he fancies me. He's never away from the door.'

He said, 'I just heard a noise, I thought there might be somebody in your house.'

Like a fucking burglar playing the banjo? 'When I'm robbing houses' – *dinky-dinky-dink-a-dink-dink.*

She told me about a previous boyfriend who was a kind of hippy guy, and he had rolled a joint in the house, and when he lit it there was a knock at the door and she says, 'Oh, that'll be that bloody policeman!' So he goes, *cough-cough,* throws the joint out the window, and rams the hashish behind the electric fire – one of those one-bar electric fires with the stainless steel convex to make the bar look big. So, he's shoved it behind there, and then he can't get it out. Every time she puts the fire on the house smells like an opium den and this prick comes running down the stairs. That's why it was always freezing in this house. And she always had to say, 'It's the Indian shop downstairs, it's the smell of the cooking.' 'Oh, right.'

Drugs always got me into trouble. I was doing a tour in Britain, and it was eighty-nine nights, from the tip of Scotland to the bottom of England. I'd bought some drugs in Inverness.

Inverness has usually got red deer and sheep and all that, and guys in kilts, but this – once again – was Pakistani black hashish, which is sort of the Red Bull of the hashish world. This stuff was so strong I had to smoke it in bed, because, if I didn't, I wouldn't *make* it to bed.

My roadie used to make it for me. He'd roll the joint and I'd get into the T-shirt and the knickers and get into my bed, and he'd go, 'There you go, Bill.' *Pfffft-pfffft.* 'Thanks.' Zzzzzzzzzz. And that was me till the morning – dead as a stone.

Now, I had lighting men, T-shirt guys, sound guys, all that. It was quite a crowd. And I'm the star, I'm the only one going on stage, so I've got the suite in the hotel, the big, big place. They've got like single rooms and double-rooms and all that kind of shit. But as soon as I'm 'gone', they'd be all upstairs into my room. With all the whores and groupies and mentally ill people and dogs and cats and things they'd picked up along the way. It was like Gomorrah in my room.

I would wake up in the morning and the place was wrecked. 'Oh, *shit!* I must have been stoned and got up and wrecked the place!' I would put it all together again and hope they wouldn't find out and go downstairs. 'Is everything all right up there?' 'Er, yeah, uh, fine, fine . . .'

This went on for about two weeks. I still didn't know about what was really happening. We go down to the borders of Scotland – Newton Stewart was the name of the town. It was astonishing. We did the gig, came back, *pfffft* – gone.

I think the whole of Newton Stewart was in my room. It was like a Hieronymus Bosch painting! Fucking incredible. And a girl comes over and looks at me in the bed: 'Is that *him*?'

And one of the roadies says, 'Aye, that's him.' 'Ah've never seen him *real* before! Ah've only seen him on TV! Ah'll tell you—'

Bleuuuuuuuuuuaaaaaaaaggghhh!

She vomited on my head. And I didn't wake up.

So, there was a rush of panicking weird people out of my room, pulling each other back.

I woke up in the morning: *Yawn . . .* s*niff-sniff . . .* 'Euugggh! Aw *no*! Aw *fuck* – I've been *sick*! Aw, *and* I've wrecked the fuckin' *room* again! Aw, it's in my *hair*! . . . Wait a minute. *Spaghetti Hoops?* I don't eat *Spaghetti Hoops!* What the *fuck's* goin' on here?'

And that was the end of the midnight parties.

But three women have vomited on me. I was really young with the first one and didn't know her. She just vomited on my legs. I was waiting in the street for a woman coming out of a dance hall and this fucking idiot vomited all over my legs. And I ran away! I ran off and changed my trousers and came back and the girl I'd been waiting for had gone. The lovely Violet Johnson. The following week I went and I said, 'Violet!' and she said, 'Fuck off!' Or: '"Fuck off," she hinted.'

But the last one was the best, I must say – not for me, but it *was* the most extraordinary event.

I'd become quite a big shot, and I was performing at the Edinburgh Festival, playing my banjo in a big folk concert. *Did-diddle-idly-a-did-a-diddle-dee.* I could see a girl in the audience looking at me, you know, kind of smiley and nice eye contact. So, I'm going over and looking at her and playing. Doing tricks, y'know: *Diddle-ing-ding-diddle . . .* Looking at her, y'know.

Then it's over: *Hurray!* 'Thank you very much, ladies and gentlemen!'

So, I went over to her. I said, 'How you doing? Did you enjoy that?'

She said, 'Oh, you were fabulous!'

I said, 'Oh, nice, I'm glad you enjoyed it.'

She said, 'You were so *centred*!'

'Was I?'

She said, 'What's your sign?'

I said, 'Gemini.'

She went, 'Oh, of course! You are *such* a Gemini!'

I said, 'Thanks very much.' I said, 'I really enjoy being a Gemini. I find making friends very easy. And I communicate very easy, which is handy, doing this, y'know? Life is pretty good. 'Cause when I was Sagittarius, I was really down in the dumps and—'

And she went, *'What?* You can't change your *star* sign!'

I said, 'What are you talking about? In Scotland you can! You just go up to the Post Office, you fill in a form, five pounds – *boom* – Gemini. And I'm a much happier man. It's a miracle. Oh, and I think I might be slightly taller, and all the rest is absolutely fabulous!'

Reeling her in. Reeling her in.

She said, 'I'm living in a basement with a few people, kinda hippy guys, do you want to come along, we're having a party?'

'Certainly!'

Along we went into this basement. It's dark, you can hardly see anything, there's a lot of hairy people, but that's okay, because I was very hairy myself. It was the Grateful Dead playing and all that. You would never quite know for sure, because they had one of those record players, it's just a box with a lid – in Scotland it was called a 'Dansette' – and it had a spike, and you put albums on it, and you could play one after the other on it. So, I've lowered them all down, but they slid when they were down there – *zig-zig-zig* – on top of each other. But everyone was bombed with the smoking, so although the music was going slow and distorted, they were puffing, going, 'Aw, tha's fuckin' *amaaaaaaazin*', man!'

And the guys, especially at the end, had this overwhelming desire to barbecue themselves. They did these things, like, a plastic potato bag all tied in knots, hanging from the ceiling on a piece of string, and you'd put a bucket of water underneath it – we made our own entertainment then, ladies and gentlemen! – and you'd set fire to it. And it melts and goes: *Phuuum – Splash-Fizzzzz!* 'Aaaaw, *fuck!* I'm fuckin' glad Ah came *here*!'

They had a cylinder of paper with holes cut in it, on top of the record player – spinning round with the records – and a light bulb inside of it. *Whizzz-Flash-Whizzz-Flash!* The music's still all distorted, they're still all puffing away. Brainless!

And at one point this girl says to me, 'Do you wanna go to bed?' *Pffft.* 'I certainly do!'

Now, there's several beds in the room, and they're army beds. Seven beds. And I said, 'Which one's yours?' She said, 'It's over here.' She goes over to the corner and pulls out this sleeping bag – a huge great army sleeping bag. I said to her, 'Will we both get in there?' She says, 'Oh, yeah, yeah.'

So, we're in the bag, and she's tied the hole at the top, and shoved the strings through the hole. I'm getting a wee bit *scared*. And I'm a bit 'bomb happy' as well – paranoid. We're kissy-kissy, and we're all sweat, sliding around, I don't know *what* I'm touching, it doesn't *feel* the way I remember things, and at one point she goes: 'Uhhh!'

'Are you okay?'

It's Stygian darkness – I can't see her. My hair's wet now.

'Are you *okay*?'

'I'm fine, I'm fine. It's okay, it's happened before, it's nothing.'

'Are you *sure*?'

'Yeah, fine.'

Kissy-kissy-touch-touch-feel-feel-feel.

'Uhhh! Uhhh!'

A double!

'What the fu—? *What?*'

It wasn't long before the 'Uhhh! Uhhh! Uhhh!' *treble*! I said, 'Ah, come on, what's goin' on here?' And she said, '*Mmmmmyyy jaaaaawwww . . .*' I thought, 'Oh fuck! I'm gettin' out of here!' But she's turned and twisted around, so I'm now at the bottom of the bag. In pitch darkness! And she's halfway up between me and the wee hole at the top. I can't *see* anything!

I'm thinking, 'How did you get yourself into *this*? An hour ago, there were people *clapping* for you, and shouting "Hooray, how clever!" And now you're in a *bag* with a woman having a *fit*!'

I'm trying to remember the Scouts, y'know – what you *do*.

'Er . . . Ooh, you put a *pencil* in the mouth . . . Where am I going to find a fuckin' pencil in here? Oh, no . . . no . . . she'll bite it in half . . . I'll just go see if I can find the hole . . .'

So, I'm just crawling on top of her trying to feel my way. And she's going, 'Uhhhhh . . .' And I'm just going over her. And that's when the first wave hit:

Bleeuuuuuuuuuuuuuuuugggggghhhhh!!!!!!

'Oh *fuck!*' I'm already covered in sweat and now *this!*' It's like Scotch broth! 'Fucking hell!' And I can't find the hole, and it's all over my face. 'Oh shit!'

Eventually I find it, just when the second wave hits:

Bleeuuuuuuuuuuuuuuuugggggghhhhh!!!!!!

'Oh my GOD!!!!'

I've got the hole, and I've got my fingers through, and I'm going: 'Help! Help!' I can't get the string in! She's put it outside! *'HELP!'*

And a big hippy came in, with a big hat on. 'Oh, *what*? Oohh, *man*! Hey – come an' see *this*! There's a *giant maggot* in here!!'

And then the third wave came:

Bleeuuuuuuuuuuuuuuuugggggghhhhh!!!!!!

And it was squirting through the hole!

He says: 'Ah think it's giving *birth*, man!'

CATS AND DOGS

It's a nice leisurely thing, to relax around the house with your wee cat or dog. They're nice creatures. They can help you unwind. But they do tend to divide people. You do tend to be either a cat person or a dog person.

I've got nothing against cats at all. But I've never trusted them. There's just something sneaky about cats that I really don't like. Any animal that stays where it is when you move house is a little bastard. It doesn't deserve feeding. If that's the way they want it, they can fucking have it.

Kevin, my promoter, *is* a cat lover. He's got this hypochondriac cat that cost him thousands. He takes it to all kinds of very expensive specialists. It's a lazy bastard, this cat. I've said to him, 'There's two ways out of this: one is to throw a dog in the room and see how fit the fucker really is, or the other option is a canvas bag and a canal – watch it spring back to life then!'

I'm a doggie kind of guy, myself. I like doggies. I've got two Labradors.

I bought all those books telling you how to train them. There's these monks in New York – the Monks of New Skete – who breed dogs, they've written two very good books on that. They're really into teaching the humans as well as the dogs, and building the relationship between the two. It's fascinating stuff. I learned a lot from them.

My dogs were okay at sitting and staying and how to come around on one side of me or the other side of me, and running and stopping and all of that. They're fine. But no book I've ever bought teaches you how to stop them sniffing people's crotches. That's what I'd really like to learn how to make them stop doing, but I've never found any helpful advice. My dogs are forever going up to people and doing that: *sniff-sniff-sniff!*

'Oh for goodness sake! I'm *so* sorry! I guess they're pleased to see you!' It's so embarrassing.

In Scotland they're up people's kilts at the back. A big wet nose suddenly pressed up against the inside of a bare thigh. It's a terrible habit. And you stand there and go: 'Oh, I'm awful sorry about that!' And people laugh and say: 'It can probably smell *my* dog!' Which makes you think: 'Oh? *Oh!* Oh, okay. Fair enough. Live and let live. We'll draw a discreet veil over that. And you can trust me never to tell a soul.'

But dogs are nice. My dogs are nice, and they're very clever, too. As a matter of fact, all dogs are clever. When did you last see a dog stepping on a human shit? I rest my case.

They're good things. And they have some great attitudes.

I envy some doggy things. Like sex. Dogs have a season And I think that would be good for *us*. You see, when they're not in season, they just get on with it.

It's a weird life: 'Sit! Stand up! Go for a walk! Sit! Stand up! Eat your dinner! Lie down! Sit over there! Come here! Go for a fucking walk again! Have a piss! Go for a walk! Catch the ball! Lie down! Stand up! Catch the ball! Eat your dinner! Go over there! Lie down! Try not to fart!' Their life's all planned, and they're happy with that.

And then one day: *sniff . . . sniff-sniff . . . sniff-sniff-sniff . . . Doinnng!* The penis is up like an antenna!

Sit!

'Fuck you!'

This power emerges from somewhere. It changes them. Now, *I* would like that. I wish *we* were like that. Because I was never ever any good at chatting women up. I don't know if I was lousy at it and saying the wrong things, or being too funny or silly, but I couldn't read the signs. I didn't know when it was working. When a woman was on my case, I didn't see it. I couldn't get the message. My friends used to tell me: 'She's *fuckin' mad* for you!' 'Who?' 'That one over there!' 'What one??'

You see, everybody lied about sex and I believed everything they said. 'Hey, Billy, I'll tell you what you do: you blow into their ear and their knickers fall off!' I'm at the movies, arm round a girl: *phhhhooooooo!* 'What the *fuck* are you doing?' Have a look at the floor: nothing. 'Lying bastard!'

A season would be a good thing for us all. For the chatting-up inept department.

It would be hard, though. You'd maybe have to spray your wife, and the doorstep, because the garden's full of guys going, '*Aaa-ooooooooooh!*' 'Go on, get out of here!' You've got your daughter locked in a room upstairs. Guys at the door – *ding-dong* – 'Hullo, is ya daughter in?' 'Fuck off!'

But for the *single* guys it would be such a godsend. You see, it's not easy being a man. Men are under pressure. With a dog's sex life, they just grab the first one that's passing: 'Yeah, you'll do!'

SEX, CONDOMS AND MASTURBATION

The world's gone fucking bonkers. Have you noticed this? The world's changing. Values are changing.

They've got films on television urging us all to wear condoms! I don't even *like* them! I *hate* the buggers!

I mean, in the past, if your mother had found one of them in your pocket, she would've had a *coronary* – but *now*, there's mothers forcing them on you! 'Have you got your *condoms*?' 'Aw, Mother, for fuck's sake! I'm with ma girlfriend!' 'Here! *Have some!!*' 'Fuckin' leave me alone!'

I personally dislike them. I don't like the *smell*. Why are they such a *horrible* smell? It smells like burning rubber, doesn't it? Or maybe that's just me!

Please don't be embarrassed. I like talking about sex and stuff. I *like* sex, and I like to *talk* about it. I like it as a *subject*. I think it's very funny. And the older you get the funnier it becomes, it's quite extraordinary.

But I'm not one for reading about it, or looking at pictures of other people doing it, or going to see movies, and I certainly don't want to watch other people doing it. I find it really uncomfortable when you *hear* someone else doing it. You know, in the room next door, when you're staying in a hotel, and there's somebody bashing away next door? I feel very uncomfortable. It's quite extraordinary how differently other people do it, isn't it? How the noises they make are different from yours?

I remember I was in Perth, Western Australia, and I had jet lag – the hell of all diseases. Jet lag, for those of you who've never experienced it, it's like three in the morning you go: BOING! 'Good *morning*!' You know how normally you go: 'Aaaaw . . . what's the time . . . oh, Jeeeeesus . . .' With jet lag, you're awake: BING! '*MORNING!*' It's a *dreadful* feeling. 'Aw, shit, I'm awake . . .' And sometimes you lie down and think, 'I'll try to go back to sleep,' and your brain says, 'What are you doing? Why're you lyin' down? It's *morning*, IT'S MORNING, IT'S MORNING, IT'S MORNING!'

So, I'm sitting up in my Y-fronts. 'Ah, shit, what am I gonnae do?' There was no all-night room service. I'd read all the pamphlets in the room. I thought, 'Oh Christ, I haven't anything else to read!' And I had a box of chocolates – now this is an unusual thing for me, because I've never bought a box of chocolates, except for people's birthdays and stuff, but somebody at the airport had said, 'Welcome to Perth – here's some chocolates.' 'Oh, thanks very much.' So, I had this box of choccies.

I had them on that wee shelf by the bed there, and I was sitting up, and I looked and thought, 'Well, there's the chocolates . . . Oh, I cannae eat the chocolates . . . *Chocolates*, aye . . .'

So, I thought, I'll play a game. I shut my eyes and I put my hand in the chocolates, and I found that sheet inside, and I threw it away. And I thought, 'Right, let's see if we can find a coffee cream without a map here . . .'

The banana ones are a dead giveaway, you always get that, that's your starter for ten. On the second, I always blow it, I always get the ginger one that's cunningly disguised as a toffee. They know that everybody hates it, but they've got a big mound of ginger that they have to get rid of. There's always two gingers, and one fucking coffee, and that's another thing! I *hate* the ginger, I really do. It doesnae *belong* in there! It's like putting chilli, or carrot, or something else that's weird in there. It doesn't belong beside all the cherries and straw-berries. *Bastard* of a thing!

Anyway. The upshot was, I ate every bloody one. A whole pound. And I thought, 'Oh, *fuck*, what have I done?' Even the nut crunch and the cherry cup. Everything. My stomach was a wee mound, sitting there in ma Y-fronts.

I was still wide awake. I would go for a walk, but I don't know where I am.

Then they started. Next door.

There were sort of *growlings* at first. I thought actually someone had broken in and was eating the person next door. There was a lot of: *'Grraahh-hummm-mmmnnaah-mnaaaaahhhh . . .'* I thought it was a fucking *lion* eating a woman!

And then a certain *rhythm* came into it, y'know? *'Oo-oo-ah-uh-uh! Ooh-ah-uh-uh! Ooh-ah-uh-uh!'* Sounds like they're *rowing* the bed down the fucking corridor! *Ooooh-Ahhhh! Ooooh-Ahhhh! Ooooh-Ahhhh!* They've obviously got a burst pipe, and they've got room service mending it.

It was more of that and his headboard started to hit the wall behind me. BANG! *Oooh-Ahhh-Oof-Oof-Huh-Huh-hah-Oof-Oof-Hoh-Hah-Oof-Oof-Oof-Ooooof . . .*

I thought, 'Jesus, that's different from me – I don't do that.' He was a very uppy and downy person, obviously one of them – *pound-pound-pound*. I'm more your *loooong* type.

And then *she* started.

Oohhh-Ha-Aaah-Aaaaahhh! Ooooh-Eeeeh-Ooooooh . . . !

She's obviously thought, 'I'd better look *interested* here.' He sounded a bit big and hairy, and he's obviously got a medallion on: *'Uuh-Uuh-Uuh-Uuh-How-Do-You-Like-THAT? Female orgasm? Just you fuckin' hang on here – I've got a fortnight's*

holiday, I can do this for fuckin' DAYS! G-spot? We'll get tae
fuckin' L-M-N-O-P-Q . . .'

So, they were giving it plenty. And I thought, 'Oh, my God.
I'm full of chocolate!'

The noise is deafening. And then she starts: 'Yes! Yes!' –
Uuh-Uuh-Uuh-Uuh – 'YES! YES! *YES!'* And I'm hammering on
the wall: 'Will you stop asking her that fuckin' question?! Let
us all get some *kip* in here, ya fuckin' *madman!'*

And she's saying: 'More! More! More! MORE!' And he's
saying: 'What do you think this is – a fuckin' *telescope* I've
got here?'

Don't talk to me about sex. And these *condoms.* Smelly
bloody things!

Ian Dury was on an information film about them years
ago, and he pulled a condom on to a plastic willy, which is
fair enough. But I don't have a plastic bloody willy. And I'm
sure Ian Dury didn't have one either. My God, you don't want
to put your willy in a vice to put the bugger on. It's all moving
about, in the dark, and you're all sweaty . . .

And that brings the other problem in: *when* do you put
the bloody thing on? At what point in the proceedings does
the point get covered?

If you're in the middle of proceedings –

'Ohh . . . Ahh . . .'

'Just a minute, stop, stop, stop – I've got this *thing* over
here, right? Carry on yourself, I'll be back in a minute – of
course I do, don't be ridiculous, *course* I love ya, I've just got
this thing over here, one of them condom fellows, er, I'll tell
you what, I'll shake the bed till I come back – . . . Found it,

found it! Got it, here we are! Aw, how do you *open* these bastard things? Come *on*, ya bastard! Aw, fuck, jeez, ow, that hit ma filling there! Come on, ya bastard! Oh, jeez, I've dropped it! Okay, found it, *found* it . . . Just get most of the fluff off it . . .'

Pffffffffffff!

And you realise then, in picking it up and getting it out the packet, you've pushed the top *through*, so it doesn't unroll anymore, it's inside out, and it's jammed on your willy there. You have to just *grab* it and go for it.

So, you end up: your willy's half an inch long and seven inches wide!

Another thing is masturbation.

(Whenever I talk about this on stage, I can see men in the audience going, 'Aw, *no*! Please change the subject! Oh, Billy, I'm with a *girlfriend* here, give us a break! If I laugh, she'll know I've *done* it!')

It's a weird thing, masturbation. Because I read in a magazine recently that sixty-eight per cent of all British men masturbate on a regular basis. And I thought, well, okay, I'm quite prepared to believe that. But how do they know? Did it show up on the Richter Scale or something? I mean, how can they possibly *know*? Because anybody *I* ask never does it. 'Do you?' 'Fuckin' *what*?? Coh! I'd rather cut ma fuckin' *hand* off!!!'

But I thought I'd change it for this occasion and give you a more grown-up and practical guide to more fulfilling masturbation. Because I have found a new method. I read it in a book – I've never tried it. Here's what you do.

Because you're *driven* to it, really. I mean, you could be watching *EastEnders* or something, or *Neighbours*, and you think, 'That's it, I've lost the will to live, I'm gonna go off and jump off somethin' high. On the other hand . . . I may have a wee wank before I go.'

So, what you should do first of all is find a quiet place where you won't be disturbed. Because it's hardly a spectator sport. And it's quite *exceptionally* difficult to find an excuse for what you're doing if you're caught in mid-masturbation. I mean, just think about it – what do you say? 'Er, I wuz, er . . . I wuz just countin' ma willies!'

It really is awful, being caught in mid-masturb. But now I am going to give you the excuse if you do. This could improve the rest of your life no end.

Now – and this is point number one – you must be *quick* with the excuse. You're in mid-masturb—

Oh, the word 'wank': I must explain that. I don't know where it comes from. I've asked many, many people. My personal theory is it's those army beds. You know those metal beds you get in the army, with springs on it? I think that's the noise they make, isn't it? *Wank-wank-wank-wank-wank* . . .

I have travelled the highways and byways of this planet. I have never met a bed that goes: *masturbate-masturbate-masturbate-masturbate* . . .

So, you're in mid-masturb and the door bursts open.

And it's your nosy brother: '*Uuhhh!!* What *the fuck* are you doin—'

You don't let him finish the sentence! *Don't* let him complete! *Don't* give him the joy, the satisfaction! When he goes, 'What the *fuck*—', come in immediately with this: '*Thank God you're here!*'

That *deeply* upsets them! That's a three-steps-back shocked and amazed.

He's thinking, 'Thank God I'm here? What d'yer mean? *I thought he was havin' a wank.*'

'Thank GOD you're here – and not a minute too soon!'

'*Really?* Er, so what's the fuckin' story?'

'You'll never believe this.'

'Er, no . . . probably not . . .'

'I was walkin' across the bloody room there, when the biggest fucking hairy spider you ever saw ran oot from underneath there and I thought, "*What the fuckin' hell was that?*" A HUGE bugger the size of a soup plate! It came scelping towards me and right up the leg of me troosers! I thought, "Jesus Christ, it's way up the leg of me troosers!" And you probably remember – only last week I was reading that book. D'you remember?'

'Eh? Er . . . what book was that?'

'*Tarantulas and their Wily Ways.*'

'No . . . ?'

'You fucking *mentioned* it! You said, "What the fuck are you reading *that* for?" I *remember*! And it said in the book, it said: "There's nothing tarantulas love more than to sink their teeth into people's testicles"! And I thought, "*That's* what the bugger's up tae! It's away up the leg of ma troosers to sink its teeth into the family jewels!" So, before you could say Jack Robinson I'd whipped the tweeds doon – and not a second too soon! It was up like that: raising its horrible hairy legs and baring its teeth. The bastard, its fucking teeth were poised to bite, just as you walked in the door! And I was desperately trying to shake it off: *"Get the fuck outta here!"'*

MULTIPLE ORGASMS

It's not easy being a man. Men are under pressure.

It's the Women's Movement. Women these days are *demanding* things. *'Give* me things! *Give things* to me! Do *exotic* things, and *plenty* of them!'

'Tonight, I think I'll have multiple orgasms, thank you!'

'Fucking hell! W-why, w-what's that?'

'Go for it, my boy – plenty of *orgasms, I'll* tell you when to stop!'

No sooner had we found the clitoris, than we were in search of the G-spot. I don't think you can find *that* with a fucking wetsuit and a diver's helmet! I know *gynaecologists* who don't believe in it!

It's *difficult* to be a man. I mean, the Men's Movement in America has taken the country by storm. People are all meeting and wailing about the injustice of it all. They're hugging each other in sympathy.

You see films of the Women's Movement and they're terrifying: 'We want *this*! And *that*! We *demand* a share in *that*, and most of *that*! Some of *this* and fucking all of *that*! Less of *that*, and more of *this*, and fucking *plenty* of *this*! And another thing, we want it *now*! I want it *yesterday*! I want fucking more *tomorrow*! And the demands will all be changed by then, *so fucking stay awake!*'

Stay well awake, yes – but you'll probably *remain* awake, because you'll be fucking sleeping in a wet bed!

The Men's Movement. The cameras have gone to meetings of the Men's Movement. They are all crying. 'My father wouldn't talk to me . . . *sob!*'

I don't know what the fuck has been happening! We used to be hairy hunters: 'I am *Man*! The Hunter! Therefore, I'm going to get pissed!' It made sense to us!

But modern sex and this effect on sex is devastating. Now, the most awful thing we are subjected to, as men, is this *longevity* of sex.

It's shagging away for a fortnight. That's surely not the idea. I don't think it was supposed to be like that. Like press-ups: 'twenty-nine, twenty-eight . . . forty-seven, forty-eight . . . ah, *fuck,* roll on morning!' Trying to distract yourself and keep going by thinking about Russian tractors. 'Who won the Scottish Cup in 1953 . . . Name the team . . . Henderson, McDonald, McCallum . . .' Twelve condoms on, in case you feel anything.

You don't hear a *man* shouting, 'Yes! *More!*' It's the woman. 'More! *More!* MORE! Oh yes! *More!* More of *that*! MORE! *FASTER! FASTER, FASTER!*'

You're wheezing away there: 'Oh, Jesus Christ!'

'*Faster, faster!* That's IT! *Faster, faster!!!*'

My arse is just a *blur*!

'*FASTER! FASTER! FASTER! That's it! That's it! FASTER! FASTER! FASTER! FASTER!*'

The fucking sweat is *blinding* me.

'Move your leg. Move your LEG! *Faster!* Move your *other* leg. That's it! Now bring 'em in, bring 'em in! Now up on one elbow, one elbow! *Faster! Faster!*'

You're shattered. You've been on cross-country runs less gruelling than this. But still she goes on:

'Say something, *something, something!* Say something *sexy*, something SEXY, something *SEXY*! Faster! Something sexy, something SEXY! *Swear!* Something *fucking sexy!*'

You're now checking the carpet, to see if any of your tattoos has slid off!

'*FASTER! FASTER!* Something sexy! *Something sexy! SOMETHING SEXY!* Move your *knee*! Move your *elbow*! Move your *nose* . . . ! *YOU'RE LOSING THE ERECTION?!*'

THERE'S TOO FUCKING MUCH TO REMEMBER!

It's unfair.

SEXUAL PERVERTS

Have you ever thought about being a pervert? I don't mean that in the sense of: 'I'm fed up – I think I'll be a pervert tomorrow. I think I'll nip oot and get ma willy pierced – put a safety pin in it or something.' I don't mean it quite like that. I mean it more along the lines of: have you ever wondered if a pervert lurks somewhere inside you? Because I read a . . . thing.

When you do these long tours, like I used to do, eventually you've read all the papers, all the monthly magazines and all the weekly ones, as you're travelling and killing time between gigs. So, out of boredom, you start buying the more bizarre magazines, and eventually I weakened and bought one of *those*.

There was an article in it about sexual perversion, and I couldn't believe what I was reading. I mean, I didn't even know that there were so many types. I'd heard of all the usual ones – leather and rubber and all that kind of stuff, and bearded guys dressing up as nurses, all of that. But there were things in this article that I'd never heard of. I couldn't believe my eyes. 'Sellotape freaks' – what's that all about? There's guys being covered in Sellotape and then getting it all ripped off – 'Yippee! Woo-hoo!' They must be totally hairless by now.

And I thought to myself, 'I wonder how they ever got around to *that*?' Even to them just *thinking* about it, you know? I mean, surely it didn't first occur to them as they were watching *EastEnders* one night. 'Ah, I'm fed up . . . I think I'll cover myself in Sellotape. Get the wife to rip it off later – see how it feels.'

Maybe it started with a wee piece of Elastoplast. He rips it off and then thinks, 'Cor! I think I'll get a bigger bit!' *Rip!* 'Corrr!!'

When I was pondering these rather bizarre things, it made me start thinking, 'I wonder where they meet each other?' I wonder if there's a bar somewhere? You know, where people stood about, all dressed in Sellotape, with German officers marching in and out, and bearded guys dressed as nurses wandering around. And if they don't go out with the gear on, if they just go out in straight clothes, how do they approach one another? I imagine somebody coming up to you at the bar: 'Er, excuse me, I don't like to butt into your conversation or anything, but, um, could you see your way clear to giving me a thrashing outside?' I doubt that would work.

It's like the two Glasgow guys, coming home from work one night. One says, 'I'll tell you what, as soon as I get into the house, I'm going to rip the wife's knickers off!' The other one says, 'What for?' He says, 'The elastic's hurting ma legs.'

I think you should be warned more at school about sexual perversion. They should at least tell you a wee bit more about it. Because the first experience you usually have of it is somebody feeling you up at the pictures, isn't it? It's usually a wee man in a boiler suit. I think if you knew more about it, you wouldn't worry about yourself so much.

It's like the girl going to the psychiatrist. She says, 'Look, I've got a bit of a problem.'

He says, 'Well, I'm your man. What is it?'

She says, 'I think I'm becoming sexually perverted.'

He says, 'Really? My goodness. Jings, even. What form does your perversion take?'

She says, 'Well, I'm a bit embarrassed by it, really, you know? I'm frightened you'll laugh at me if I tell you.'

He says, 'Look, I'm a professional. I have ethics. I don't laugh at anybody. Now don't be silly. Tell me what it is.'

And she says, 'Well . . . I like people to kiss me on the bum.'

So he says, 'Oh, for goodness sake! You're wasting my time! There's nothing wrong with a wee kiss on the bum! Och, I'm worse than you myself!'

And she says, 'Ah, yeah, right, sure, you're only saying that to make me feel better, aren't you?'

He says, 'No, no, I'm telling you the truth – *I'm* worse than *you*. In fact, I'll show you if you like.'

So she says, 'Okay, then, yes: show me.'

He says, 'Right. If you would take your clothes off and go to the other end of the room there, and stick your head under the carpet . . .'

She says, 'Aw, come on! *What?* You're having me on!'

He says, 'No, honestly, this is my *thing*.'

She says, 'Oh. Well, er, okay then.'

So, she goes to the other end of the room, gets all the gear off, goes down on her knees and puts her head under the carpet. And she's thinking to herself, 'Hey, I think I've knocked it off – I might get a kiss on the bum out of this!'

She's under there for two and a half hours. Nothing happens. The neck's aching, the bum's getting cold. And she's thinking, 'Wait a minute here – what *is* this?' So, she slips her head back out of the carpet and has a wee look, and there he is at the other end of the room, fully clothed, puffing on his pipe, sitting there reading the paper.

She says, 'Ah-*ha*! See! You *were* having me on! You *were*! You haven't done a single thing!'

And he says, 'Oh, haven't I? I've just had a shit in your handbag!'

6.

A Life Worth Living

'I do stray sometimes into political incorrectness, and I do not fucking care one bit . . . I'm telling a joke! Shut the fuck up and get a life!'

THE AGE OF BEIGEISM

We need to battle against bland people these days. The Beige People. They are intent on turning the world into one great massive bore. You mustn't be different, you mustn't be daring, you mustn't be dangerous. You must just bow down and be beige. Well, not me, and I hope not you! We have to resist this fucking madness.

I was in Belfast a while ago – this is a great example of how Beigeism is taking hold of our culture: some fucking idiot in a cardigan in an office with a memo pad, trying to think how else he can screw things up for everybody else.

I'm in Belfast, five o'clock in the morning, and I hear this sound: *'Beep! Beep! Beep! Beep! . . .'* What the fuck? I woke up, I thought, 'Christ, the place is on fire!' I looked up at my smoke alarm: nothing wrong with it, it was just blinking happily, merrily. *Sniff-sniff.* No smoke. Look out the door: nobody naked, going off their head. Then I checked the alarm beside my bed to see if some fucking sales rep's left it set for five in the fucking morning. Nope. I look out the window, and there's a truck reversing up the lane behind the hotel: *Beep! Beep! Beep! Beep! . . .*

There's a *beige* decision if ever I saw one! Some little numpty: 'There's a truck reversing. Dangerous. Should make a funny noise like *Beep! Beep! Beep! . . .*'

Now, you know as well as I do, five o'clock in the morning in lanes behind hotels – they're thronged with children, positively *thronged* with them! Especially wee *blind* ones who can't see fucking great big trucks coming. It's only right they should go *Beep! Beep! Beep!* so they can hear us.

Yet the same fucking truck, doing seventy miles an hour, going *forward*: not a *cheep* out of the fucking thing! I'm sure they kill *many* more people when they're going forward.

Beigeist bastards!

The Beige Mob. They're controlling the planet. They're at the controls. Make no mistake about that.

You sing to your children: 'Oh, the big fire engine goes ding-a-ling-a-ling.' No it fucking doesn't. It *used* to. Now it goes *NEE-NAW! NEEE-NAAW! NEEEEEE-NAAAAAAW!* Were *you* consulted about that? *I* certainly wasn't! I don't remember the memo.

'We're thinking of changing that wonderful ding-a-ling-a-ling to a fucking nerve-jangling NEE-NAW. How do you feel about that?'

Not one fucking note did I receive!

We're never consulted on anything! The word 'AMBULANCE' is written backwards now. I don't fucking need that. I can fucking recognise an ambulance! I'm not fucking stupid! I don't need the fucking thing in reverse to recognise it in the mirror, thank you very much. Fuck you!

If you think it's a good idea to change them, try the song

again: 'Oh, the big fire engine goes *NEE-NAW! NEEE-NAAW!'*
See how *your* fucking child behaves. Fuckers!

I was listening to the radio in a car, in Melbourne, a while
ago, and I especially hate pop station fuckin' DJs – drivellers,
bluh-bluh-bluh! I fucking hate them.

'Hey, and at two o'clock we've got Willie Smillie who's doin'
the Golden Oldies and a competition: What height is Stevie
Wonder? And at three o'clock, Big Harry McNally – oh, it's
a good show, it's Easy Listening!'

I thought, 'What? "Easy Listening"? What the FUCK is
that?' Listening *is* easy! You stay awake and it happens in
fucking *spite* of you! 'Easy fucking Listening'! What are you
talking about, ya dick?

Now *there's* a beige expression for you: Easy Listening. I
want a fucking *Difficult* Listening show! 'Now at three o'clock,
it's the Difficult Listening Show, with Billy Connolly – take
it away, Bill!' 'Thanks very much . . . um, we've got a great
show, lots of stuff . . . some great tapes . . . Um, Frank Zappa
and other people . . . and some good—' 'Turn it *up* a bit – I
can't *hear* the fuckin' thing!' 'It's right up at twelve – it won't
go any higher! Fuckin' difficult to hear, in't it!'

This is what you have to do! Battle against the Beigeists.
Make the world the way you want it. Set things right.

ON SWEARING

People say it's a limited vocabulary that makes you swear.
Well, I don't think so. Because I know at least – oh, my God

– a hundred and twenty-seven words. And I still prefer 'Fuck'.

You see, I've never found the English equivalent for 'Fuck off!'

It isn't: 'Go away!' Because 'Go away!' kind of *dissipates*, doesn't it?

'Go awaaaaaaaayyyy!' 'Oh, go away! . . . Shooo! . . . *Shooooo!!* . . . Go away! . . . *Go awaaayyy!*'

Whereas in contrast: *'FUCK OFF!'*

It always works.

THE WALKER

There was a Glasgow guy and he was out for a walk. And he was doing 'out for a walk' sort of things. Personally, I'm not a great 'go for a walk' person. But he was, and he was doing whatever 'go for a walk' people do.

'I'm oot for a walk, walking. Oh, a *tree!* I'm glad I came. Ooh, and there's a *bird*! What a walk this is turning oot to be!'

And he's walking along some cliffs, and the sea was pounding on the rocks way down below. 'Ooh, sea pounding on rocks! What a walk this is!' And then he slips and falls off. Straight over the top. And he's hurtling down towards the sea, grabbing handfuls of fresh air as he goes. 'Help!' he's crying out. 'Help! Help! – I have fallen in mid-walk!'

There's a bush sticking out from the side of the cliff – a wee bush – and as he's passing, he reaches out and just manages to grab hold of it, and now he's hanging there. 'Help! *Help! HELP!* Anybody up there? *Is there anybody up there?'*

From out of nowhere, this deep, warm, compassionate-sounding voice replies: 'Yes, my son. I am up here. I am everywhere.'

Now the walker guy, holding on grimly to this bush, is a bit baffled by this, but he shouts back up: 'Er, look, eh, I was up for a walk there, and I slipped on something, and I fell doon here. And now I'm hanging on to this wee bush here. I'm just hanging on!'

And this mysterious voice says: 'I know. I know all things. I see all things. I am the father of all men.'

And the walker guy is still hanging there, his arms are really hurting now, and he's getting more than a bit irritated by all of this strangeness. 'Look,' he shouts. 'I don't think you quite understand. *I'm hanging on to this bush!* And my arms are aching! And my hands are getting sore! *I cannae hold on much longer!'*

And the voice replies: 'I know. And your arms will get even achier. And your hands will get even sorer. Until you can stand the pain no longer. And then you will let go, and plummet to your death on the rocks below. But fear not. For you shall join me in heaven.'

Upon hearing this, the walker guy is silent for a few seconds. And then he shouts:

'Is there anybody else up there?'

TATTOOS

I'm forever searching for proper individuals. People who resist being beiged.

So, I went to see a tattooist. And we were talking about tattoos – as you will, when you're in a tattooist's shop, you're kind of drawn to the subject – and about the best tattoos that we'd seen.

Now, the best tattoo I had *heard* of – I didn't see it – was on the radio. They had a competition in Los Angeles for the best tattoo, and you had to phone in and describe it.

And I *laughed*!

The girl who won it, it was down on her pubey bit, and she had the Tasmanian devil. And she had a lawnmower, and she would shave a wee strip that he'd done!

And we laughed. Especially about a tattoo on the radio. But you see, being British, I'm no stranger to that. I grew up listening to the radio. We had a fucking *ventriloquist* star on the radio! A ventriloquist!

I'm sure it was just two guys. They'd just show up:

'Hullo, Archie!'

'How are you doin', Bobby!'

I wonder if they bothered bringing the doll in at all! 'Ah fuck it, leave it at home!'

'How are you getting on?'

'Aye, no bad.'

'It's nice to see you.'

'How's things?'

'Aye, well, the weather's nice.'

What the fuck was *that*?

And do you know what I heard once on British radio? For the Queen's Jubilee? I *had* to switch it on, I saw it in the *Radio Times* – and I should have recorded it, because nobody believes me. A BONFIRE! On the RADIO! I'm sure it was just a guy with a bit of cellophane, going: *crackle-crackle-crackle-crackle* . . .

And do you know, when I was a boy, there was a programme called *Workers' Playtime*. It was a variety show, and they'd do it for the workers in their lunchtime. They'd all be sitting there in their overalls, eating their sandwiches and drinking from their flasks, and these people would be dancing and stuff in front of them. At least with the dancing you could *hear* it on the radio: *ricky-tippy-tap-tap* . . .

But they would have other stuff like *trapeze artists*, and all you could hear were people going, 'Ooooh! Aaaahhh!' And jugglers: 'Oooooh! Whoah! Ahhhh!' Magicians: *Deedeedeedeee* – 'Eh? *Dahdahdahdah* – Oh? *Deedeedumdedeeeeee* – A-hah!'

It was beyond belief!

So: I was talking to the tattooist and we were talking about the best tattoos. And he said he'd never actually seen his favourite, either, but he told me about it. It was at a tattoo convention.

If you've never been to a tattoo convention, go. You don't need to *get* a tattoo, you're not forced into it. But you'll see the most exotic human beings in the world. They are the least *beige* people on the planet. They are pierced in places you've never been touched. The piercing of the clitoris is pretty fucking special, don't you think? Can you imagine being down there and somebody's got fucking wind chimes hanging?

So, he'd been to this convention in Hong Kong, and he met

this Chinese tattooist. They got talking about their favourite tattoos and the Chinese guy told him about his friend, in the 1950s, who had tattooed a Scottish guy. He was a soldier. And on his back he wanted: 'Scotland Forever!' and a big thistle. So, he tells the guy, 'I want "Scotland Forever!"' – 'Ah, ah' – 'and a big thistle, right?' – 'Ah! Thistle! Thistle . . . Big Thistle . . .'

'Do you know what a thistle is?'

'Ooh! Thistle, yes – *foo-fu-fu-fu-fu-fooooo!*'

'No, no – That's a *whistle*! I mean *thistle*! It's the national flower of Scotland, it's a jagged fucker, it's purple and green and it's very nice. A THISTLE.'

'Oh . . . Thistle?'

'Look, have you got a bit of paper and a pen? Here, give us that.'

Scribble-scribble.

He draws his best impression of a thistle and he hands it back to the man.

'Oh!! *THISTLE!!* Ah-ha!'

So, he sits down. Five hours . . .

Somewhere, my tattoo guy says, there's a guy walking around the Earth with 'Scotland Forever' on his shoulders. And a big pineapple.

He must be one of those Hawaiian McDonalds.

THE CRUCIFIXION

This story is about a girl in Glasgow who worked in a printing works. And she made a terrible misprint one day. In the Bible.

A Life Worth Living

And because of her misprint, people to this day think that the Last Supper was in Galilee. When in actual fact it was in Gallowgate. In Glasgow. Near the Cross – *hahaha* – near the *Cross* – ah, forget it!

So, seriously, the way the Last Supper *really* happened . . .

You see, it was impossible that it could've been in *Galilee*, because in those days nobody really knew where they were anyway. They used to wander aboot saying to each other: 'Where are we? What's the name of this place? I wish an explorer would come and tell us where we are!'

The Last Supper actually happened in a small tavern known as the Saracen Head Inn . . . quite a popular place for cocktails of an evening.

The way it really happened: all the apostles were there, drinking wine and tearing lumps off the Mother's Pride. Singin' and shoutin' and bawlin': *'We are the Christians! – oh oh – Intae these Romans!* Give us another glass of that wine!' They were awful scruffy, the apostles, in reality.

But this wee apostle came up to this big apostle, and he said, 'Ach, what's goin' on here? You told me the Big Yin wuz comin' in! Nah, giz a break, ya said the Big Yin wuz comin' in but he's no, d'ye know what I mean? Eh? I think he's giz us a body swerve, know what I mean?'

The bigger one says, 'Now, look, son, I've been in this game a wee while now, and I'm tellin' you, if the Big Yin says he's comin' in, he'll make an appearance. You stand there wi'me, kiddo, and giz us another glass of that wine.'

'What would he need to come in here for anyway, eh? He's probably out doing them miracles. He doesnae need to come

285

in here. He can sit in the hoose wi' a big bucket full o' water and change it into wine like that himself! Doesnae need tae come into a boozer! Aw, giz another glass of wine.'

Then the door opens. And in he comes: the Big Yin.

'Helloooo, there, boys!'

He's in a long dress and the casual sandals. And the aura, all roond.

He says, 'Hello, there, lads, and how are youse getting' on an' that?'

And the wee apostle comes up and says, 'Ah thought you weren't comin,' Big Yin, ya know? Ah thought you weren't gonnae turn up.'

And he says, 'Ah nearly wasnae turning up, sonny boy. Ah've been up all mornin' doin' miracles an' I'm knackered! Giz a glass of that wine! Ah'm nae kiddin', son, Ah'm *knackered*. Jeez, the miracles Ah've done this morning – Ah'm *KNACKERED!* Take a look out that door – there's nothin' but deid punters walking up and doon wi' their beds under their arms, all pleased wi' themselves!'

He says, 'There was a joker up there this morning came up tae me, and says, "Are ye goin' tae cure my boy?" Ah says, "Aye, what's up wi' him?" He says, "He's deef and dumb, like, y'know?" Ah says, "Nae problem." *Wallop-wallop!* "There ya go." You know what the boy's first words are? "Is it all right that I'm a Protestant?"'

So, after a while, they're all drinking the wine, and wandering about, screaming and shouting. They all sat down – they sat down round this big table, because they were having trouble standing up at this point, you see. They all sat down

– you might have seen the picture – and the Big Yin's holding on to the table. He's *steaming*! He's fearing in case he falls out the window at the back!

They're all sat down. They're all singing songs and talking and drinking the wine and tearing lumps out the bread. And the Big Yin says, 'Hey, wait a minute! Best of order here!'

Silence.

And the wee apostle's sitting opposite. He says to the bloke next to him, 'Hey, I hope he giz us one of yon stories, eh? Aw, those stories are magic! I lap 'em up, so I dae! See the one about his father up in the sky? What a story yon is, eh? Aw, haw! Aw, the punters with the wings an' all that? *What a story!* Hey, Big Yin, giz us a story!'

'Shut yer face!'

Bang!

And his face was shut. For it is written.

He says, 'Open yer face!' He says, 'Right – let that be a lesson to ye!'

The wee guy says, 'Aye, all right. That's terrible, eh?'

He says, 'As a matter of fact, Ah'm not going to give youse a story today. Ah'm going to give youse a prophecy.'

'Oooh! D'ye hear that?' says the Wee Yin. 'D'ye hear that? *Prophecy,* eh! Nae bother tae the Big Yin, eh? Prophecies an' *everythin'*, just like that! What's a prophecy anyway?'

The Big Yin says, 'Look, a prophecy tells ye what's gonnae happen the morra.'

They say, 'What – aboot three-thirty the morra?'

The Big Yin says, 'See *you*, Judas – you're getting on ma tits!'

He says, 'All right, all right, all right . . . So here's ma prophecy: see right into this boozer today – you might've noticed there was a wee chicken standing ootside the door. See, before it goes cock-a-doodle-doo three times, Ah'm for the off! One of youse gonnae shop me!'

And they say, 'Wait a minute—'

'No, no, one of youse is gonnae shop me, and two of them big Roman police are gonnae wheech me right oot of here – right intae the jail! And Ah'm gonnae do a one-night lie-in, me with ma good dress on, too, and Ah'm gonnae get up in the mornin' an' say to myself, "First offence – Ah'm only on probation, nae further." But a big Roman's gonnae come into ma cell and say, "Probatium? My Arsium!" Ya know how they talk, these Romans? "Probation? Nah, Big Yin. I'll giv ye yer sentence, come here. Look at that windae." So, we'll look through the windae. He'll say, "See that big lump of wood doon there?" Ah'll say, "Aye." He'll say, "Well, get yer shoulder under it and take it up to that hill up there, would ye?" Ah'll say, "Aw, wait a minute! Ah was only kiddin' on Ah was a joiner!" He'll say, "*On yer way!*"

'So away Ah'll go. Got the wood on ma shoulder. Ah'm just aboot to set oot. He'll say, "Hey, where are *you* goin'?" Ah'll say, "You told me tae go tae the top of the hill." "I'm not finished with you yet, Big Yin."

'*WALLOP!*

'Jaggy bunnet, right on the heid!

'Ah'm sayin', "Aw, *noooo,* come *on*! Ah just had these split ends done this *mornin'*!"

'"On yer way!"

'So Ah'm away up the hill, kiddin' on Ah don't care.

'About a third of the way up, somebody's been oot there with a big Alsatian. It's done a big jobbie right in the street. Guess who stood in it! Didnae know when. Well, Ah'll tell ye somethin', that dog must have had a severe attack of the di-holier-hi-hay. Another twice, doon Ah went – *wallop!*

'At the third time Ah'm setting still kiddin' on Ah don't care. A big joker on the pavement, he'll say, "Hey, are you all right there, Jimmy?"

'Ah'll say, "As a matter of fact Ah'm not."

'He'll say, "D'ye fancy a wee hand?"

'"That's a good idea – get yer shooder under the other end."

'"What's yer name, anyway?"

'"Simon's the name – I just ran out of pies."

'So, the two of us will bring it up the hill. Get to the top and he'll sort of crawl away home. Ah parked the wood on the grass. Well, Ah'm knackered, like, havin' done that. Ah'll fancy a wee kip, but Ah won't want to lie on the wet grass wi' a gud dress on, ya know? "Ah'll hang up ma kit on this dod of wood here," and Ah'll lie doon.

'Wake up an hour later. *"Wait a minute!"* Some joker's been up an' nailed me tae the wood! Stole ma gud dress and pawned it! Lyin' in ma Y-fronts on the wood! They'd stuck a wee notice on the top: "MAD TONGS RULE, OK?"

'So Ah'll be lyin' there, freezin'. And two Romans'll come up the hill: *"We are the Romans, we hate the Christians!"* And they'll come right up, and one'll say tae the other: "Hey, look at that! What'ya make of them Christians? There's one of them stuck to a big dod o' wood!" The other one says, "Och, Ah don't know what tae make of 'em at all. Come on, let's stick him in that hole over there for a laugh."

'So, they'll stick me in this big hole. Ah felt such an eejit. Ah'll say, "Aw, come *on*, Da, giz us a *break!*"

'All the locals are all gathered roond the bottom. They're all wantin' me tae dae somethin'.

'They're all sayin', "*Dae somethin'! Dae somethin'! Dae one of yon holy tricks!*"

'"It's *miracles*, ya mug, you!"

'"All right, dae one anyway!"

'That's when Ah'll do the last miracle.

'But after a while they get bored and shot the craw, an' Ah'll be up there wi' myself again, until this wee Roman comes up the hill. He's about three feet high, carryin' this spear about six feet high. He's goin', "I am a Roman . . . I hate the Christians . . . Come to think of it, I even hate the Romans . . . Ah'm just a little jobbie . . ."

'He'll come right roond in front o' me.

'"Aye?"

'He'll say, "Aye, yer all right?"

'"Nope."

'"Nights are fair drawin' in, eh?"

'"Aye."

'"See this spear?"

'"Ah cannae keep ma eyes off it."

'"Well, Ah'm gonnae stick it right in yer body!"

'"Aw, man, don't be stupid – *Now wait a minute!*"

'Ah could've put the boot on 'im but Ah'll not be able to

get the foot away, y'know? Ah could've hooked him but Ah'll not be able get the arm away. So, Ah'll pee on him:

'*Pssssssssssssssshhhhhhhhhhhh!*

'He'll go away, sort of pissed off if you know what Ah mean.

'Then a couple of chinas'll come up and get me doon off the wood, take the nails oot. Carry me doon the hill and plunk me in an old air raid shelter. Ah'll be lyin' in there like a pound o' mince.

'As if Ah could dae anythin' aboot it, they'll roll a big stone in front of the door. And you know me, Ah'm that scared in the dark tae. But in the mornin' a couple of chinas of mine – unknownst tae youse, ya bunch of scruffs – will turn up with the good gear on, the wings an' everythin' – a couple of fairies, like, y'know – roll the stone away – ye never know the strength of these people! – roll the stone away, get me oot, and say: "There ye go, Big Yin – away up tae the sky an' see yer father!"

'So Ah'll be up in the sky, sittin' on a cloud wi' ma da, and Ah'm lookin' doon, and Ah can see y'all, sittin' in the boozer all sayin', "Where's the Big Yin?" "Ah don't know!" "Did you go up?" "Yer kiddin'!"

'The door's gonnae open – *BANG!* – and Ah'm gonnae walk in. An' you're gonnae say, "*You're* no the Big Yin!"

'Ah'm gonnae say, "Aye, Ah *am!*"

'You're gonnae say, "Well, where's the holes in yer haunds?"

'An' Ah'm gonnae say, "There they are!"

'You're gonnae say, "*They're* no *holes!*"

'Ah'm gonnae say, "Okay. Haud up yer fingers. Cop yer whack for the chib mark under the semmit!"'

Just then, John stauns up an' says: 'Aw, wait a minute, Big Yin. We *like* you. We've *always* liked ye. An' we know that you chipped in more for this carry-oot than anybody else. But see, when you've got a few of these cheap wines in ye, your patter's *rotten*, so it is!'

NEW AGE NONSENSE

Astrology? That's right up there with feng shui and fucking aromatherapy and all that other pish! Because, you know, I don't believe in any of that shite. I think it's bollocks, I really do.

Feng shui. Move the chair and you'll be happy. Aye. 'No, it's the movement of *energy*. Mmm, yes. The *flow* of *energy* through your—' *Get fucked!* Fucking flow of energy! I'll fucking kick your arse! 'There's a flow of energy, mmm, move that, mmm, that's much better – that'll be fifty quid!'

It's fucking nonsense.

I saw some new age dick come on TV the other day. She's like twenty-two years of age. 'I'm an expert in feng shui.' Yeah, right. When you're twenty-two you're not an expert in any fucking thing!

And she's got a specialism within her specialism. Oh yes, of course, she has. Her specialist specialism is: 'Clothing feng shui'. That's what she's into. Clearing up your wardrobe. That's not *feng shui*! 'Ooh, blue, no, no, that goes there, and throw that out, and put that there . . .' That's just *tidying up*! For God's sake! That's not fucking feng shui! Shui feng fucking nonsense!

And aromatherapy, that's another one. Aroma-fucking-therapy. Give me a fucking break. 'Smell yourself better!' Fuck off!

All you have to do is look at the people who do it. They're all: 'Mmm, yes, mmm, it's ancient, yes, mmm, it goes back to Egypt.'

Oh, does it? So does fucking *slavery*! We're not taking *that* up. Fucking idiots.

'Oh, and lavender – it makes you relax, mmm, lavender!' No, it fucking doesn't! I've been in the south of France where *they grow* lavender, loads of it, in fields. Nobody was relaxed. They were all working, digging stuff, driving tractors. No one's lying about going: 'Ahhh, fuck, so much lavender here . . . Oh, I cannae fuckin' stand up . . . I cannae stop fuckin' yawning!'

It's fucking nonsense. Pish! It's crap and junk.

I'll give you an example. This is aromatherapy at its fucking best.

There's a huge smash on the motorway. A *huge* crash. Seventy trucks are on fire, there's wheels and bits of truck everywhere. A hundred and twenty cars, fifty motorcycles, all blazing and bits of limbs everywhere. And one pedestrian, who caused the whole fucking thing chasing his cat across the motorway. There's blazing, smoke, wailing, hundreds of people on the sides of the motorway: 'Ooooh, *fuck*, look at this!' 'There's a *leg* over here!' 'Where? Ooh, fuck, don't make me look!' *Bluuuggghhh!* There's fire engines, ambulances, paramedics, police, flashing lights, helicopters. Fucking mayhem.

And through the crowds comes a guy: 'Let me through – I'm an aromatherapist!'

I don't think so!

A truck driver, lying against the wheel of his truck, his leg's over there, just the stump sticking out his overalls.

'Aaaaaagggggghhhhhh!!!! Help!'

'Listen, I'm going to rub this lavender on your earlobes, you'll relax, you watch this!'

'Eeeaaaaaaggggggggggggghhhhhhh!!!!!'

'Ah, just you take it easy, now' – *rub-rub-rub* – 'Do you feel the difference?'

'Eeeeeeeaaaaaaaaaaaaaaaaaaaagggggggghhhhh!!!!!!!!'

'Here, I've got another thing here, watch this. This is tea tree oil. I'm going to rub it on your stump here. There you go . . .'

'EEEEEAAAAAAAAAAAAAAAAGGGGGGHHHHHHHH!!!!!!!!!'

'You see? See how you're leaning back? That's you relaxing!'

'Aaaaggghh! Aaaaggghh! I'm not fuckin' relaxing! I'm tryin' to reach ma leg – I'm gonna *fuckin' hit* you with it!!!'

PARENTHETICALLY SPEAKING

The world in general is a wonderful place, but there are still some people who fuck it up and make life awful for other people. And I think one of the types of people who should be slapped into place forthwith are the people who use their fingertips to signify quotation marks.

Where the fuck did *that* come from, that stupid wiggling of the fingertips that people do when they're punctuating in the air, when they want you to understand 'the incredibly complex concept' that they're saying something in quotation marks? Who on earth was the moron who first thought of doing that? Whoever it was, they ought to be horsewhipped.

'Yes, I believe they're – *wiggle wiggle* – "married", if you get my drift.'

'Mmm, I've heard that they're – *wiggle wiggle* – "having problems", if you see what I mean.'

Fuck off!

You want to grab their fingers, squeeze them really, really hard, jam them up their own arse, and shout, *'Fucking stop it!'*

I hate it.

'Mmm, Billy Connolly, yes, I believe he's a – *wiggle wiggle* – "comedian", supposedly.'

Do shut up!

When anybody does it to you, punctuate everything you say when you reply to them. Stick the finger out for a full stop, add a little curve for a comma, do both for a semi-colon, a vertical swish and a point for an exclamation mark, and so on and so on. Do the whole lot. Give it back to them with both barrels, it really fucks them up. 'You know – *point, curve* – I was saying that to my wife only yesterday – *point* – I said – *wiggle wiggle* – Darling – *curvy line, point* . . .' See how they cope with that, the bastards!

They need to be slapped into place.

COMPUTERS

People keep saying to me, 'Email me.' And I keep saying, 'No, I fucking won't!' I don't know how to do it. I don't have one of those silly fucking things. I can't do it. I'm not 'computer literate'. And I have no fucking desire to be. Don't feel sorry for me.

I write with a fountain pen. I'd like your address. I don't want your 'dot-com-double-you-double-you' pish. 'How am I driving dot com' – Go fuck yourself Dot. Dot. Dot.

I think the whole thing is a desperate con.

I used to go to the airport: 'I'd like to fly to Glasgow, please.' 'Certainly, Mr Connolly!' *Whizz.* A ticket would come out from under the desk, they'd take a ballpoint pen – 'What's your name?' 'Connolly. Billy Connolly.' 'How are you paying?' 'Cash.' 'Certainly.' *Ching!* 'There's your change.' Then they would say: 'What seat would you like?' And they would have a cut-out of an aeroplane behind them, with all the seat numbers on it. 'I'll have 17F.' *Bish-Bosh.* Stuck it on your ticket. Done!

It was fucking perfect!

They couldn't allot that seat again because it isn't there; it's now on your ticket. There's just a hole where it used to be. Perfection!

So, they fucking changed it. They fucking had to change it!

Now they're typing for fucking *days.* And you're standing there losing the will to live. *Tappity-Tappity-Tappity-Tappity.* Then they stop, scowl and do that single one, you know, pressing with one finger repeatedly as though they're trying to unblock something. *Tap-Tap-Tap-Tap-Tap.* And then they're off again for another burst: *Tappity-Tappity-Tappity-Tappity.* And then they'll go: 'Do you *have* to get the 2.15?' 'Well, that's the flight I would like, yes.' Then they're back to the typing for another few minutes: *Tappity-Tappity-Tappity-Tappity.* Then they look to one side and say: 'John?' And this other guy, further down, is typing for somebody else along there. 'Yeah?' 'When you put XYL, oblique 7, dot dot dot, do you have to put 3PFOG?'

Now I've lost it completely.

And he goes: 'Oh no. Is there an "r" in the month?' 'Oh, I forgot about that!' 'Well, it's BRMG206 dot-dot-dot 7 oblique 5, then.' 'Of course!' *Tappity-Tappity-Tappity-Tappity.*

Then it doesn't work. It's frozen. So, they just stare at the screen and rub their chin for a while. Then they try that one-finger thing again for a bit. *Tap-Tap-Tap-Tap.* And eventually they call for help again, and the other guy has to excuse himself from his own customer and come over. And the two of them are typing away on one machine now, and nothing much is happening. *Tappity-Tappity-Tap-Tap-Tap-Tappity-Tappity . . .*

And the other customer, the one they've abandoned, is looking over at me, as if it's my fault, and muttering, 'Aw, *you*! Fucking Connolly! Fucking big shot, eh? Oh, yeah, they all run to *you*, they don't run to *me*! I'm working in Saudi Arabia for six fuckin' months, that's all! But *you*. Probably homosexual, show business – velvet troosers, a sure fucking giveaway! I've a good mind to whack you on the side of the head, ya great poof!'

It's a fucking nightmare.

And, while I'm on the subject of computers, wait until you hear *this* one.

I was in Australia some time ago, I'm watching TV, and this guy comes on and says, 'It's astonishing! It's absolutely *astonishing*! Because of the microchip, you can now get the whole *Encyclopaedia Britannica* on one CD. And it fits in your pocket! The whole *Encyclopaedia Britannica* in your *pocket!*' And he left it at that. He didn't go on to mention that it's fuck-all good to you in your pocket! That you need thousands of pounds of equipment to play the fucking thing! Which is more expensive than a set of the *Encyclopaedia Britannica.*

Liars and bastards!

Bill Gates lives in a fortress. He's a squillion-billion-dillionaire! So why doesn't he make the fucking things cheaper, then, the cheating bastard? The fucking things should be a pound-fifty! He can afford to lose a billion or two. He could drop a squillion and not even notice!

'Oh, he does good work.' I should fucking hope so – *he's got everybody's money!*

MOBILE PHONES

Mobile phones. Aren't these the bane of the fucking world?

People with no arse in their trousers and a phone. If you walk behind them you can hear them: 'Guess where I am now!' He goes for a walk and phones home to tell everybody where he is!

I do not understand it. You see, to me, mobile phones tame you. They tame the wild beast in you. They pin you down. I mean, I always regarded my car as my ashram. It was *my* place.

'Where's Billy?'

'Where he wants to be – now get on with your life!'

But now you're always on tap. You're always *gettable*. People can get you now in your nice quiet moments that you used to love. I really don't like that, and I don't understand those people who do like it.

Some people seem to be so afraid of being alone with themselves and their thoughts that they have to be talking to someone on the phone constantly. And talking really, really loudly. It's as though they're trying to shout the quiet out of their lives. 'HELLO? YEAH! I'M ALL RIGHT, HOW ARE YOU?' And as soon as one call ends, they're desperately trying to call someone else before the silence settles back. 'HELLO?' It's madness.

But unfortunately, it affects all the rest of us. Because this unending noise is inflicted on you while you're trying to mind your own business.

I've had it on aeroplanes. The guy beside you: 'Hey, is that you, John? . . . Aye, no, the phone . . . Yeah, March . . . Oh, just put them in that cupboard on the left . . . Twenty-six . . . Friday!' You want to join in: 'Aw, come on – Thursday! Twenty-one!'

Now I say to them: 'Do you think you could do that somewhere else?'

'. . . Sorry?'

'Do you think you could take your phone somewhere else? Instead of shouting it all over me?'

I don't have a phone, personally. I don't have a mobile phone. But we *were* the first family in the street with cordless pyjamas.

But this guy. He can't believe that I don't want to have him intrude into my space with his stupid foghorn voice and his stupid little comments. 'Take the phone somewhere else?'

I said, 'Just take it the fuck away from me! I don't care about your twenty-six or your Fridays. Bugger off!'

STUPID QUESTIONS

We often say things to each other that don't make any real sense. It's as if, over the years, you get worn down by the stupidity of it and you just come to accept it.

Your mother starts it all with the first stupid question of your life. And you're too wee to say, 'That's a fucking stupid question!'

The first stupid question that your mother asks you is: 'Where did you lose it?' That is the most stupid question in the history of the human race. 'Where did you lose it?' 'Er, I don't know. It's lost – that means I don't know where it fuckin' is!' 'But where?' 'I don't fuckin' know!'

Another one you often hear is when you'll be talking to people, and they'll say: 'Can you tell us in your own words what happened?' 'What, do you think I've got my own *words*? What would I want with my own words? Who would I talk to?' The next time somebody says, 'Tell me in your own words' – do it. 'Ow, splagmik debree, magrayba kalu a bagawap.'

I was touring in Kuwait recently. I was really pissed off – I thought that after all the hostilities there Kuwait would be all burning and shit, you know, and I'd be like Bob Hope turning up in the camouflage clothes and all that. But the fucking place was hoovered, it was spotless.

There was a British guy there who said this really stupid thing. He said, 'Watch out for the secret police.' I said, 'Oh, aye, yeah, I'll try and do that, yeah.' How in the name of Christ do you watch out for the secret police? How stupid is that?

There's a whole list of stupid things people keep saying to you. Like those guys who point at their wrist while asking for the time. I know where *my* watch is, where the fuck is yours? Do I point at my crotch when I ask where the toilet is? No!

What about when people say, while you're sitting there watching a film: 'Did you see that?' Of course I didn't, I paid ten quid just to come to the cinema and stare at the fucking floor!

Then there are those fools who always say, 'Can I ask you a question?' You didn't really give me a choice there, did you, sunshine?

Or there's that other stupefyingly dumb one where people say straight after you've just found something you've been searching for: 'Oh, it's always in the last place you look!' Of course it is! Why the fuck would you keep looking after you've found it?

And there's that old one that really does my head in, when they say: 'Ah, you just want to have your cake and eat it too.' Too fucking right I do! What good is a cake if you can't eat it? It makes no sense at all!

Why do we put up with this nonsense?

I was in Los Angeles recently and there was a sign that said: 'To the Braille School'. Who the fuck was it for?

Then there's all these strange and stupid phrases that get used these days quite deliberately. Like, when I was watching that wee war recently – it was on CNN – and the main two phrases I learned from it were 'smart bombs' and 'friendly fire'. Neither of which made sense to me. I thought bombs were things you put in bombers, and they would fly away and drop them somewhere. But now, apparently, there's no need for that. With these so-called 'smart bombs', these fucking things arrive in your street in a taxi. They ask people where you live and all of that. You're reading the Sunday papers. *Knock! Knock!* 'Who is it?' 'Bomb-a-gram!' *Boom-whoosh!*

And then there's 'friendly fire'. What a concept! So you're lying on the stretcher, your bollocks are missing and there's an ugly gaping wound where they used to be, and you'd love to give it a wee caress but your arm's missing as well – but you have the consolation of knowing that your *friend* did it to you. And that makes you feel just fucking dandy!

We're far too tolerant of all these words. We need to remember how stupid they are!

AMERICAN CINEMA

I went to the movies the other night in New York to see *Hide and Seek* starring Robert De Niro. And I loved it. But the experience of watching it in this place was weird.

I was up at 42nd Street, at the pictures. Of course, nobody else calls it 'the pictures' anymore, but I go way back. Actually, I used to hang out with a guy in Glasgow called Frankie McBride, who was a movie fanatic. I'd go to his house and his father would always say, 'He's away at the talkies.' That's how fucking old I am! 'He's away to the magic lantern show' – there's a guy running around the theatre with a photograph and a torch!

But anyway, this New York cinema, this 'multiplex' place: I was shocked and horrified by the experience.

First of all, I find I'm on the *sixth* floor! I gave this guy my ticket, which is number nineteen, and I said, 'Where is that?' He said, 'Ah, that's on the sixth floor.' And I thought I'd heard him wrong. 'The *sixth* floor?' I started going up on the escalator and, sure enough, I had to go up six of them. Six escalators! And of course escalators are always made worse by the fact that nobody *walks* on them, they just stand there, preventing you from getting past them, the pricks!

Eventually I got up to the sixth floor of this building. It was incredible. I went to the place where you get all the stuff to eat. I just wanted some ice cream.

'Can I have some ice cream?' I said. 'We don't have any,' the guy serving there said. I said, 'What? It's the fucking *movies*! The movies with no *ice cream*? What is *that*?' He was completely unmoved: 'Oh, we don't have it in the building, sir.' Then he said brightly: 'We have pizza' – fucking pizza! – 'Thin crust pizza, thick crust pizza, stuffed crust pizza, deep dish pizza . . .' And on and on came this big list of other shit, including things like hot dogs, hamburgers, cheeseburgers, nachos, tacos, waffles, barbecue flatbreads, pizza flatbreads, buffalo chicken flatbreads, 'Bavarian pretzels', chicken wings, chicken thighs, chicken breasts, chicken bites, chicken tenders, mozzarella sticks, fries, curly fries, mega fries and popcorn. I said, 'Oh, I'm sorry, I had my mind set on a plate of fucking *stew*!'

What do people in America eat at movies these days? No wonder they're as fat as fucking pigs! There should be a health warning on a *cheesecake* in that country. It's time they all smoked and lost a bit of weight!

My advice to you, if you want to lose a bit of weight: don't eat anything that comes in a bucket. Buckets are the kitchen utensils of the farmyard!

There's nothing more discouraging than sitting waiting for your movie to come on, and somebody comes into the row with a great big armful of fucking stuff. And a bucket of Coca-Cola to go with it. 'Excuse me . . .' It's fucking raining popcorn and butter.

'Could I have more butter in my bucket, please?'

'Do you want the Large Bucket, Sir, or the Family Trough? You could sit it between the four of you and tuck in hands-free!'

Eat at home! *Eat at home!*

WE DON'T BELONG IN THERE

I've never understood it. We don't *belong* in there. We've no fucking business in the water.

The sea's full of shit anyway. I saw it on TV. Morecambe! There's nothing makes me swim faster than pink toilet paper beside me. We've got no fucking business in there!

The things that live in there don't like us. They have made it absolutely *plain* that they don't! They sting us, fucking some of them *nip* us, some of them fucking *burn* us, some of them like to *eat* us, or they have arms that *stick* to us and fucking *drown* us! When are we going to take the *hint*?

We are not fucking *welcome* in there.

The stones are covered in slippery stuff, you fall and hurt your arse. It's fucking wet and it's uncomfortable and fucking freezing!

It's the truth!

Our species spent fucking thousands of years getting out, and the first thing we do is run back in. You see them, buying that fucking gear. They buy it in the Fulham High Street, there are things in the back, and masks, and they get down there to the water, and they see a hole, they go, 'What's in there?' and they put their hand in: 'Ow, yer *bastards*!' they say.

That's not a bastard, that's his *house*! How would *you* like it, eating your Sunday dinner, an' a big fucking hairy arm comes in the window? You'd jab it with a fork.

'Fuck off!' you would say, and rightly so!

MODERN REVENGE

I was listening to Radio Four one afternoon. They had a programme on about revenge, and it was very interesting. There was a woman on it who was discussing the subject, and she said that women these days are much more into revenge than men are.

Men still tend to lash out, she said. 'Ah, you fucking bitch, have some of that!' Wallop! That sort of thing – instinctive nasty stuff. But she said that women are much more inclined to think, 'My day will come. You will be sleeping, and I'll have a bread knife!'

And to illustrate this she told a story about a woman in London who lived with an airline pilot. He sounded a real bastard; he may even have been a cunt. He phoned her one day from South Africa and said, 'Listen, bitch – get your shit out of my house by Friday. I've got a new bitch moving in.' Sounds like a rascal to me, a real ruffian!

Well, of course, she was shocked and broken-hearted. And she collapsed in tears and was in a terrible state. But eventually she recovered enough to be able to pack up her stuff, and was about to move out when she discovered that her stereo equipment, with the big speakers and all, was far too heavy to carry; she realised she'd have to come back and get it separately. So, she was writing a note to that effect when she got this idea.

She nipped out to the fishmongers and bought a bag of shrimps and then she went back, unpicked the hem on the curtain in the main room of the house, put a line of shrimps in, and sewed it back up again. Then she left a note that she'd be back the following Friday to collect the stereo unit.

The following Friday she shows up again. He's at the door: 'Oh. You're here for your stereo. It's in the living room. Er, listen, when you're in there, see if you can smell anything. I've noticed a kind of weird smell in there.' She says, 'I will.'

So, she gets her stuff. He says, 'Did you smell anything?' She says, 'No.' Her nose should have grown like Pinocchio's. 'No, nothing at all.' And then she left.

Six weeks later, she bumped into him again in a local store when she was out shopping. 'How are you doing?' she asked. 'Oh, I'm in fucking misery,' he groaned. 'Even as we speak the plumbers are up in my living room pulling up the floor-boards. They think there's something dead under the floor. And the police have shown an interest – they're coming to dig the garden up tomorrow.' She says, 'Ah, that's a shame.' And she walks off.

Six more weeks later, and one of the neighbours told her he'd moved away. And taken the curtains with him.

UN-BEIGING YOURSELF

There are ways to un-beige yourself.

One of the ways to start is to go to some place where there are still rebels in action, just like at a tattooist convention or somewhere like that. Because that establishes how beige you currently are. You go: 'Aw, no, for fuck's sake, I am so fuckin' beige! I am *beige* – people think I'm fuckin' *beige*! I'm a *beigest*. I'm a fully qualified *beigest*!'

And there are many ways, and many, many acts, you can do – you don't need to get scarred for life, you don't need to get pierced – there are lots of things you can do.

Here's a great one. Take on The Beige at source. Subvert The Beige Society on their own patch. Because they always love to have *buffets*. Salad buffets.

The Edinburgh Festival is fucking awash with salad buffets at lunchtime. 'Oh, do come to our salad buffet with the Lord and Lady Mayor, and we'll have a salad buffet, and we'll talk shite all morning. We'll all try to look artistic. Bring your corduroy trousers.'

Oh, yeah. That makes you look artistic: you wear your fucking corduroy and a cardigan. 'And some corduroys and lots of fucking pamphlets. And sit around with one leg going round the other one. Twice. That's terribly fuckin' artistic. And we'll bore each other shiteless about Art. And we'll have a salad buffet. A *salad* buffet!'

Well, I went to one of these, years ago, and they're fucking *impossible* things. Because they give you stuff on this paper plate, you get your tomatoes and your wee radish and your spring onion and your bits and pieces, all on a bendy plate. You spend the whole day trying to balance the food and stop it from rolling off the plate. And then you get a drink that you can't fucking balance because you're already trying to balance your cherry fucking tomato . . .

Here's what you do. To un-beige the entire event. It was shown to me by three fabulous actors, who are still my pals today. You get the plate of 'buffet' and you get the drink. The first thing you do is fucking drink the drink. *Unk-unk-unk!* Put the glass down. Now, the three or four of you, you get together in a sort of horseshoe shape at the buffet table, close enough to cover each other so you can't be seen from behind.

You whip out your willy, and you put it on the plate. You then get plenty of . . . salad stuff . . . but not a big mountain. The trick is not to *hide* your willy. It's to have it *lurking* in the undergrowth. A bit of olive oil drizzled over the top. Nice.

Don't even *think* about the balsamic vinegar! Your eyes will be crossed for fucking years! The only cure is to shove your willy through your legs, like that guy in *Silence of the Lambs*. Make yourself a mangina!

Owwaaahhuuuaaahhh! Turn round and get your mate behind you with a fucking fire extinguisher!

Phhhhhhffffftttt!

Whooowaaaaahhhhhh!

So. You've got it here, your willy, resting on the plate, nestling in the rocket-heavy undergrowth. And then: you mingle. Just walk around nice and casual, holding the plate comfortably at crotch level, occasionally picking up a leaf on which to munch. Do that as you partake in the chit-chat.

'I saw your show last night' – *munch* – 'It was *excellent*. Who *designed* that? I thought the *design* was *extraordinary* . . . You should be so *proud*, my *God*' – *Munch-munch* – 'And I believe you put it on for just a pound fifty for the whole thing? It didn't show, it was *excellent*. Mmm, who wrote the songs?'

And then you dare each other to go and talk to someone who looks very important – you pick the victim for your friend. You go, 'Right, you go and talk to *them*!'

'Aw. Fuck *off*!'

You see, because they get the big shots there. It might be . . . Sophia Loren!

'Right, go and talk to Sophia.'

'Ah, fuck *off*!'

'Nah, you *must*! It's part of the *game*, you beige bastard, you!'

'Oh, okay, okay . . .'

You see one or two people panicking halfway there, losing their nerve. Ramming it back into their troosers and zipping up. Then they've got that unique walk, with the olive oil cascading down the inside leg.

Or one of you will say: 'Right, go and talk to the lady mayoress . . . And talk about salad.'

'Oh, come *on*!'

'No, you must!'

'Okay . . . Fuck it!'

So you try to amble over, very casual, still picking up the odd piece of leaf from over your willy:

'Hello . . . Lady Mayoress . . . the caterers have done us proud, haven't they?'

But you have to watch for those wee white plastic forks. They're *unbelievably* sharp. And very weak at the neck. Where it joins the body. You know? Because I actually hit John Gielgud in the neck with a new potato. I stabbed it and it went – *chiii- boom!* 'Oh! *Whhhhat* on EARTH happened there?'

So you're chatting away to the mayoress: 'Yeah, the caterers have done us proud. It's a lovely salad!'

And you can see the lady mayoress doing this double take, glancing down at the plate, looking back up, glancing down again, all with that 'Did I just see . . . No, I couldn't have!' expression on her face.

I was banned from the Traverse Theatre in Edinburgh for having my willy in a gin and tonic! That's taking it, I confess, that's taking it a bit far.

But beigeness must be confronted.

Actually, I was trying *not* to be thrown out: 'That's right – throw me out! You didn't know I was disabled – that's how I drink!'

So, you can see the lady mayoress checking you out. And you can see her puzzled thought bubble saying: 'I didn't see *sausage rolls* when I was at the buffet table . . .'

Now, you have to beware of the fork. You don't want to risk that lunging down at your plate. Because jealousy knows no bounds. She might try and whip your own fucking willy off the plate with a white plastic fork.

Shooom!

Aooooaaaahhh!

You'll end up with a row of wee holes along your willy! You'll be pissing like a *fountain* for the rest of yer life! You'll have to go and see specialists.

Not medical ones.

Probably clarinet players.

SHOUTING AT WILDEBEEST

I don't think I'm old. I don't *feel* old. But I've noticed certain distinctive changes coming over me recently.

My hair's changing colour. I've got the winter plumage on now. And at the back it's gone a sort of Turkish hooker blond, which I must say suits me down to the ground.

My nose hair is accelerating, for reasons best known to itself. I used to cut it once every thirty years. Now it's, like, twice a month. Presumably the body knows what it's doing. *I'm* very baffled. I wonder what's going to happen to me that's going to need long nasal hair to deal with it.

I test myself every now and again – to see how old I'm getting. I test myself to see how long it takes to get out of a bean-bag chair. You're like an upturned turtle, flopping about – you can be lost in there for *days*! You have to wait until someone wanders into the room and finds you.

But the most terrible thing I found recently was that I tend to make a noise when I bend down. I don't know how long I've been doing this. But I caught myself the other day going: '*AaaaaeeeeeeeeeaaaahhhhhhhhJesusChrist!*' How long have I been doing *that*??

But one of the most disconcerting things I've found myself doing recently is: shouting at the television. It's crept up on me, as a phenomenon. It started out as just *talking* to the TV. I was sitting on the couch one day, in Los Angeles, watching the local news, when a minor earthquake happened. And the newsreader in the studio, she felt it, too. So, she looked up and said, 'What was that?'

And I actually heard myself saying back to her: 'I don't know.'

Well, that was bad enough. But after a while I started *shouting* at the TV. Really angry shouting. At the news, current affairs shows, political interviews, anything like that. Like they could *hear* me, but I kept on doing it anyway. '*Rubbish!* Liar! LIAR! Answer the *question,* ya dirty bastard, *answer the question!* You know?

But now I've been taken to shouting at animals on television. And it's a grade down, it's a step down the ladder, I feel.

It was a documentary about wildebeest. Wildebeest in the Serengeti Plain of South Africa. David Attenborough, one of those guys, you know, was narrating it. And it didn't take me long to conclude that the wildebeest are a particularly stupid animal. They were standing around there, eating grass. Thousands of the buggers, you know, just standing around, eating grass. And there's lionesses creeping up on them.

The leader of the wildebeest looks up – *munch, munch, munch* – '. . . Do you hear a lion? . . . Thought I heard a lion there . . . Just got a "liony" kind of feel about this place, y'know?'

And there's a particularly stupid wildebeest about four back, and he goes: 'Did you say lion? I've never seen a lion, what are they like? I heard they were beige. Is that right – are they beige? Kind of camel hair colour?'

And the leader goes: 'Hey *you* – eat the fucking grass and shut up and do as you're told!'

'Excuse me for being fuckin' born, by the way! Coh! For asking a question about a lion you get a mouthful of fuckin' abuse!'

Meanwhile it cuts back to the male lions, and they're all lying under a tree, scratching themselves, playing cards, you know, smoking and all of that. And then it cuts back to the female lions – they're now about six feet from the wildebeest. The leader one's sneaking up, doing that shoulder number.

'*Waaaauuuuuuggghhhh! Fuckin' lions!*'

'W-where? Where's the fuckin' li—'

BANG! BOOF!

It's on the ground, they've split it open, they're into its ribcage, there's lungs and stomachs flying out, blood everywhere, its back leg is still trying to run . . . And there's another wildebeest standing there watching them doing it! 'Oh . . . look at them eatin' that thing . . .'

And I'm screaming at the telly: '*Run, you fuckin' idiot!* If they look up, you're fucking *history*! You see that *dust*? That's every fuckin' wildebeest in *Africa*! Run after them – *they know somethin' you don't!*'

'I'm nae a fuckin' wildebeest!'

I've now come to the conclusion that wildebeest don't know they're wildebeest. For there are no mirrors in the Serengeti Plain. You can be anything you like.

You *ask* a wildebeest: 'Are you a wildebeest?'

'Are you fuckin' *kiddin'*? A *wildebeest*? I'm one of them stripey things over there! Too fuckin' right, oh aye! When one of them lions looks up, I'll just fuckin' fly away!'

INCONTINENCE PANTS

I was looking at these ads for incontinence pants.

Now, I don't want to laugh at incontinent people. It must be terrible, right, being incontinent. You know, you get all dressed to go out and then: *phisssssshhhhhh!* Ah, no! You can't buy white clothes, you can't buy grey suits, you go: *phisssssshhhhh!* Jesus Christ! Because, let's be honest about this: young people are incontinent, too, you know. It strikes at all ages.

Suppose a young trendy guy, he sees the advert and thinks, 'Right, that'll do me – give us a pair o' them!' And when he gets them, he steps into them, pulls them up nice and high, ties them securely at the waist, and ties them equally securely below the knees. Done!

Looks in the mirror: 'They're the very fellows fer me! They're see-through plus-fours! Just the job at St Andrews!'

So, he pulls the trendy baggy troosers over the top of them and he's off to the discotheque, giving it a bit of that, striking poses, leaping around, full of confidence as he flirts with all the ladies. 'Hey, how're you doin'? What's your sign? Sagittarius? Oh aye, half man and half horse, aye – a licence to shit in the street, that's good . . .'

Phisssssshhhhhh!

He cares not a jot! It's all being safely contained in his new and special pants.

Phisssssshhhhhh!

He's still dancing away, singing as he goes: *'Saddle up and ride your pony . . .'*

Phisssssshhhhhh!

'Aye, ha-ha-ha . . .'

Phisssssshhhhhh!

He's sending gallons down each leg!

Then the design fault starts to show itself. He's full up. He starts walking slowly and awkwardly like his feet are carrying weights. From resembling John Travolta boogying on the dancefloor he now looks like Buzz Aldrin shuffling about on the moon.

'I'll take you home in a minute . . . I'm . . . just goin' tae empty ma underwear . . .'

Goes to the toilet, loosens the things at the legs, and then: *whoooooooooshhhhh!*

Incontinence pants: good idea, needs more work.

HEALTH ISSUES

Now at this point, for those of you who have been reading for a long time, I'm going to explain my health issues to you.

I've got Parkinson's Disease. I wish he'd fucking kept it to himself, but there you go.

The Parkinson guy, I got my daughter to google him. He's James Parkinson, who studied at the beginning of the nineteenth century. It used to be called Shaking Palsy. Fuck, I'm glad *Parkinson* showed up!

It affects the left side of me, mostly. It affects the way I walk and my left hand shiggles about. You'll notice – maybe you won't, but you probably will – my left hand climbs up.

When I'm talking about something else, it thinks I'm not noticing it, and it climbs up. And the strangest thing is, if I look at it, it dashes away guiltily. Lately it's been climbing up and I've just ignored it, and it's come up and joined the other one. I look like Saint Teresa or somebody like that.

So that'll happen sometimes. I just ignore it.

I met Ian Holm, the actor, who also suffers from it. He has had it longer than me. And he said, 'Do you shake much – your hands?' I said, 'No. When I'm nervous, when I'm tired, they shake a bit.' He said, 'Oh, yeah, they probably will.' He said, 'I'll give you a bit of advice. If it shakes just stick it in your pocket.' He forgot to mention he meant the *jacket* pocket.

Which was strange, because he'd told me a wee funny story before that. He was in an art gallery, at the Royal Academy in Piccadilly, for a big art exhibition. He was looking at a big nude, on his own, with his hand in his pocket . . . 'Hey, get the fuck outta there!'

If you find Parkinson's funny, you're going to love the cancer!

I've had prostate cancer. It's over now, I got the all-clear. They ripped it out and I pee like a racehorse now. I went back to the doctor after about two months for an appointment, and he started to ask me very personal questions.

He said, 'Can you still achieve erection?'

I said, 'Oh, yes.' I'm thinking, 'Don't ask me to show you, please!'

He said, 'Because we have various pills and potions, you know, and we have a little class for penile rehabilitation.'

I thought, '*I'm* not sitting in a circle wanking with *strangers*!'

And everything's in working order except that when I have an orgasm I don't ejaculate. Because that's what the prostate does. And it's not there anymore. So, nobody in my house sleeps on a wet patch.

I'll tell you one thing that might have the men in the room crossing their legs. I went back to work – I think I went back a wee bit early – I was doing a film about death and funerals and stuff. We were in New Orleans, and I got quite painful in this department. I went to the hospital and the guy said, 'I think we'll have to flood your bladder and have a look.' I said, 'Sure.' So, he put me on this big table, naked, and there was a beautiful Jamaican nurse, holding my penis. She was really nice and very beautiful, and I'm trying to get in touch with my penis, and I'm saying to it, 'Don't fucking MOVE!'

The doctor came with these three silver things over his arm – catheters. He said, 'This is for the water,' and he put it in my willy, shoved it in, and started to flood it. And I got an overwhelming desire to piss up in the air. I thought, 'Oh God, please don't pee over the nurse!'

And he said, 'This is the camera and the light,' and it went in. He said, 'Would you like to watch this?' I said, 'Sure.' A big screen lit up on the wall. Just like the one you have at home – those big buggers. It was like an aquarium, it was really strange. The seaweed swaying in the bottom. It was mostly pink. And with the light on the camera he was pointing out points of interest. He said, 'This is your sphincter.' I said, 'What's it doing *there*?' Because I thought your sphincter was your bum hole! But apparently you've more than one sphincter.

I kind of like my bum hole. Because it's a circular muscle. It's very interesting the way it works, like a lens in a camera.

Well, the tour went on. 'This is this and this is that . . .' And he was down among the seaweed, and he came upon a piece of white plastic and a piece of metal, both the same size. And both of us at the same time said: 'What the fuck's *that*?' They'd been left in from the operation; they'd got loose and gone adrift. He said, 'Oh, we'll have to get *that* out of there.' And I said, 'I couldn't agree more.'

So, he sent in this other thing. Snapping. And he was working it. It's a bit like those things at the funfairs, you know, with the crane as you try to lift things. And every time he got near it me and the nurse went, 'Ooooohh!' And at about the fifth attempt he got both of them. 'Oh, *aaaaayyyy!*'

And he said, 'We'll have to get them out of there.' I was trying to remember the tour, but I couldn't remember any emergency exit. I said, 'Oh, God, you don't mean the way it goes out is the way it came in?' He said, 'Yes, I'm afraid so.' He said, 'Do me a favour, could you move' – it was the sneakiest thing I've ever had done to me – he said, 'Could you move the toe next to your big toe?' I went, 'Yeah, I—' and he went *sliice.*

Don't get prostate cancer.

I know you were planning to. But don't.

BY MY SIDE

I like older people. Even since I was a wee boy I've liked them. They used to play dominoes in a little park near me, in a wee shed, and I used to go and talk to the old guys. It's a love that has never really left me. I remember hearing an old guy in Glasgow, arguing with his wife, and it stays with me to this day.

He said, 'Hey, Agnes.'

She goes, 'What?'

'When were we married? What year was it when we were married?'

'1911.'

'1911? Fucking hell . . . 1911 . . . That was only three years before the fuckin' war came. Aye. We had three bairns. I went away and fought in the war, didn't I? Away fighting in a place I couldnae even fuckin' spell. And there was nights I was a frightened person. But you know what got me through it, Agnes? I knew you were by my side, every step of the way.

'1918 they let us oot. Couldnae get a job. Fuckin' unemployed. As we marched proudly intae the Twenties, and the National Strike. I didnae go on strike myself. I was fuckin' unemployed at the time. It wasnae easy. But I got by, with you by my side, every step of the way. Standing by my side.

'Intae the Hungry Thirties we went. We managed to get through the Depression without eatin' any of the children. As we proudly marched towards 1939 and another war. They gave me a steel helmet and a big stick and told me to keep the Germans out of Sauchiehall Street, which I did to the best

320

of my ability. 'Cause I knew that you were beside me, every step of the way.

'1945, they let us oot and I couldnae get a fuckin' job. They said I was too old. Struggled forward for five years, got the pension. We soon tired of the Caribbean holidays and the mad parties. Settled down to a life of starvation with occasional trips to hypothermia. Aye. And you by my side, every step of the way.

'And here we are. What are we? . . . Nineteen-fuckin'-eighty-seven! My God. We're in the middle of a recession, whatever that might be. Feels like a depression to me. It might be a typin' error. And you're still beside me, every step of the way.

'D'you know, Agnes, I was thinkin' . . . You're a fuckin' *jinx*!'

DEATH

Us Scots have a peculiar idea of death and funerals and all that. As a matter of fact, there's an old saying: 'There's more fun at a Glasgow funeral than there is at an Edinburgh wedding.' And it's true.

Especially after the woman or the man has been buried away, or burnt – no, not 'burnt', but 'cremated', 'disposed of'. The party afterwards is great. Of course, they're all maudlin at first, all 'Sob! It's terrible, I don't know what I'm going to do!' 'Here, have a large one for a start and we'll see what happens!' – and by the end of it they've forgotten who it was they've lost!

You see, death has always fascinated me. My own, in

particular. Not so much the *process* of dying. I always wondered where I was going to be when it happened. I mean, you could be really caught if you die in the wrong place. You can't say it wasn't you! You'd have to say to the bit of stuff: 'See, if I die in here, will you put my troosers on, write me a suicide note and throw me out the window?'

But this death thing – and especially cremation, being burnie-wurnied – I don't fancy that much. I went to a funeral once – a burying one – and I thought, 'My God, what a terrible thing to do to people!' It looks really horrendous when you're at one, you know?

And then, right after that, I went to a cremation. That intrigued me, because they put the coffin on a plinth thing, and the minister was over on the other side. I had no idea, I'd never been to one before, you see. I was watching the coffin and I was thinking, 'I wonder what happens to it? I mean, surely to God they don't set fire to it right in front of you?' You know, like they flambé steak in a restaurant.

So, it's sitting there on this thing and the minister says, 'Well, we'll have some prayers now. Let us pray: O God who is high in heaven, take our friend into your hands, and show him . . .' I looked back . . . and it was away!

I thought, 'Oh, come on – what happened?' But I was afraid to ask anybody, I didn't want to appear naïve. But obviously it went off into this thing, down to the vault below. I felt a bit cheated.

I waited and I waited and I waited, and eventually somebody else died. I went up to *that* crematorium. I thought, 'Right: I'm gonnae *watch* this time.' So, I'm waiting and watching – I'm not going to be conned by this 'prayers' business into looking away!

This was a different kind of ceremony. The coffin didn't go down – it went along a ramp thing. It's sitting there, and I'm watching both of them, the minister and the coffin. 'Let us pray . . .' I thought, 'Right. Here we go.' 'O God, who is high in heaven, please take our dearly beloved . . .'

Whirrr.

I thought, 'You wee hypocrite!' He didn't even look at the button! 'Please keep him' – *press* – 'safe in your care . . .' An expert. He's done about fourteen that day, you see. So away it went – *whirrr* – through a curtain – *whirrr* – and then the curtain shut.

And I was listening: nothing. I was expecting a wee man to come through the curtain and go, 'Have you got a match?'

Well, you see, the whole thing was quite horrific. It was raining outside and I came out feeling lousy. 'God, what was *that?*' I think they could do a lot to cheer the place up. I mean, they're supposed to believe the guy's gone to heaven, aren't they? I mean, surely, if they're true believers, they're quite *happy* about that. But no, they're all peely-wally and eating sausage rolls that they don't even like.

It needs a bit of a rethink.

They could do a poster campaign: 'COME ON IN, FOLKS – COME AND SEE ELIZABETH FRY!' You know, a wee bit of humour injected into it. 'COME ON IN AND WATCH ROBERT BROWNING!' You know? 'COME AND SEE CAPTAIN COOK!' 'COME AND WATCH HOW RABBIE BURNS!'

It would cheer it up.

AND IN THE END . . .

They have a saying in Scotland: 'You're a long time looking at the lid.' And of course it's true. So, I say: embrace the here and now and make the most of the moment, because you'll have a long time looking at the lid.

I've been asked how I would like to be remembered, and my answer is: as a good laugh. 'Here lies Billy Connolly: A good laugh.' That'll do me.

And instead of having a stone somewhere to commemorate my life, I would rather have it made into a table on an island in Loch Lomond. Somewhere for the fisherman guys to have their tea on. Somewhere to put their cups on.

That would be practical. Like at picnics. Picnics are uncomfortable things; your arse is at the same level as your cup. Eventually you'll knock your cup over and spill it all over your sandwiches. So, I think it would be nice to have a wee table for the fishermen. A useful gift from me to them.

Growing old, it's hard, of course it is. But the good things are still there. The love you have for people is still there. And, with a bit of luck, the love they have for you is still there, too.

And I'm very lucky, in as much as I've made a bit of a mark. And that makes me think, 'Well, I must have done something right.'

That keeps you company when you're older. The fact that, when you were creative, you created well. That thought is a great companion.

So, what else should I tell you in conclusion? I think only this.

Acting your age is about as sensible as acting your street number. You can volunteer to take life seriously, but it's going to get you anyway. It's going to win against you in the end. It's harsh, and you can either break down and complain about how miserable your life is, or you can have a go at it and survive. I think that's the basis of it all.

And laugh. Always look to laugh. Nothing else will ever keep you going like laughter.

So, thank you for laughing with me. And please do keep it up.

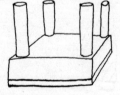

Acknowledgements

It's taken me a long time to come around to the idea of publishing this book, but I'm glad I did.

Thanks to everyone at Two Roads for their help in making it happen – especially to Nick Davies. And thank you to Kate Craigie, Al Oliver, Alice Herbert, Yassine Belkacemi, Jess Kim, Megan Schaffer, Amanda Jones and Lisa Highton. And to Graham McCann, Jacqui Lewis and Linda Carroll. Thanks to Jaimie Gramston for his great photographs. Thanks also to Washington Green Fine Art, for their continued passion representing my other career, and to Andrew White and his team at Castle Fine Art who have introduced my art to a new audience.

Thanks to Pamela, Supreme Goddess and Empress of Everything. I'm sorry I frequently maligned you on stage in the service of a good laugh. I usually cut that stuff out when you came to the show, but now there's no escape. God knows you've tried to rein me in over the years, but I'm not gonnae apologise for what you thought I shouldn't say, because actually I'm not sorry about anything I said on stage – it always felt right at the time.

Finally, thank you beyond words to everyone who came along to my shows over the last fifty years. It's been totally brilliant.

Love and cuddles, Billy